Paramount

My Side of the Road

Dorothy Lamour

as told to Dick McInnes

Prentice-Hall, Inc., Englewood Cliffs, New Jersey

Book design by Joan Ann Jacobus
Art Director: Hal Siegel

The author expresses appreciation for permission to reprint excerpts or quotations from the following works:
Wide-Eyed in Babylon by Ray Milland. Copyright © 1974 by Ray Milland. By permission of William Morrow & Company
Hollywood Director by David Chierichetti published by Film Fan Monthly in their Curtis Film Series. Copyright 1973 by Film Fan Monthly
Light Up Your Torches and Pull Up Your Tights by Tay Garnett with Fredda Dudley Balling published by Arlington House. Copyright 1973 by Fredda Dudley Balling and/or Tay Garnett.
Photographic stills from Paramount Pictures reprinted by Courtesy of Universal City Studios, Inc.

Dorothy Lamour: My Side of the Road
by Dorothy Lamour as told to Dick McInnes

Address inquiries to Prentice-Hall, Inc., Englewood Cliffs, N.J. 07632
Printed in the United States of America
Prentice-Hall International, Inc., London
Prentice-Hall of Australia, Pty. Ltd., Sydney
Prentice-Hall of Canada, Ltd., Toronto
Prentice-Hall of India Private Ltd., New Delhi
Prentice-Hall of Japan, Inc., Tokyo
Prentice-Hall of Southeast Asia Pte. Ltd., Singapore
Whitehall Books Limited, Wellington, New Zealand
10 9 8 7 6 5 4 3 2

Library of Congress Cataloging in Publication Data
Lamour, Dorothy,
My side of the road.
Includes index.
1. Lamour, Dorothy, 2. Actors—United States—Biography. I. McInnes, Dick. II. Title.
PN2287.L243A35 1980 791'.092'4 [B] 79-26300
ISBN 0-13-218594-6

This book is lovingly dedicated to my dear mother, Carmen, one of the main shining lights of my life. She was always there when I needed her, and her loving spirit still surrounds me . . . .

And to "My Bill," my beloved husband, lover, confidant, and my best friend who made my life beautiful, my dark moments bearable; who stood by me at all times and gave me the greatest happiness a woman could wish for. His presence is still with me in anything and everything I do, and his deep love enriches me now and forever . . . .

And to my three wonderful sons, John Ridgely Howard and his lovely wife Karen; Richard Thomson Howard and his charming wife Denise; and William R. Howard IV.

And last but certainly not least, my wonderful little Scottish Terrier Coco, whose personality and warmth have helped me fill a bit of the void in my life since losing my mother and my Bill.

Acknowledgements

A lot of good friends contributed to the making of this book. Some graciously gave of their valuable time to be interviewed and to share their memories with me. Others helped with the typing, loaned photographs and sheet music; still others shared their professional know-how, and some supported me with undying friendship, faith and loyalty. I send them all a heartfelt *Mahalo*, which means "thank you" in the Hawaiian language.

Alvina Arnold
Gordon Arnold
Patrick Baldauff
Gen. Lucas V. Beau
Mrs. John C. Bogan, Jr.
Harold Bolin
Storer Boone
John Bowab
Jane Jordan Browne
Mary Burnfin
Bob Carlisle
Allen Cahan
USAF Chaplain Elmer T. (Mike) Carriker
Gene Casey
Bing Crosby

Cass Daley
Audrey Descher
Doris and Andy Durkus
Margaret Ettinger
Henry Fonda
Don George
Ward Grant
Dorothy Gulman
Andy Hanson
Edith Head
Bill Holden
Earl Holliman
Bob Hope
Bill Howard IV
Ridge Howard
Tom Howard
Len Hughes
Louise Lester
Pauline Kessinger
Tom Korman Associates
Tracey Lee
Raymond Lendway
M. M. Frank Liberman
Leo Lynn
Dorothy Mackaill
Fred MacMurray
Lt. Col. F. W. McCarthy
Dick McInnes
Judy and Lauren McInnes
Ray Milland
Adele Miller
Sam Mineo
Lloyd Nolan
Ben Pearson
Ted Pettit
Harry Ray
Fred Schmidt
Mrs. George Seaton
(Phyllis Loughton)
Dow Sherwood
Maurice and Alice Shinners
Gordon Sichi and co-workers
Jimmy Stewart
Glenhall Taylor
Andre Verges
Charles Wisdom
Don Wortman
Adolph Zukor

Contents

1. The Road from New Orleans

My first road began in the charity ward of New Orleans' Hotel Dieu Hospital on a very cold December 10, 1914. Instead of the laughter and congratulations of grandparents and aunts and uncles, there was only my father beside my mother's bed, holding her hand and beaming as the nurse brought in their new baby girl.

The year before, you see, my mother—Carmen Louise LaPorte—had eloped with John Watson Slaton, something that in those days was unforgivable. Both sides of the family had wanted a big wedding, and Dad's parents were so angry that they cut him off without a cent. He had to go to work as a waiter, but wages weren't all that high in 1914, and tips were even worse.

As a member of the Girl Scouts. (The uniforms didn't include stockings, so each Scout bought her own)

When I decided to make my first personal appearance, my parents had no alternative but the charity ward.

I've always put a lot of stock in prenatal influences. My mother, who had always had a secret desire to be in show business, would say to my father, "If this baby is a girl, I'd dearly love her to be a great singer or actress." Years later, I would tease her about that. Yes, I became an actress and singer, but *great*? Of that, I was never sure.

Mother always went to the "flickers" as often as she could afford it. A few months before I was born, she went to see *Braveheart* with Rod La Rocque, who played an Indian brave in love with a white lady named Dorothy, portrayed by Vilma Banky. Rod told Vilma that in his language, "Dorothy" meant "Gift of God." Mother vowed that if her baby was a girl, she would be Dorothy. She later added my middle name, Mary Leta, in honor of my two grandmothers. But when my father went down to City Hall to register me, he was so excited that he got the names mixed up. My birth certificate came out as Mary Leta Dorothy Slaton. I've been called Dorothy or Dottie all my life, although my passport still reads "Mary Howard [my married name], also known as Dorothy Lamour."

Within a few short days I became involved in the old mistaken identity gag. The nurse brought Mother her baby to breastfeed, then left. Suddenly Mother saw that instead of her own baldheaded baby girl, she was feeding a dark-haired baby who turned out to be the son of an Italian lady. Lord knows where I was dining at the time, but to this day I love Italian food!

Mother and Dad really tried, but his family caused so much pressure that soon my parents' marriage began to crumble. Finally they decided on divorce, which in those days was just as shameful as an elopement. But my mother always talked about "her Johnnie" in glowing terms; I think she loved him until the day she died.

Mother's sister Jeanne Deshotels invited us to move in with her and her four children. Mother was the youngest of nine children, and since Aunt Jeanne was eighteen years older, I always called her Grannie.

My cousin Jeanne Deshotels (Aunt Jeanne's daughter)

recalled that even at age three, I had been quite a ham: "One day we found you out in front of the house, dancing and singing for the other neighborhood kids. At the end of the number you took a big bow and even curtsied. Where you learned to curtsy, I'll never know."

Jeanne also told me I livened up the masses at the St. Louis Cathedral. Once, watching the altar boys light up the candles at high mass, I got so excited that I jumped up and did a very jazzy version of "Ja-Da." Another time, when the altar boys walked down the aisles with the candles burning, I felt it was most appropriate to sing "Happy Birthday."

When I was five years old, the week before Thanksgiving my mother took me to see a movie. She didn't have enough money to admit the two of us, so she went for a walk until the audience let out. After the movie, they had a live talent contest—and when they asked the contestants to come up, guess who was among the first to reach the stage?

Either the audience was impressed by my youth and boundless energy, or they thought I looked the hungriest, but they applauded me the most. I sang and danced my way into first prize—a basket of groceries.

With Thanksgiving a week off, those groceries were like a gift from heaven. But as I was leaving the theater to find my mother, a big boy (to a five-year-old girl he looked like a giant) grabbed the coveted grocery basket, and ran. I chased after him, but to no avail—my very first prize was gone forever. Mother tried to comfort me by saying that obviously the boy had needed those groceries more than we did, painting such a vivid picture of his poverty that soon I felt like a Good Samaritan. I had done something good by letting the boy steal my prize!

That seemed to be the end of my show biz excursions. I then became involved in the business of being quite a stubborn little tomboy and doing my share of fighting with the other children. One time, the class bully threatened that if I didn't shut up, he would break my wrist. I dared him, and he did. I hoped that someday I *would* learn to keep my big mouth shut, but that was never to be.

Mother had met a man named Clarence Lambour who

wanted to marry her, but despite her divorce, she was still very much in love with Dad and had vowed never to marry again. But one day something happened to change her mind. Although my fathers' family strongly objected to the marriage, they felt they should be taking care of me. They felt that it was not possible for a woman to raise a little girl alone when she was working as a waitress for five dollars a week plus tips. They certainly didn't know my mother well! They wanted to give me singing and dancing lessons, which they felt Mother couldn't afford. Politely but firmly, she refused their help. One afternoon, they attempted to entice me into their car. "Dottie!" yelled one of our neighbors, who had been watching, "Don't get in!" I ran into the house, and they drove off.

Mother was so upset about the incident that when Clarence asked again, she agreed to marry him—but only if they moved away from New Orleans so I could be safe. And if we changed my last name to Lambour too, my father's family couldn't find me again. Dad, who felt very bitter about his family's interference, came around on my birthday with a gift of white stockings. But Grannie didn't trust him because of the kidnapping attempt, she wouldn't let him in. Mother didn't know about this until years later; when Grannie told her, she broke down and cried.

Clarence, Mother and I moved to Houma, Louisiana, but as I began to mature, Clarence directed more of his attentions toward me, and started treating Mother very badly. As much as she hated to go through another divorce, she finally had enough of his abuse. We packed up and went back to New Orleans to our family. Mother quickly filed for divorce, but we kept the Lambour name.

Around age ten, I started to develop into a fairly good basketball player. Then came one of the big games with the whole school watching (including some of the boys I liked). While I was taking a jump shot, my bloomers fell down to the court. I vowed never to show my face (or anything else) on the basketball court again. Instead, I joined the Girl Scouts, which I still think was one of the best things that ever happened to me.

Even then, the Girl Scouts organization did a great deal to help young girls grow up properly.

Our Girl Scout camp, Camp Covington, offered a life-saving course. In those days we didn't have a pool: we swam in the river that ran by the camp. And instead of having us rescue people, our instructor would heave a large rock in the river. I was so proud of having "saved" my rock, that I carried it all the way up the bank, promptly dropped it, and broke my toe.

My long hair became my trademark in the early films, but from the way I cared for it, I'm surprised I didn't end up bald as the day I was born. I'd had very blonde hair as a child, but when it started to darken, Mother decided to "help" keep the lighter color. A so-called friend told Mother to rinse my hair with Marchand's Golden Hair Rinse, claiming it was just like a lemon rinse. To my mortification, my hair turned bright red! For weeks I wore a scarf until we could get my natural color back.

Then on my thirteenth birthday I got my first permanent. We had no money for a trip to the beauty shop, so I went off to the beauty school and got one for nothing. Tight curls looked good on Mae Murray, but for months afterward, the boys at school called me "Pineapple." I kept cutting the curls out; and when they were finally gone, I decided to let my hair grow long and keep it that way.

Mother had always felt cheated that she had never finished school, so she was doubly determined that I go to college. Even though history wasn't my strongest subject, my favorite teacher was a lovely redhead named Mae Carey, and I wanted to teach history just like her. But first I had to *learn* history—so Mother paid Miss Carey one dollar a week to tutor me. She was also paying a dollar a week for my music lessons. She thought that since my hands were my best feature, I should play the piano. But with typical teenage logic, I chose the saxophone instead. The only piece I ever really learned to play was "Russian Lullaby," which the neighborhood eventually came to hear several hundred times.

As teenage girls so often do, I needed a new dress for a school function—but we had no extra money. So my mother took a last loving look at the sheer living room curtains and ingeniously cannibalized them into a dress for Dottie. Until we could afford new curtains, she carefully put up newspapers in their place—and other children, who can be rather cruel about things like that, used to say, "If you want to read all about it, just go over to Dottie's house and look in her living room window." Even now, I have an abiding love for the nice curtains and drapes my mother couldn't afford.

Those years were rather rough financially, but Mother always held open house for my friends every Sunday. Everyone was welcome to come in and eat her homemade noodles and chicken creole. She never ceased to amaze me with her unselfish kindness, but she was still working hard at Martin's Restaurant for the sum of $5 a week. Finally I forged her signature to a form giving me permission to quit school, so I could begin a series of jobs. I knew it would break her heart that I wouldn't be going to college, but better a broken heart than a body exhausted from overwork.

My first endeavor was selling real estate junkets. I was the one who dropped by the house to talk you into going on a short trip, with all expenses paid, of course—to look at some terrific property. I wasn't too successful at that, but selling radios door to door wasn't my cup of tea either. When a family friend offered to send me to Spencer Business College, I jumped at the chance. If I was the secretary to a millionaire, I could travel all over the world and then I could *really* take care of Mother! Although I never became the secretary I'd dreamed of, I did learn to type quite well, a skill that comes in handy even now, since I type all my personal correspondence.

I was now 15 years old, and my best friend was Dorothy Dell Goff, an incredibly beautiful blonde. (Florenz Ziegfeld later talked her into dropping the "Goff" for professional reasons.) Having won the coveted title of Miss New Orleans, Dorothy's next step was the International Beauty Contest in Galveston, Texas. With her persuasive manner, she talked the sponsors into having three others accompany her—Dorothy's mother, Ma Goff, her sister Helen, and me!

My first trip away from home was enhanced by the

excitement of seeing my best friend win the Miss USA title and then go on to become Miss Universe. We were all hoarse from cheering. Then, inevitably, the job offers came pouring in. Florenz Ziegfeld wanted her in his *Follies,* Earl Carroll insisted she join his *Vanities.* But it was Fanchon and Marco who came up with the best offer.

Vaudeville was then in its twilight, but Fanchon and Marco used to send live entertainment "units" all over the country to supplement movies—much as the Rockettes would do in later years. Each unit was called a "Fanchon and Marco Idea." Dorothy was offered the starring role for one particular idea called "The American Beauty;" as the reigning Miss Universe, she would work with a group of the contest runners-up.

But loyalties were stronger in those days, and Dorothy swore she wouldn't take any job that didn't include her sister and best friend. Neither Helen nor I was tall enough for Ziegfeld or Carroll, so Fanchon and Marco won all three of us in one package. Since there was no Miss Louisiana that year, I inherited the title for the purposes of the show; Helen became Miss Mississippi. Our first step would be Hollywood, California.

I had a little difficulty talking Mother into giving me permission to go, but since Ma Goff was going to chaperone us, she finally agreed. I recently ran across a diary that I kept during that tour, and there's no better way to describe that period of my life than to share my diary with you.

September 21, 1930

We opened at the Pantages, Hollywood's largest and and best theater. The dressing rooms are perfect. This theater is owned by Mr. Pantages, the notorious Greek who was in a recent scandal, but his two handsome sons, however, run the theater. [One of them, Lloyd, and his sister Carmen became close friends of mine in later years.]

Our show, much to our surprise, was a huge success. The people flocked to see it and instead of being lost among the gorgeous women of Hollywood, we stood out like fresh roses among a lot of withered orchids. Hollywood is hungry for fresh girlhood instead of artificial beauty. They want a new face and a fresh smile—someone who hasn't "gone Hollywood."

One evening as an added attraction, Sally Eilers, star of "Let Us Be Gay," made a personal appearance in a white satin evening gown with white orchids. Named the most beautiful brunette in the "Ziegfeld Follies," Miss Eilers was accompanied by Bill Haines and by her husband Hoot Gibson. But Bill Haines was a great disappointment to me—typically Hollywood, and a complete flop! Sally Eilers' stage presence was poor and when she was finished, she ran off the stage like a child.

September 25, 1930
Long Beach, California
West Coast Theater

We opened here today, and it's a regular summer resort. Our hotel, the Grand Pacific, is joined right to the backstage entrance—very convenient. There's a place called The Round Table where you pay 45¢, order your entree and take all the pie, cake, salads you can eat. [I defy you to find that place in Long Beach today, or anywhere else for that matter!]

September 29, 1930
Hollywood, again!

We're here for a two-day layoff. Today Ma Goff and I are going to stay home to wash our clothes. Dot's going out tonight, so Helen, Ma, and I are going to Warner Brothers' Hollywood theater to see "Dawn Patrol" with Richard Barthelmess and Douglas Fairbanks, Jr. Tomorrow night we're going to Grauman's Chinese to see the Four Marx Brothers in "Animal Crackers." I'll bet it's a scream.

October 2–4, 1930
Fresno, California
Wilson Theater

Everything here's marvelous except the town. . . it's full of hicks. The Union Oil Company gave a parade the last day, and we were asked to appear in it. As a reward, each girl was presented with a bouquet and a box of candy.

We carried the flowers in our finale at the theater, a very pretty sight.

October 5–7, 1930
San Jose California
Sainte Claire Hotel
Fox California Theater

San Jose is a very beautiful town; so is the theater. Our act seems to be a drawing card for this week's bill. I've waited since I arrived for a letter from Kully [a boy that I had met in New Orleans; he was a musician and he traveled a lot] and as yet, none has come. It's our second-to-last day here.

Hooray!!! I just got a letter from him, and he might be home for Christmas. [As you can probably tell, this 15-year-old was in love for the very first time.] . . .

October 10–16, 1930
San Francisco, California
Fox Theater

This is the dirtiest, crummiest, spookiest place I've ever been! The fleas eat people alive! Although there are quite a few interesting things and places here, I don't like it. We visited the famous Golden Gate Bridge and Chinatown. This theater is beautiful. It seats 5,000 people. [Years later, I'd make a personal appearance there with Skitch Henderson on the bill, and fill all 5,000 seats.] This week, we're having a beautiful prologue of Joan of Arc. I'm supposed to be a French maiden. What a costume!

October 17–23, 1930
Oakland, California
Leamington Hotel
Oakland Theater

Oakland is a pretty nice little place, not at all like its sister city Frisco. We were introduced at a luncheon given by the Chamber of Commerce the first day we were here. The fourth day, a young man from the press took us through the campus of the College of California. We also took a drive through the high hills, which was breathtaking. Good-bye, dear old California!

October 25–26, 1930
Salem, Oregon
Elsinore Theater

There's nothing to say about Salem. It's just a little country town.

October 30–November 5, 1930
Portland, Oregon
Sovereign Hotel Apartments
Broadway Theater

Portland is grand! We were shown through the Jantzen Swimming Mills, and each girl was given a swimming suit. The next day we left at 9:00 to ride around Mt. Hood and along the Columbia River. Had dinner in a little log cabin up in the mountains. We even stole apples and ran. Gosh, we had fun!

November 6–12, 1930
Tacoma, Washington
Rhodes Hotel
Broadway Theater

Tacoma is all right. Nothing to say about it. Oh yes, the box office was held up the other day.

November 13–19, 1930
Seattle, Washington
Fifth Avenue

A pretty nice place. On our last night in Seattle, an Episcopalian reverend had a church service for show folks at 11:10 and afterwards they had a party, games and refreshments. A lot of cute boys and girls were there from the cast of "New Moon" and a few other popular shows.

November 22–23, 1930
Yakima, Washington
Commercial Hotel
Capitol Theater

There's nothing to say about this place except there's "Indians Running Wild." Kully sent me a whole box of gum, and boy are we chewing! That's the sweetest lil' old boy living!

November 28–30, 1930
Butte, Montana
Grand Hotel
Fox Theater

The altitude—7,500 feet above sea level—is so high that it's got everybody sick. The town is terribly dirty. Next Thursday is Kully's birthday, and I tried to get something nice for him, but the people in the stores here look at you as if you're crazy. I had to send him some initialed handkerchiefs. He's going to meet me in Milwaukee. Hooray!! Thursday was Thanksgiving, and Charlie and Nell arranged a dinner for the company. We had an awfully nice time. We leave here Monday night for Joplin, Missouri, a four day's ride!

December 7–9, 1930
Joplin, Missouri
Connors Hotel
Fox Theater

This is a little town, but it seems pretty nice. A fellow here, Billy, has been pestering me to death. Just because he's got money, he thinks he owns the world and everything in it. He pretends to know Kully, but I don't believe him because he says a lot of things I know are falsehoods. Well, I'll not believe a word until I find out from Kully's own lips. I'd believe Kully before anybody else.

When we changed trains in Denver, Jimmie [the stage manager] had a notice from the main office telling us about our "idea" closing. Gosh, what a blow! When we stopped at Wichita, Kansas, I wrote and told Mother that I'd soon be home. Dorothy and I had a heck of a fight, because she was embarrassed that the show was closing and didn't want anyone to know.

December 10–24, 1930
St. Louis, Missouri
Melbourne Hotel
Fox Theater

Today's my birthday, and I've traveled all day. When

we arrived a short while ago, I received a cake from Mother and a beautiful robe.

December 11. I went to the post office to get a package, and it was from Kully—a beautiful crystal necklace! Thoughtful boy! Tonight I spoke to him over the phone. He didn't seem so nice, but I'm taking his word—he says *he's been asleep for hours. He's to call again Saturday night.*

December 13. He called me tonight, and he's as sweet as ever, if not sweeter. There's no use in denying it to myself or anybody else that I —— —. [I didn't want to write down "I love him."] Some day I'll tell him. I'm to let him know when I'll be home so he can call again. Mr. McReynolds took us to about every high-class night club in the city. He gave every girl a $5 gold piece for Christmas.

December 23. Tomorrow night at 11:30 I'll leave for good old New Orleans. I've got to pack tonight and wait for my long-distance call at 11:00. The night we closed, Al Wohlman, the M.C. at the Fox, had to make apologies to the audience because everyone had tears in their eyes. What a troupe! I dearly love every one of them.

December 25–30, 1930
New Orleans, Louisiana
HOME!!

Christmas night I arrived home, and Mother and family met me at the train. It was a pretty lonely trip, but I looked back over the past few months and realized how much I've seen and learned. Although I didn't return home a "howling success," I can very easily say that I'm the same good girl who left New Orleans five months ago.

January 8, 1931
Home

Today I spent the day with Olga and had a little sneaking suspicion that Kully would come in today instead of Friday or Saturday, so I called Grannie to see if I had a letter. A card was there from him saying that he'd be in about Wednesday in the P.M. *I made my friend Olga take me there instead of home, and to my greatest surprise and joy, there he was!*

Bliss and everything good that goes with it!! Kully told me tonight that he loved me, and though I knew it before, it sounded like magic to hear him say it.

February 25, 1931

Kully left and oh, how I miss him. I expect within the next few short years to become Mrs. Carl H. Anderson. Let's see if I'm right, huh? I'll let you know. . . .

After our Fanchon and Marco tour, Dorothy Dell decided to go with Ziegfeld after all. She became a *Follies* star, and in April 1931 I landed a one-week job in Mangel's Beach and Style Show at Loew's State Theater. Wearing an 1890 bathing suit, I was billed as "Miss Way Back When." When the audience's votes were tallied at the end of the week, I was voted their favorite and received a big silver loving cup. This time, there was no bully to take away my prize.

Sonny Moore, a neighbor of mine who wanted to be a great photographer, used me as his practice model. We were always in his studio taking pictures. Some of the shots were quite good, too, and somehow the artist Jules Cannert—one of the judges at the beauty contest in Galveston two years before—got word of one of Sonny's pictures and did a sketch of it, making a few minor changes—but it was obvious that it was me.

Someone—and I never did find out who—submitted Cannert's picture in the 1931 Miss New Orleans contest. The local paper ran the picture with the banner headline, "She Decides to Run!" I hadn't even thought about the contest seriously until I read that newspaper, but now I'd wondered, Why not?

I knew all beauty contests featured a bathing suit sequence, so Mother borrowed money to buy me a proper suit. But I didn't know I also needed a dressy afternoon frock. I arrived for the contest at the St. Charles Hotel, wearing a light blue linen dress with a white applique flower on it—total cost $2.98—and was mortified to see all those filmy chiffon dresses.

Sobbing with embarrassment, I fled to the phone and told my mother that I wanted to drop out of the contest.

"You're *in* it now." Mother said. "Once you've started something, you must always finish it."

That was good advice, and I've always tried to follow it since. Determined to make the best of it, I went back to the dressing room and as I opened my overnight bag, out dropped a horseshoe! I don't know how it got there—it certainly wasn't there when I arrived at the hotel. But the horseshoe worked: I was named Miss New Orleans of 1931! When I was awarded the loving cup, I didn't even bother to return it to have it engraved.

I never discovered who entered me in the contest or who put that horseshoe there, but wherever he, she or they may be, thanks a million! That horseshoe is still in my den today, framed in a shadow box, still bringing me good luck. The cup, still not engraved, sits with my horseshoe in the den.

Off to Galveston once more for the International Beauty Contest "Dedicated to Beautiful Girlhood," I ended up one of five finalists competing for the title of Miss USA. If I won, I would then compete for the Miss Universe title with other girls from all over the world.

In 1931, beauty contests had different rules than they do today. For example, you were not allowed to have a hairdresser, and couldn't wear any makeup at all. I was very nervous, feeling I looked very pale and wanting so much to feel "prettier," I dipped the tip of my little finger in lipstick, rubbed it on my lips, and then wiped it off. You couldn't really see it, but I felt much better. However, one of the judges came right up to me, drew a white handkerchief from his breast pocket, and touched it to my lips. It came away with just a trace of lipstick, and I was disqualified for the Miss USA crown.

I was crushed and terribly embarrassed—but the day wasn't over yet! I was *still* Miss New Orleans and entitled to attend the big ball that night. When another one of the judges asked me to dance, I slipped on the heavily waxed floor, knocked him down, and ended up on top of him, laughing so hard that I couldn't get up. I still laugh when I fall—I guess it beats crying!

Listening to the other girls talk about the places they

came from, I did get a case of wanderlust. Every city sounded so much better than New Orleans in 1931 that I wanted to take my mother and get out.

My favorite radio show at the time was Ted Weems and his Orchestra, then broadcast live from Chicago. While listening to it one night, I decided it would be Chicago for me! The problem was convincing Mother to pick up everything and move to a strange city. Finally one day, I took the remains of my contest winnings down to City Hall and bought two seats on the train to Chicago. (Don't ask me why you had to go to New Orleans City Hall to buy a train ticket, but you did.) It was cheaper if you sat up all the way, so I bought "sit-up" tickets.

When I arrived back home, Mother was still at work in the restaurant. I packed my one meager suitcase and left a note:

> *Dear Mother,*
> *I've gone to Chicago. Here's your ticket. I feel there will be more opportunities in Chicago to improve our financial situation. I'll be waiting for you in the Illinois Central Station. Please take the next train.*
> *Love, Baby [her nickname for me].*

It may sound drastic, but I knew that was the only way I could get her to leave New Orleans. So, armed with two dollars and three Hershey bars, I went to the station.

Aboard the train I sat next to a kid who had no money at all, so I shared my Hershey bars with him. I put away the two dollars to spend on a room for Mother and me and spent my first night in Chicago right there in the railroad station. Mother got off the train the next morning, and after a tearful but happy reunion, I took the first steps on the biggest road of my life.

2. That Toddlin' Town

In the Twenties and early Thirties Chicago was one of the music capitals of the world. Hal Kemp, Kay Kyser, and a young man named Herbie Kay had scored at the famed Blackhawk Hotel. Wayne King was holding court at the Aragon Ballroom, and Jan Garber was packing them in at the Trianon Ballroom. Sherman's College Inn was filled with the sound of Ben Bernie's music; and Horace Heidt was hitting high notes down in the Gold Coast Room of the Drake.

The town and the people in it moved much faster than the folks in New Orleans, and there was excitement in the air. But adrenaline doesn't feed two hungry ladies. Mother was hired as a salad maker in the tea room at Mandel Brothers Department Store, and I started work in the back of an Army-Navy store. A

Neiman-Marcus gave me this dress after I modeled it at a fashion show in Dallas (I liked the braided look and used to wear my hair like this)

little old lady and I would mend second-hand uniforms and athletic supporters for resale, but the pay wasn't much. One day I would bring coffee cakes and the elderly woman would bring milk; the next day I'd bring milk and she, the cake. That was our lunch. In an exciting city like Chicago, that kind of dullness was too much for me, so against my mother's wishes, I took a job as a waitress in the restaurant of the Allerton Hotel. But I was too young and thin to handle those heavy trays. "Honey," the hostess-manager finally said to me, "you're just too frail for this job. Maybe you should find something else." She even sent me home with a note explaining to Mother why she had to let me go. Mother was actually relieved; the only reason she had consented was because we did need the extra money.

In between job interviews, I would run off to the beach of Lake Michigan to get tanned. One afternoon a girl told me that the huge Marshall Fields Department Store on State Street was looking for attractive girls. I went straight up to the executive offices and asked for the manager.

The secretary looked up sweetly. "Which one, honey? We have nine of them here."

I was finally sent to a Mr. Kettler, who to my joyful surprise hired me as a uniformed elevator operator. (In those days, elevator doors weren't automatic; someone had to pull them open.) My immediate boss was Donald Singleterry, whom everyone called Terry; I was trained by Mary Utzinger, still a close friend to this day. The job was easy, but my weekly salary of $17 just covered my rent, lunches, and bus fare. I was constantly kidded about my worn, rundown shoes, but even with my employee's discount I couldn't afford new ones.

Mother and I would scrimp and save for our only luxury—the movies. Any Joan Crawford film was a must. In *Letty Lynton* (which I saw ten times) she wore the most magnificent clothes; Robert Montgomery and Nils Asther were her co-stars. Shortly after the film opened, they came out with "Letty Lynton" dress at $15. I put a dollar down and paid my dollar faithfully each payday until I could take it home with me. I didn't look like Joan Crawford, but then, who else ever did?

One afternoon a young man got into the Marshall

Fields elevator and didn't get off, just riding up and down. When there were no other passengers aboard, he came up from behind, grabbed me in a bear hug, and tried to kiss me. Finally I pushed him back and yanked open the elevator door. When he lunged forward, I stepped to one side, and out he went. Believe it or not, that man went to the superintendent's office and complained! But after I told them my side of the story, they threw him out of the store.

One afternoon I had clocked my fiftieth round trip to the top floor of the store when a voice from the back of the elevator said, "Hello, Dowie." There was only one person who had ever called me "Dowie"—a nickname she gave me when we were kids. I spun around and there stood Dorothy Dell, who had come to Chicago with the *Follies* and had slipped into the elevator unnoticed, wanting to surprise me.

Being a Ziegfeld star had made her even more beautiful than when we had been friends in New Orleans. She was with Dorothy Gulman, a good friend of hers who was in charge of public relations for the Morrison Hotel. (It's been torn down since, but it was very popular with everyone who came to Chicago in 1931.) It wasn't easy with three Dorothys running around Chicago together, and it got even worse when we all became friends with bandleader Arnheim's wife Dorothy; and then there were four.

I enjoyed listening to Dorothy Dell's show business stories, but still had no burning ambition to join her. I'd already had what I considered a bad "show business" experience: One day on the bus to work, a guy came up to me and said, "Gee, you're beautiful. I'm a commercial photographer, and I'd like to have you pose for me."

I was still too naive to tell a line for what it was. And since I was making a mere $17 a week running that elevator, I said yes. He gave me his card. It should have given me some hint when I read that his studio was located in a hotel. As soon as I walked in, he informed me that I would be posing in the nude. I very quickly informed him that I most certainly would *not* and ran out of there—highly insulted, hurt, and scared. Needless to say, I didn't talk to many strangers after that and had a very low opinion of most "show" people.

When Dorothy Dell moved on to Milwaukee in the *Follies*, Dorothy Gulman, Mother, and I went to see her. We all three got drunk on hamburgers, of all things. The more we ate, the sillier we became. That was a time of innocence when having a good time simply meant laughing a lot.

Dorothy Dell went on to Hollywood, accepted a contract at Paramount Pictures, and co-starred with Victor McLaglen in her first film, *Wharf Angel*; her next was *Little Miss Marker* with Shirley Temple and Adolphe Menjou. (Ironically, when it was remade in 1949 as *Sorrowful Jones*, another good friend of mine starred in it: Bob Hope played Menjou's role, Lucille Ball played Dorothy's role as Bangles Carson, and little Mary Jane Saunders stood in for Shirley Temple.)

After Dorothy D. left for Hollywood, I continued my friendship with Dorothy G., who had a suite at the Morrison Hotel with room, food, and beverage paid. Once in a while I would stay over with her and we would live it up, ordering all kinds of bizarre breakfasts (our favorite was Chinese food). For an elevator operator, it was delightful!

"You really should be in show business," Gulman was always telling me, but I would just poo-pooh her. The extent of my vocal training was singing along with Ruth Etting recordings, but Dorothy felt sure that I could sell a song and get a job with an orchestra. Then she heard that the Balaban and Katz Theaters were looking for girl singers. Barney Balaban and Sam Katz had a chain of theaters that booked movies and live shows. Gulman felt that this a good chance for me and arranged for an audition.

The only time I could go was during my lunch hour. Because I didn't have time to change, I had to wear my uniform. Four men—Mr. Balaban, Louis Lipstone, and two press agents, Bill Pine and Bill Thomas—listened to my vocalizing, then to Dorothy Gulman, who told them that I was available at $35 a week. "Thirty-five dollars a week?" they said, almost in unison "We wouldn't give her thirty-five cents!"

Barney Balaban became Chairman of the Board at

Paramount; Lipstone, the head of the music department; and Pine and Thomas, very successful producers. A few short years later, while lunching at the Paramount commissary with those very same gentlemen, I reminded them of that audition. I had long since traded in my elevator operator's uniform for a sarong, I was number one at the box office, and I can assure you they were paying much more money than thirty-five cents a week. So if you're an aspiring performer, take heart and never mind those awful auditions or terrible reviews!

One of Gulman's publicity accounts was the famous Chez Paree night club. Her contract let her bring a guest with her to dinner any time, so we used to eat there quite often. There we ran into several of Chicago's "questionable aristocracy," but they never seemed to bother us.

When Sophie Tucker returned from Europe to play the Chez Paree, Gulman was assigned to pick her up at the train station, and I rode along. Sophie's heart was just as big as her waistline, and she always brought gifts for everyone whenever she came back to Chicago. Realizing that she didn't have something for me, she pulled out a lovely hand-embroidered hanky from France. I never forgot that little gesture of kindness. Every time I work with a group of people, I make sure that they receive some kind of reminder from me when I leave.

I was then making extra money by doing some commercial modeling—fully clothed, needless to say. Marshall Fields paid me fifteen to twenty dollars for a layout. I modeled some knitted suits and dresses that remained the rage for years—and so they were still running those ads, with no identification of the model, ten years later, when I had become the Sarong Girl for millions. But to Marshall Fields I was still an anonymous Jane Doe.

Gulman had been broadcasting "Celebrity Nights from the Morrison Hotel" on radio, meeting nearly every celebrity who came into town. Again Gulman took me with her when a young singer arrived to promote his newest film. The crooner's brother, Everett, was also his manager, and we had to talk to him first—whereupon Everett asked me out to dinner.

I looked across at Gulman to be sure it was all right.

"Okay, Everett," she said, "but you be careful with her. She's an innocent girl, and if you give her any trouble, I'll take care of you."

Then the singer himself came in. In case you haven't guessed by now, his name was Bing Crosby. That was our first meeting, but I don't think I ever reminded him of that night. As another bit of irony: Everett took me to dinner at the Blackhawk and introduced me to the bandleader, Herbie Kay, who was to become my first husband.

Another of Gulman's clients was Georgia Glenn, whose radio show featured beauty tips from celebrities. Georgia herself had a Southern accent you could cut with a knife, so she asked Gulman to be the stand-in hostess on the air pretending that *she* was Georgia. One day I came on the program as Miss New Orleans which was Gulman's first mistake. Whenever the two of us began to giggle at something, we'd find ourselves unable to quit. And right in the middle of the interview we started chuckling and just couldn't hold it in. Soon we were both laughing so hard that Gulman gasped, "Damn it! Will you stop it?" You have to remember that in 1939 Clark Gable created a mild uproar when he voiced the word "damn" in *Gone with the Wind.* And this was 1931! Live! On the air! Needless to say, Georgia and friends were cancelled.

But Dorothy Gulman hadn't learned her lesson. One afternoon she called me frantically. A guest had just disappointed her and couldn't make that evening's Celebrity Night from the Morrison Hotel. As Miss New Orleans, could I go on instead? This time my stint would be different: I would sing "Dancing on the Ceiling," for which Dorothy herself would coach me.

Now Dorothy Gulman was a wonderful friend, but an equally terrible singer. (And still is—I recently asked her to sing a chorus of "Dancing on the Ceiling," and she was still terrible.) That night on radio, when she announced me as the visiting celebrity, I was so nervous I kept forgetting the lyrics, faking it as much as I could. Finally the announcer, who could see what was happening, mercifully went to a station break.

What a fiasco! The studio audience wasn't booing as I

joined Dorothy at the "celebrity table," so perhaps it wasn't as bad as I thought it was. We weren't yet back on the air. Then up came a tall, very handsome man I had seen before, the night I was out with Everett Crosby.

"I'm Herbie Kay," he reminded me, "and I'm looking for a new girl singer. Will you come over to the Blackhawk and audition for me? Here's my card with the address." And then he was gone.

Herbie Kay was one of the country's most popular bandleaders with a very successful Sunday night nationwide radio program called "The Yeast Foamers," sponsored by Fleischmann's Yeast. I figured he must be out of his mind. "What do you care?" Dorothy Gulman asked. "This is a good break!"

She loaned me her best dress—a black satin skirt with a sea-green top and a light blue jacket. On my way to the Blackhawk, I was so terribly nervous that I slipped and fell, splitting the jacket seams. But I had no time to change, so in I went, torn jacket and all. The next thing I knew, I was standing on the bandstand in front of the orchestra.

"Dorothy," Herbie asked, "do you have any music with you?"

"No."

"What songs can you sing?"

"I don't know."

"Well," he said sarcastically, "can you sing 'Tiger Rag'?"

"I think so."

"Well," he said, definitely disgusted by this time, "then sing it."

I'd neglected to tell him that I knew only one line.

"Hold that tiger! Hold that tiger! Hold that tiger! . . . " But now he became amused and made me sing it over and over as he moved around the room to see how my voice carried.

I'm not exactly sure why, but I got the job as the female vocalist for Herbie Kay. Going out on the road with him, I joined the company of some heavy names: Dale Evans was singing with Anson Weeks' Orchestra. My old radio friend Ted Weems featured a pretty brunette named Marvel Maxwell (who later went to Hollywood and became a pretty blonde named

Marilyn Maxwell). Weems also hit it rich with a young singer called Perry Como. Ginny Simms was getting started with Kay Kyser's Band, while Russ Columbo was singing along with Gus Arnheim's Orchestra. Betty Grable, who would become a very dear friend of mind, was getting her start with Ted Fio Rito's Orchestra, one of several bands that also featured girl trios. Ted's was The Debutantes, Gus Arnheim had The Three Cheers, and Fred Waring had The Lane Sisters—Lola, Priscilla, and Rosemary. The Lanes were the only singing trio I can think of who went on to make any impression in movies, but not as singers. They made a series of films for Warner Brothers including *Four Daughters* and *Four Wives*, with Gale Page serving as the fourth sister.

At the same time, two very talented brothers were warming up in the studio orchestras of top radio programs. It wouldn't be long until they formed their own band, The Dorsey Brothers Orchestra. Also standing by in the wings were Frances Langford, Alice Faye, Georgia Gibbs, Connie Haines, Janet Blair, Jo Stafford, Harriet Hilliard (Singing with Ozzie Nelson's Band), Tony Martin, Dick Powell, Buddy Clark, Nick Lucas, and later still, Dick Haymes, Mel Torme, Peggy Lee, Doris Day, Rosemary Clooney, Helen O'Connell, Tony Bennett, and Merve (with an "e") Griffin, the boy singer with Freddie Martin's Orchestra.

To get some information about my first tour, I went up to the MCA booking office—approximately the size of a closet, with a huge desk in the center that took up most of the space. But from that little acorn of a room would grow a huge forest called Universal City Studios. In that tiny office I first met Jules Stein and Lew Wasserman, now the top men at Universal.

Norman Steppe was the booker. Whenever he started to map out a road tour, he would clear off his large desk, exposing a map of the United States under the glass. He would place his thumb on the first date and then spread his hand until his little finger touched down on a spot—which was where the tour would end. You must remember, these tours were accomplished without benefit of freeways, turnpikes, and usually even paved roads.

They promptly told me I wasn't old enough to work

without a work permit. Mother went with me to get one. She wanted to accompany me on the tour as well, but there just weren't enough accommodations, and I wasn't earning enough to support her on the road. (Subsequently I found out that Mother had been so proud of my new job that she no longer thought her job as a salad maker was fitting, so she quit. She had some rough times, but never told me about it until much later.)

That first day of the tour, when we all met at the Merchandise Mart Building to board the band bus, I was dressed all in white—a white pair of bell-bottom trousers with a white blouse and a white beret. No wonder the guys in the band treated me like an innocent little sister. Off we rattled to Quincy, Illinois, and then on to such stops as Keokuk, Burlington, and Rock Island.

Each night after we finished a gig, I usually ran out to the band bus, curled up at the back, and dozed off. It took the guys a long while to load their instruments, so by the time they were finished, more often than not I would be fast asleep. One particular night in Dubuque, Iowa, I was half asleep when I thought I heard someone chuckle. Then I heard, "Dottie, Dottie. Wake up."

In a kind of daze, I stood up. "You have to walk over the bridge to the next state," the musicians told me, leading me off the bus. "If you don't, we could all get arrested for violation of the white slavery law."

I'm not too sure I even knew what white slavery was, but I dutifully got off the bus and started walking the bridge over the Mississippi River. The Mississippi is very wide, and they must have felt sorry for me. Soon I heard one of them start to laugh, and another guy said, "Get back in the bus. We were only kidding." I could have killed them, but I've always been blessed with a good sense of humor. Lord knows I needed it when I came to doing the "Road" pictures.

I still had no burning ambition to be in films, but whenever I'd walk into the room, just to embarrass me, the band would strike up "You Oughta Be in Pictures." I would just laugh it off. Me in pictures? No way!

During intermission breaks I had the opportunity to

sing a couple of songs with the piano player, so I began to work on a medley. When we first started the tour, I had been wearing a black satin skirt and a white jacket with mutton sleeves to match the guys' black tuxedos and white Eton jackets. It was a nice outfit, but for my new medley, "Bill" and "My Man," I bought a more glamorous evening gown from the wife of one of the band members. The medley was a big hit with the customers.

Ironically, the "Bill" who was to become "My Man" was still far in the future. Right now, I thought I was beginning to fall in love with Herbie. He was a great guy, good looking and talented—and also eleven years older than me. I suppose I mistook gratitude for love, but I was one very happy young lady.

The day we arrived in Dallas, Texas, I was walking through the lobby of the Baker Hotel when I noticed the placards announcing that Herbie Kay and his Orchestra with Dorothy *Lamour* would be appearing in the hotel ballroom. They had left the "B" out of my name! I was still staring at the sign when Herbie walked in.

"You know something," he said, "that looks pretty good. Let's keep it that way."

Such a simple statement changed my whole life. "Dorothy Lamour" has 13 letters in it, and thirteen seemed to become my lucky number thereafter. I even signed my contract at Paramount on a 13th after I had done a screen test on a 13th. (Superstitious? Not me.)

One afternoon Herbie and I were sitting in the dining room of the Baker Hotel when the waiter asked to take our order. "Young lady," he said, "would you like something?"

I looked up and answered, "Give me a Coke."

"Dorothy," Herbie said a moment later, "have you ever heard of the word 'tact'? T. A. C. T?"

"Yes," I said.

"Well, the tactful thing to say would have been, '*Please* give me a Coke.' Don't forget, baby, the people you meet going up are the same ones who meet you coming down. The difference is that coming down, you meet them faster."

Mother had always taught me to be polite—and he certainly had a point. I never forgot that chastisement, and from then on I worked very hard to preface a request with "Do you mind?" and "Please" and always end with "Thank you." It takes such a little time, but it means so much.

In Dallas, I also became the owner of my second evening gown—in payment for a fashion show I did for Neiman-Marcus—and discovered my so-called sex appeal. I wasn't very popular with the ladies, because their dates would stop dancing and come over to watch me sing. Soon the guys in the band started referring to the customers as "your fan club," and I began to enjoy the attention.

In Houston, we were at the old Rice Hotel. I had just finished a luncheon session in the Roof Garden and went downstairs to the front desk to pick up the mail. There was a letter from Dorothy Dell. Though she was now a big star in Hollywood, we were still writing each other and I was very happy about her success.

I stepped into the elevator and opened the letter to find that she had enclosed a piece of sheet music from the next picture she was shooting. She thought "With My Eyes Wide Open I'm Dreaming" was perfect for me and wanted me to have it before anyone else started singing it.

Two of the guys from the band got on the elevator with me. "Did you hear about Dorothy Dell?" one of them asked. "She was killed last night in an automobile crash in California."

Stunned, I ran into my room and called Ma Goff, who confirmed it: Dorothy had been dating a Beverly Hills doctor. On the way home from a sneak preview in Pasadena, their car went over an embankment. Both were killed instantly.

Jack Oakie was her co-star in her last film, *Shoot the Works.* Years later, he told me that one of the hardest things he ever had to do was go to work the next day and do some dubbing to Dorothy's image on the screen. Even today, whenever I hear "With My Eyes Wide Open I'm Dreaming," I think of Dorothy Dell and our wonderful friendship.

On our band's night off we'd pop over to catch someone else's act and Herbie introduced me to a lot of other performers. While in Houston, we went to Galveston to see Phil Harris. Ted Weems told us that although his new wife had been in some movies, he was going to keep her at home, "barefoot and pregnant." I remember Kay Kyser as a very kind gentleman with a wicked sense of humor. And whenever we were in Chicago, Herbie would take me to the South Side clubs, where I had my first taste of Duke Ellington and Cab Calloway. (Good music still excites me, and I think the work of Paul Williams, Burt Bacharach, and Marvin Hamlisch is the best of the new lot.)

Tiring of his own arrangements, Herbie decided to go after a whole new sound. He had heard of a great band at the University of Indiana, and when we went to hear them, Herbie decided they were perfect for what he wanted. He hired them all. Naturally he had to fire his old musicians, but he kept me.

The new band had been run by Charles "Bud" Dant, and Ronnie Spangler. (Spangler has gone to play music in heaven, but Bud is still a big man in the music field in Hawaii.) We went to the university to rehearse, and visited Hoagy Carmichael's house nearby. "Stardust" was then at the top and he played his new song, "Little Old Lady," just for us.

While playing in Denver's Metropolitan Hotel, we also did a nightly half-hour radio show live from the ballroom. It was what was called "a sustaining program," meaning there was no sponsor; it was used mostly as a promotional gimmick. After the first show, Herbie received a telegram from his old Sigma Alpha Epsilon fraternity brother: *Liked your program. Your girl singer has a lovely voice. Who is she? Signed, Rudy Vallee.* I was terribly flattered, but had no way of knowing that Rudy Vallee would soon become very important to my career.

In Denver, I met Charles Boettcher, whose family owned the Brown Palace Hotel, a big newspaper, the railway system, and practically everything else. (Later, in 1942, he would introduce me to Air Force Captain William Ross Howard.) Not long after, our band was playing a hotel in St. Paul, Minnesota, on the night that Prohibition ended. Suddenly the teacups and flasks disappeared, and we could hardly be heard over the pop of the champagne corks!

Herbie was still treating me like a little sister. I felt I was desperately in love with him, and to me, our relationship began to look hopeless. Finally I told him that I wanted to leave the band and try to make it in New York. What I didn't know was that he was indeed in love with me, but he'd always disapproved of orchestra wives traveling with the band. After all, if he wouldn't let his men bring *their* wives, he certainly couldn't let me accompany him. In fact, he was just as frustrated as I was. But Herbie seemed to understand and even suggested that I look up Rudy Vallee—maybe he could be of some help to me.

So I bid him a tearful farewell, stopped in Chicago to pick up Mother and off we went—this time on the road to New York.

3. New York, New York

On the train trip from Chicago, I had stars in my eyes, and a foreign object in one of them! I just couldn't wash it out, no matter what, and by the time we arrived at Grand Central Station, I was a sight with a sore eye. An ophthalmologist we found in the Yellow Pages told me it was a piece of steel that he could remove in the office, but I would have to wear a black patch over my eye for a few days. Emerging from the doctor's office, I felt like a female version of columnist Floyd Gibbons, who was famous for his eye patch.

Mother and I now had to find a place to live within our very limited budget. We stopped at a brand-new hotel with a large sign: NOW TAKING RESERVATIONS. Naturally, my first question was "How much?"

The "sweater girl" look that Hathaway dreamed up

"Our rooms start at forty dollars . . ." the room clerk replied nonchalantly. I thought it a bit high, but it was a nice hotel and spanking new, to boot. Then he finished the sentence: ". . . a day." Aghast, Mother and I literally ran out of the lobby. I turned back to read the name of this expensive castle—the Waldorf-Astoria. I knew I'd never be able to afford a place like that!

We walked to every hotel in the telephone book without finding one that suited both us *and* the budget. Tired, disgusted, and slightly heartsick, we found ourselves alongside St. Patrick's Cathedral. We went in and asked for guidance, and came out feeling much better and ready to conquer New York again. But like any red-blooded American females in New York for the first time, we took time to look in the store windows along Fifth Avenue. That first day was the beginning of a lot of window-shopping sprees for Mother and me.

Finally we discovered the Chesterfield, a pleasant hotel that looked respectable enough for two ladies—and its rates were reasonable. Located right near Broadway, it was an impressive address to give to our friends in Chicago and relatives in New Orleans.

I hadn't seen much live theater at that time—the closest I had come was seeing Dorothy Dell in *The Ziegfeld Follies* in Chicago—but I had read a lot about the Great White Way and the Broadway theater district. Helen Hayes was then starring in *Victoria Regina,* Leslie Howard and Humphrey Bogart had received raves for *The Petrified Forest*, and Katharine Cornell was playing Juliet to newcomer Maurice Evans's Romeo. Also in that show, in a minor role, was a young man who would become one of my favorite leading men—Tyrone Power, Jr. (he later dropped the Jr.). Fifteen-year-old Montgomery Clift was a hit in *Jubilee,* starring Mary Boland, and Billy Rose's *Jumbo* starring Jimmy Durante was the last attraction to play the famed Hippodrome before it was torn down. The great Tallulah Bankhead was reviving *Rain,* and the Gershwins had just opened *Porgy and Bess.* It would be many years before my name would be up there in lights, and frankly, it never even entered my mind. I just wanted to get to work and make some money.

Our room at the Chesterfield was very small, with a double bed and small chest of drawers. There was only a narrow rack for hanging clothes, but then, we didn't have that much of a wardrobe—just two changes of clothes, one to wear while we washed and dried the others for the next day. Of course, my two evening gowns lent the room a touch of class.

Mother and I used to sleep late so that we could get by with just one meal a day. When we arose, we would go to the Automat and each have our cup of coffee and a glass of orange juice, splitting one order of bacon and toast between us. One day a gentleman came to our table and asked if I'd ever had my hands sculpted. I thought this was another "modeling" line, but he was legitimate; he even asked Mother's permission and insisted that she chaperone me. Mother always felt that my hands were one of my best attributes, so she agreed. I did it, but when I never got paid for my time, I decided never again to listen to any more modeling offers.

A deposit had been required on our $15-a-week room. Our finances were already going down, and I really had to find work. Then Rudy Valley called me. Herbie had written him, giving him our address. His orchestra was playing at Broadway's famous Hollywood Restaurant, and for his occasional engagements at large, elegant social parties—usually at the Waldorf-Astoria—he used a different band. He said he could use a girl singer and asked if I'd be interested. *Would* I? The position paid only $15 a night, but that would pay our rent for the week. I accepted immediately.

Rudy turned out to be a good friend, taking me around to other important places to help me get work. One night he brought me to El Morocco and introduced me to John Perona. With us we happened to have Rudy's accompanist, so I "auditioned" for Mr. Perona on the spot, singing a couple of songs that didn't impress him one bit.

"No," he said emphatically, "I can't use her." But Rudy told him that before long he would be returning with me and that I'd be a very big star. (On a visit to New York a couple of years later, I ran into Rudy, who again steered me to El Morocco. Rudy looked slightly like the cat who swallowed the canary as he told John, "This is Dorothy Lamour. Remember? You turned her down a couple of years ago.")

Another night Rudy and I went to the Stork Club to meet Sherman Billingsley, a charming, friendly man. After my audition he smiled and asked how much money it would take to get me to sing there. I probably would have done it for nothing, but I knew I had to earn a salary. With Herbie I had made only $45 a week; Rudy paid me $15 a night—but this *was* the Stork Club. I was about to ask for $75 a week when an inspiration hit me.

"Well, I don't know, Mr. Billingsley," I said. "What would you suggest?"

"Would one hundred twenty-five dollars a week be all right with you?" I nearly fainted!

I really had stars in my eyes when I read the paper the day of the opening: *New Star Sings at Stork Club Tonight* sang out the headline, but even then, press agents took a few liberties. "Dorothy Lamour, prima donna, begins an engagement at Sherman Billingsley's 'New' Stork Club, where she will be starred in an intimate Continental revue. Miss Lamour will be introduced by Rudy Vallee.

"The singer has just completed a record-breaking engagement at the Edgewater Hotel in Chicago. Miss Lamour was discovered in New Orleans where she was chosen as Dorothy Dell's alternate in the International Beauty Pageant in 1930. The prima donna joins the lavish revue that features such favorites as the Vercille Sisters, George Owen, Armand Valleria, and others. Andy Kaltoy and his orchestra provide music."

Rudy had arranged for me to go on at the Stork between his shows at the Hollywood so that he could introduce me. He even brought his portable sound system (and they were rare then) and his pianist for me to use. Now, that's a friend for you!

The room was packed. Rudy and Sherman had invited the cream of New York, including the top government, society, and theatrical elite. Rudy gave me an absolutely beautiful intro, saying that I would be the next Ruth Etting of the radio and screen, and the spotlight fell on the table where I was sitting.

I started to get up, and one of the gentlemen at the table pulled out my chair. Briefly, I started to sit back down—but there was no seat! I landed right on the floor with my fingertips desperately clutching the edge of the table. The spotlight was still on me, of course, and to make matters worse, standing nearby was the cigarette girl, a good friend of mine. When her giggle got me started laughing, I had to be picked up off the floor.

This pratfall got the evening off to a funny start, but didn't spoil it. Instead of working just two weeks as we had agreed, Sherman held me over for several more.

There was a story with pictures in the *Sunday Mirror* headlining "Four Gals Who Bring Pulsating Rhythm Into Gay Spots: Loretta Lee, vocalist featured with George Hall and orchestra in the Hotel Taft Grill; Helia Slavinska, featured dancer in the revue Follies Bergère at the French Casino; Dorothy Lamour, singer, adds to the popularity of Billingsley's new Stork Club; and Vivian Vance, charming songstress, entertains in the Continental Grill of the St. Moritz." (Did you know that TV's Ethel Mertz was a songstress? And a good one too.)

During that engagement I got to know Walter Winchell (we used to rhumba together), Postmaster and Mrs. James A. Farley, the Rockefellers, and last but definitely not least, a man who became a lifelong friend—J. Edgar Hoover.

In addition to my salary, Mother and I were invited to have our nightly meals at the club—and Sherman always insisted that we order the best of everything. Thanks to the Stork Club, Mother and I were able to move to slightly more elegant surroundings—the Great Northern Hotel on 57th Street. I was even able to save a little money—not enough to retire on, but still it was something.

After so many years, Mother still painted a touching and respectful picture of "her Johnnie," my real father, and it was obvious that she still cared for him. One day she found that Dad's family had been living in Birmingham, Alabama, and she wrote to a minister at Birmingham's Christian Science Church. From him she learned that my Dad's father had passed away and that my grandmother and aunt had moved to Houston. Through friends, she heard that Dad had remarried and had moved to

Denver; the final, sad word was that he had been killed in a plane crash near California's Lake Arrowhead.

I can still see Mother's face as she told how sad it was I didn't get to know my father. The tears rolled down her cheeks as she talked about what a wonderful man he was. At the New York Public Library, we looked up the newspapers from the day after Dad was killed. We both silently read the story of the plane crash and then closed the book on the past.

When my engagement at the Stork finally ended, I knew I would miss the club's elegance and excitement. It wasn't easy trying to line up my own jobs, but I quickly found another at Dan Healey's nightclub; Dan was married to Helen Kane, the "Boop Boop a Doop" girl. This job didn't pay as well as the Stork, but Mother and I had grown accustomed to having a roof over our heads and food in our mouths. Nor did this club attract the cream of New York, but I'd heard that a lot of show folks dropped in.

I had been working there less than a week when I noticed that a particular group of shady-looking men came in every night, always taking the same table. Mother and I decided that they must be gangsters. One night they got into some kind of argument, and one of them reached into his hip pocket as if going for a pistol, and that's all Mother and I needed to see. We grabbed our purses and ran out of the club, all the way back to the Great Northern. I was so scared I didn't even go back to pick up my paycheck. I often wondered if Mr. Healey ever knew what became of his new girl singer.

It was the custom then for singers like myself to visit men in the music publishing business, who would give us the latest sheet music for free. It helped us get new material, and it helped the publishers to have their songs being sung. One publisher, Abe Frankel, advised me to get an agent. So I visited a man who had once come to see me when I was singing with Herbie; he'd told me to look him up if I ever came to New York. After a lengthy discussion, I decided to sign with him. Even though he's deceased now, I'll hold off on his real name and call him John Doe—for reasons I'll get to later.

The first job he got me was at One Fifth Avenue, a

small but classy nightclub in a hotel bordering on Greenwich Village. Each of the two pianos had a mirrored pole beside it. The pianists, billed simply as Jules and Joe, were Jules Monk (who later became quite famous with his own successful club, The Upstairs at the Downstairs), and Joe Lilley. Also on the bill were Dorothy Sara, a noted handwriting analyst, and Melvin Pahl with his "Pianologues." I was the featured *chanteuse.*

Bob Hope was playing on Broadway then, and he used to drop in at One Fifth Avenue once in a while. He tells people that I was a "beautiful chantootsie with a sultry voice" and that he threw his first nickel at me as I sang against that mirrored post.

I really thought my agent was going to be good for me, but I had no idea he was making all kinds of professional enemies for me. He was certainly nice enough to me and did get me work by signing me up with the National Broadcasting Company Artist's Bureau, NBC's own theatrical agency. (The government later made NBC dissolve it because they naturally could use their own clients on the air, creating a monopoly.) To build up my name, the Bureau manufactured a radio program called "The Dreamer of Songs," which aired at 11:00 P.M. Mondays, Wednesdays, and Fridays over the NBC-WJZ network. I would do the first show at One Fifth Avenue, catch a cab to NBC's brand-new Rockefeller Center Studios for the radio show, and then taxi back downtown for my second show at the club.

NBC put out a brochure announcing that "Glamour Comes to Radio" with five gorgeous pictures of me captioned "Dorothy GLamour" with the *G* crossed out. The description was pure press agent wizardry: "Dorothy Lamour . . . In her name alone, there is a significant charm; it lends itself to an auspicious acrostic when linked with glamour, for Dorothy Lamour is glamour incarnate! . . . In the limpid beauty of her person is embodied all the silken allure and mystical enchantment of the eternal woman . . . To see her is to look upon a scented loveliness that holds the dark flame of a tantalizing ecstasy or the delicate aloofness of some exotic flower . . . The svelte sorcery of all this is transfused into her singing . . . In her voice, there is the haunting quality of a whispered intimacy and the soft delight of warm persuasion . . . It may have the velvet sheen of a caress or the plaintive sigh of tremulous longing . . . Her song may be touched with petulant abandon or the receptive languor of a southern night . . . We invite you to share the new thrill that follows in the luminous wake of Dorothy Lamour's singing . . . You can hear this new and glamorous radio personality on Monday, Wednesday, and Friday evenings over the NBC-WJZ network."

Can you imagine trying to live up to that description?

My agent thought I should spread some of that glamour around town to the places where I should be "seen." Lindy's was one of the "in" places where the glittering stars of Broadway went after their shows, and the press followed to get their news items. I remember seeing Billy Gaxton, Victor Moore (I later did *Riding High* with him), the great Mark Hellinger and his *Follies* wife Gladys Glad, and Walter Winchell. Eleanor Powell had just gone into pictures, and I'll never forget the sight of her and her mother, both in brand-new mink coats and squealing in delight at the marquee of a big Broadway movie palace with Eleanor's name in blazing lights. Bill LaHiff's was another in spot: there I met a most charming bouncer who went on to open his own restaurant—Toots Shor. The spectacular Blue Room had all-blue mirrored walls, and I often watched Helen Morgan, my personal favorite, singing in her own club, The Stables. Years later I tried to talk Paramount into letting me do *The Helen Morgan Story*. But they weren't yet making that kind of film biography; it was one of my few dreams that didn't come true. Mother and I also enjoyed Harry Richman, Texas (Hello, Suckers!) Guinan, Fanny Brice (nobody sang "My Man" quite like her), Gertrude Niesen, Ethel Merman, and Jane Froman. (People used to tell me I looked like Jane, but didn't have the character in my face that she had.)

Dorothy Mackaill was one of Hollywood's most elegant and glamorous blondes, equally at home on stage or the screen. (One of her biggest Broadway hits was *Personal Appearance*, which I later did on the road in 1977; Mae West adapted it for the screen and called it *Go West, Young Man,* Randolph Scott played the young man.) I was too shy to get to know Dorothy when I first saw her from afar in New York, but we have since become the best of friends. She lives at the Royal Hawaiian Hotel on the beach at Waikiki. I go there every year before Christmas, and we play gin rummy around the clock. She is one wicked player, and she usually beats me.

Since my agent knew Bert Lahr, we would occasionally go to his apartment on Central Park South, where he would perform for all his friends. To my surprise, I discovered that nervous quality of his was no mere *schtick*; he would get that way any time he had to perform. As he did a number for us one night, he grew so jittery that he pulled all the buttons off his jacket.

When my engagement at One Fifth Avenue ended, I landed a two-week spot at the Club Navarre on Central Park South. The stars of the show were The Yacht Club Boys, a very funny comedy group. (Later on we did a film together, *Thrill of a Lifetime,* and one of them, Jimmy Kern, went on to become a director at RKO.) The Y.C.B.'s loved to tease me, especially when I was singing a serious song. They would come bounding across the stage, sit down, and try to break me up by pulling me from one of their laps to another, while they made up funny lyrics to my music. The Club Navarre was a favorite of most comedians, and Bob Hope showed up frequently. He always laughed the most at the Boys' antics, and I've always wondered if that's where Bob got the idea to have me play "musical laps" in the "Road" pictures and all the other films we later did together.

Bob introduced me to his girlfriend Dolores. Now Mrs. Hope, she is still beautiful, talented, and considerate. One day, years later, she came on the set just in time to see me really get upset with Bob over something. Dolores just looked at me with that glint in her eye, and said, "Dottie, just thank your stars you aren't *married* to him and have to put up with him at home, too!"

One night while we were broadcasting "The Dreamer of Songs," a very distinguished-looking gentleman came to the studio. Everyone seemed to be particularly attentive to him. When I came off the air, I was introduced to Louis B. Mayer. The MGM mogul told me that he enjoyed my show very much and that he would like to make a movie test of me. There was one catch—it had to be shot in California. "So if you ever come to Hollywood, please look me up."

Being practical, my first thought was how I could get to Hollywood on my limited funds. Why bother? I asked myself; I knew I could never make it in films anyway. Soon thereafter, NBC told me that they were thinking of moving "The Dreamer of Songs" to Hollywood, but they never mentioned moving expenses. My agent didn't make any great effort to ask them about it, either, so weeks went by without any further talk of the Big Move West.

When Herbie came into town to do some special industrial engagements at the New York Hotel, he called me right away. I knew how *I* felt about him, but it came as a total surprise when he said he loved me and wanted to marry me. I told him I knew very well how he felt about orchestra wives, and that if I married, I wanted to be with my husband all the time: I didn't want one of those long-distance show-business marriages. We reached a compromise: if I would marry him, I could travel with him some of the time, but not *often.*

When I told my agent of this, he was furious: "You have a brilliant career ahead of you. You're giving it all up for a marriage that'll never last." But I had already made up my mind—and once I do that, that's the end of the discussion.

Herbie and I had heard that you could get married in Harrison without any delay, so we hailed a cab and told the driver, "Take us to Harrison." Unfortunately, there are two Harrisons—one in New Jersey and one in New York. We ended up in the wrong Harrison, of course, and had to drive back—unmarried. When we pulled up in front of my hotel, I saw my agent sitting in the lobby waiting for me, so we ducked in the back door and made new plans. We decided to fly to Waukegan, Illinois (Jack Benny's home town), where we knew there would be no wait. But first we stopped in Chicago long enough to pick up Dorothy Gulman, to act as my maid of honor.

Married on May 10, 1935, we spent our wedding night in Chicago. But the next day I flew back to New York and Herbie went back on the road. We told Mother, of course, but decided to keep our marriage secret for the time being. But we didn't know show biz that well. Ed Sullivan's May 15 column announced, "Dorothy Lamour flew from Broadway to Chicago and then eloped with Herbie Kay, the bandsman." So much for secrecy!

More than 85% of the reference books I've seen insist that my real name is Dorothy Kaumeyer—and it was at that time! Herbie's real last name was Kaumeyer, so I naturally became Dorothy Kaumeyer for all legal purposes. It does get a little confusing; for example, my full name would be Mary Leta Dorothy Slaton Lambour Lamour Kay Kaumeyer Howard if you keep count.

But at this point, I was just terribly happy to be Mrs. Herbie Kay. Throwing myself back into work, I wrote him faithfully every night, making plans to visit him as often as I could.

Around that time I met society bandleader Eddy Duchin, who was madly in love with Marjorie Oelrichs, a beautiful New York socialite who felt the same way about him. I could understand why: he was a real gentleman who made every woman feel very important. (Ironically, when it came time to film his life story, he was played by another of my favorite people, Tyrone Power.) Eddy asked me to do a couple of gigs with his Central Park Casino Orchestra—one in a theater in Philadelphia, the other in Baltimore. I can't remember a thing about the Philadelphia engagement, but I'll never forget my first entrance in Baltimore's Hippodrome.

Standing in the wings, I heard Eddy giving me an introduction. ". . . This young lady is only beginning in show business, but she will certainly go far. She's the lovely, talented 'Dreamer of Songs' . . . here she is—Miss Dorothy Lamour!"

I heard the band go into the beautiful strains of "Blue Moon" and as I swept on stage, my gown caught on one of the music stands and—shades of the Stork Club—down I went! The audience must have thought I was a comedy act and gave me one of the biggest laughs I'd ever received. Eddy helped me up and, daintily, I began singing.

While in Baltimore, we were asked to do a special broadcast for the American Red Cross on Station WBAL. This, the first of many charity performances I was to give, was arranged by the Baltimore *News and Post* through the courtesy of the Musical Union of Baltimore. A man known as the Globe Trotter, the radio voice of the Hearst newspapers, was master of ceremonies.

One night after finishing at the Hippodrome, we played at the famous Maryland Hunt Cup Ball, one of the most elegant social functions I had ever seen. The men looked so dashing in their pink hunt coats, and all the ladies were in evening gowns with long white gloves. I had no idea that among all those Southern socialites that evening was a man named William Ross Howard III who would become the most important man in my life. That night we merely passed like the proverbial ships in the night.

Back in New York I met two new friends: Harriet Hilliard, a band singer like myself, and Ozzie Nelson, a very successful bandleader and another fraternity brother of Herbie's (what a fraternity that must have been with Herbie, Rudy, and Ozzie in it!).

That year Nils T. Granlund, who had been a judge for many years in the annual Miss America contest, was chosen to pick Miss Radio of 1936. It was announced that, "This year Miss Radio of 1936 isn't going to be a lady. For quite a few weeks, Granny [one of Granlund's nicknames, another being NTG] has been looking over the field. And instead of picking a lady, he has selected a trinity of graces. Yep, he says, officially, three young women will combine the charms of Miss Radio of 1936. The gals picked are: Dorothy Lamour, brunette, classic type; Helen Marshall, honey blonde, the outdoor type; and Harriet Hilliard, platinum blonde, and designated as 'the perfect showgirl type.' " I'm sure the "perfect showgirl" had no idea she would grow up to be America's favorite TV mother. *Radio Guide*, an early precursor of *TV Guide,* sponsored another contest, and both Harriet and I were up for that one, too. This time I was really thrilled when I won their title of "Miss Radio." But Harriet and I remained friends throughout our competitive years, and afterward.

Finally NBC notified me to report to their Hollywood studios to continue broadcasting "The Dreamer of Songs." They hadn't given Mother or me any travel expenses, but even after Mother had thrown in her own money, our meager savings were still $45 short. I had vowed never to ask Herbie for money for my career—and I loathed borrowing from friends, so I had Abe Frankel co-sign my loan application at the bank.

Our tickets were bought, our suitcases packed, but in my heart I felt I would never remain in California. After all, I was a New Yorker now. Mother and I boarded the train in Grand Central for what we jokingly called "the jungles of Hollywood." At least we thought it was a joke!!!

4. Hollywood on the Third Try

This was my third visit to California. They say that the third time is the charm; in my case, it certainly was true. This time I wasn't one of the chorus cuties in the Fanchon and Marco troup, nor was I Herbie Kay's girl singer. I was "The Dreamer of Songs," with my own radio program.

The whole town seemed different. Movies had become the world's favorite entertainment, and Hollywood was buzzing with activity to keep up with the demand for new films. Bette Davis was *Dangerous* and had an Oscar to prove it. Herman Brix (later known as Bruce Bennett) was the "New Tarzan"; Gable and Laughton were having their *Mutiny on the Bounty*; Bill Boyd made his first "Hopalong Cassidy" film. Jean Harlow was the reigning blonde sex symbol, Shirley Temple still the nation's

One of the enormous old-fashioned cameras used to film The Jungle Princess

sweetheart; and Crawford, Lombard, Hepburn, Boyer, Cooper, and Colbert were all skyrocketing. There were two types of people in Hollywood then: those who were in pictures and those who *wanted* to be. And every day more aspiring thespians would arrive by bus, train, or plane—all wanting to become the next Shearer or Garbo, Gable or Barrymore.

No sooner had I arrived in town than NBC Artist's Bureau arranged for me to work at the famous Clover Club. Most of the clientele were in show business, so it was really like a private club where everyone could let down his or her hair and have a good time. Gambling was the club's major attraction, but they also had good food, dancing, and a floor show.

One night Louis B. Mayer showed up and once again offered me a screen test. This time it was easier to say yes, because I only had to go crosstown to Culver City. MGM already had Garbo, Harlow, Gable, Loy, Powell, Shearer, Dressler, and Beery under contract. Could Lamour join that select group? Impossible! But still, if my screen test was good . . . !

My hopes didn't stay high for long: the night before the test NBC Artist's Bureau got a call. Mayer's office was still very much interested in testing me, but wouldn't go one step further as long as I was represented by my present agent. Obviously, Mr. Doe was being his usual obnoxious self. Of course, he couldn't imagine why anyone would be saying such things, and he insisted that I honor my contract with him. I didn't want a scene, so I stayed with him—and lost the test.

One night after I finished my set of songs, I went wandering around the club and became fascinated by the famous Latin star Lupe Velez, who was putting quarter after quarter into a slot machine. She must have put at least a hundred dollars into that one-armed bandit. The Clover Club always gave you a little sack to hold your change in, and when hers was empty, Lupe turned away from the machine to get more quarters. No sooner had she left the machine than another woman walked up to it, plunked one quarter into the slot—and won the jackpot! Seeing this, Lupe let loose with a barrage of Spanish curses and hit the lady over the head with her newly filled bag of quarters. They went into a hair-pulling fight equal to the famous one between

Marlene Dietrich and Una Merkel in *The Spoilers*—until the management broke it up.

Still fretting over my lost screen test, I was introduced to Jack Votion, a gentle man with a British accent who was the head of talent at Paramount Pictures. He had a slight limp that, I later found, came from injuries he had sustained flying in the RAF. In the course of our very pleasant conversation, he asked if I would like to make a test for Paramount. A second chance! Naturally my answer was yes, but I was afraid that my agent would mess up this one, too.

This time luck was on my side because Jack went straight to Dema Harshbarger, the head of NBC Artist's Bureau. She knew what had transpired over at MGM and didn't want an instant replay; not until later did I learn that she warned my agent not to accompany me to Paramount. But that didn't deter him one bit! He insisted on coming along to the Paramount studio where I was to pre-record a song for the test.

When we arrived, we were told the test was temporarily postponed. My heart sank; to me, that meant "cancelled." Dema's office was right around the corner from Paramount in a small building on Melrose (it now houses Channel 9), so I ran right over to see her—with my agent trailing behind.

When we walked into her office, Dema told my agent that Paramount wanted nothing to do with him, that he was ruining any chances I had to get into pictures because of his rudeness and unprofessional behavior. I stood there stunned, and finally he agreed to step aside. Dema called Paramount and made arrangements for the test to be rescheduled.

Phyllis Loughton was assigned to direct the test and give her report on my possibilities—or lack thereof. She had just married George Seaton, a young writer who went on to direct such pictures as *Miracle on 34th Street, Somebody Loves Me, Teacher's Pet,* and *The Country Girl.* The first time I met Phyllis, I was wearing my hair up. She said it would be very effective if, while singing the song, I took down my hair—which reached to below my waist at the time—and brushed it. Years later she showed me a memo that she had sent to Jack after she met me:

> *Name: Dorothy Lamour*
> *Experience: Band singer with Herbie Kay*
> *Vocalist on NBC Dreamer of Songs*
> *Sings at Clover Club*
> *I would like to test her. Has a freshness and beauty that is unique. I think she has a big future and definitely will be a star.*

But Phyllis had much more faith in me than I did. After the test was shot, I called Mother and told her to pack our bags. She was going to visit relatives in New Orleans, and I needed my husband's advice. I was even considering forgetting about Hollywood and going back to work for Herbie. Determined to get away from Paramount, NBC, and everything else, I caught the next train for Denver.

I went straight to Denver's Metropolitan Hotel where Herbie was playing, but I simply couldn't talk him into taking me back as a singer. He admitted it would be wonderful for us to be together again but thought it would be a big mistake. He still felt strongly about wives on the road, and besides, he said, I owed it to myself to try for a film career.

Three days later I received a telegram from Mr. Adolph Zukor, the founder and head of Paramount, informing me that they had exercised my option: I was to report to the studio the following Monday. I was in such a state that I didn't know whether to laugh or cry—so I did both. Again I bid Herbie farewell and boarded the next trian to Los Angeles.

Having lunch in the dining car, I fell into conversation with a gentleman sitting across from me. He was on his way to Hollywood with a song-and-dance act called The Gumm Sisters; one of whom had just been signed to a contract with MGM. I met the three young girls later in the day. The one who was MGM-bound was wearing a sailor dress and looked very cute. About a year later, I went to the Trocadero nightclub for one of their Celebrity Nights. Lo and behold, that cute little Miss Gumm on the train had changed her name to Judy Garland and was knocking out the audience with her talent. (MGM had sent her to their school to groom her for what was to become one of the most brilliant, albeit tragic, careers in the history of Hollywood.)

I had wired Mother, who rushed back from New Orleans and met my train in Hollywood. We immediately looked for an apartment within walking distance of the studio—who could afford a car, or even a taxi?—and found one on Gower, right off Santa Monica Boulevard.

Bright and early that Monday morning I reported to Paramount. It was a pleasant walk from our apartment, and whenever I saw a magnificent car drive by, I was positive that sitting in the back seat was a star being driven to *my* studio. I walked past the cemetery where Rudolph Valentino was buried, then past RKO where all the RKO gals were toiling, including Lucille Ball. (Times do change: Lucy would later end up owning RKO and calling it Desilu; and now it's a part of Paramount Pictures.)

I signed Paramount's standard seven-year contract, which was divided into options. During the first year, if they thought you could make it at the box office, they took up the six-month option. Thereafter, if they were really positive you were on your way, each succeeding option was for one year except for the last one, which was for two years. and with each pickup, you got a raise. My first six-month option gave me $200 a week for twenty week's work, and the balance of my time was considered unpaid vacation. If I worked during vacation time, however, I would receive my regular salary.

Once they signed you to a contract in those days, the Paramount publicity machine really went to work. The studio told me to show up every day so they could work on a large-budget publicity campaign. They instructed Terry DeLappe, head of publicity, to give me the big buildup to stardom. So that he could write an official biography, Terry began asking me a lot of questions. Where was I born? On what date? When he questioned if my parents were still living, I answered that my father had been killed in an airplane crash; and told him how I had found an account of the accident in the New York Public Library's newspaper files. He opened his desk drawer and pulled out the exact same clipping. It seems that he had been up at Lake Arrowhead at the time, and had volunteered for the search party that found my father's plane. Here was a man who practically held my entire future in his hands, and we had a common bond without having known it.

Then we got to my name. In Hollywood, Gladys Smith had become Mary Pickford; Jane Peters was now Carole Lombard; Harriet Lake became Ann Sothern; Sarah Jane Fulks, Jane Wyman; Spangler Arlington Brugh, Robert Taylor; Ruby Stevens, Barbara Stanwyck; Lewis Offield, Jack Oakie; Margie Reed, Martha Raye; Archibald Leach, Cary Grant; Lucille Le Seur, Joan Crawford. I told him I'd been called Dorothy all my life, but the name on my birth certificate was Mary Leta Dorothy.

I could almost see the light bulb go on over his head! Sure enough, Terry said, "Let's change it to Leta Lamour!"

I gave him every possible reason why that monicker wouldn't work. After all, my original name had been built up during my radio show, and "Leta Lamour" sounded like a cheap dime store perfume. But ironically, the one argument that convinced him was that "Dorothy Lamour" had thirteen letters. The coincidences that I had signed my contract on the 13th and my test was done on Stage 13 appealed to the press agent in him—and spared me the reputation of being "difficult." I still shudder to think of it—Leta Lamour, indeed!

I must have spent half of my time with the press for interviews and with photographers for portrait sittings, fashion shots, and cheesecake. It was a busy life, but that initial $200 a week seemed like a fortune to Mother and me. Each week, with her help, I managed to save some. I never wanted to go back to those days when we didn't have any money to spare. Soon we moved to a more comfortable apartment in La Belle Tour on Franklin Avenue, a little farther away from the studio. I had saved enough to put a down payment on a Ford, which was the least expensive make at the time, and the studio signed my note for the balance. My very first car, and it was almost all mine! As I drove to the studio each morning, I wondered if the girls walking down Gower thought I was a glamorous star going to work. I certainly felt like one.

Then the studio called to say that they had decided on my first picture. After parking my car, I could hardly wait to get to the office, so I ran most of the way, then made what I hoped was a calm entrance.

Mr. Zukor, Bill LeBaron, and the rest of the top brass were waiting for me. They told me that they had tested over 250 girls for a certain role but couldn't find the right one, and so had shelved the picture. Now, after screening my test, they knew it was right for me. The picture had been called *The Jungle Queen,* but since I was so young, they changed it to *Girl of the Jungle.* I had yet to learn the plot of the film, but I frankly didn't care. All I knew was that I was going to be the star of that film!

After that meeting Travis Benton, the head costume designer at Paramount, put me in the hands of one of his assistants, a small, dark-haired lady who wore glasses. Her name was Edith Head, and who would have known that she was to become a multiple Academy Award winner? She pulled out some beautiful cotton print material and began to drape it around me. Beginning to daydream of all the beautiful gowns, glamorous hairdos, and magnificent jewels that I would be soon wearing—and of the handsome leading men who would be holding me in their muscular arms—I asked how many dresses I would wear in the film.

"Dresses?" she exclaimed. "Young lady, this is going to be a sarong!"

I had to admit to her that I didn't know what a sarong was. She laughed, and when she explained, all my hopes of a glamorous movie debut flew right out the window.

I had been embarrassed to wear a bathing suit in the Miss New Orleans contest because I thought that my hips were too big, my shoulders too narrow, and my long, narrow toes made my feet look big. And now Paramount wanted millions of people to see me with no shoes, in a little strip of cloth. I would have to wear that darned sarong all through the film!

I actually had to bite my lip to keep from crying and couldn't wait to get home. Mother assured me that it wasn't all *that* bad. I gritted my teeth and went into the studio with my head held high to start my first motion picture.

To this day, people laugh when I tell them that I have an inferiority complex. I never had much faith in myself and was always embarrassed at the things I did—and still do. In the beginning when I reported to work on the set, I was so shy that I would wear a long terry-cloth robe over my sarong and bedroom slippers on my feet. There were coffee and doughnuts for everyone; but I knew doughnuts were fattening, and I thought all coffee had chicory in it like the New Orleans coffee I despised. So while everyone else was coffee-breaking, I would just go sit in a corner.

One morning one of the men working on the set asked if I would like a cup of coffee. He was very friendly, and I was so delighted that someone talked to me that I broke my silence and started talking about my dislike of chicory. He assured me that there was no chicory in California coffee, so I accepted a cup. He told me his name was Coley Kessinger, and we discovered that we almost had the same birthday—his was December 7, mine December 10. The more we talked, the more relaxed I became.

Before long he became a little serious. "Dottie, you have such a warm personality, but because you don't talk to anyone on the crew, most of the guys think you're a snob. I've told them it's not so, but when you come on the set, you should at least say hi and make friends with tech assistants and cameramen. You'll find that the crew are very important to have as friends. They're a very loyal bunch of guys."

I was stunned to think anyone would think that I was snooty, but realized that was the way it *looked.* I followed Coley's advice, and before long the crew and I were all one big happy family. And that's the way it went from that time on.

Everybody loved Coley's wife Pauline, who ran the Paramount commissary. Even though Coley has gone to heaven, Pauline Kessinger is still my best friend, and she loves to tell a story about when I was still brand-new at the studio.

Herbie and the band were in town for an engagement, and I had the day off. The musicians in his band were my buddies, and naturally I wanted to show off a bit, so I invited them all to lunch at the commissary. The "big star" made her entrance wearing a stunning Edith Head creation trimmed in leopard skin, and accompanied by eleven men. I didn't think it necessary to ask for a table because I spotted a large, empty circular one with a huge thronelike chair in the middle of it. I went right over and sat down on the "throne" with the guys in the band around me.

Moments later, a waitress hurried into Pauline's office. "Some beautiful young lady is sitting at Mr. DeMille's table, and that's not bad enough—she has the nerve to sit in *his* seat!"

The musicians and I were all laughing and joking when Pauline came over to the table. I was so new that she didn't even know my name. "Young lady," she said, "you cannot sit at this table. It is reserved daily for Mr. DeMille."

"Who's Mr. DeMille?" I asked. "Well, no matter. If it's reserved, we'll just move to another table."

Pauline laughed every time she repeated this tale, and finally, years later, she related it to DeMille. "Shame on you, Pauline," he laughed. "I would have gladly given up my table for Dottie."

Pauline had worked for Paramount since the silent days when Clara Bow was queen of the lot. For 42 years she worked to make the commissary a major success and one of Hollywood's landmarks. Each star, supporting player, bit player, extra, writer, and executive—even visiting royalty—received the Kessinger treatment and was made to feel right at home. Both the food *and* the service were terrific—a not too common combination in studio commissaries. You knew that you were a success if Pauline named a dish after you on the Cafe Continental Menu. Among some of the dishes she served over the years which changed as the contract players came and went, were Turkey and Egg à la Crosby, Spanish Omelette à la Alan Ladd (made with eggs from "Alsulana Acres," Ladd's own farm), Bob Hope Cocktail (tomato juice, yogurt, with a dash of Lea and Perrins), English Kippers and Eggs à la Danny Kaye, Anthony Perkins Sandwich (grilled cheese and chicken), Strawberries Heston (fresh strawberries with sour cream, honey and cinnamon), Stella Stevens Special (California fresh fruit on chilled lettuce and cottage cheese and cream French dressing), and The Dorothy Lamour Salad (fresh pineapple, sliced bananas and strawberries with cream cheese, Bar-le-duc). Of course, zanies like Martin and Lewis made up their own—the Jerry Lewis Special (breaded tweed jacket with almond sauce and roasted lemon juice with peas and canned pot roast), and the Dean Martin Special (egg shells on toast with cracked crab à la 5-Iron). (When Gulf and Western bought Paramount, they decided to discontinue the commissary, and Pauline retired. I've often tried to talk her into doing a book about her many years there; it would make great reading.)

On the lot was a three-story building we called Dressing Room Row. The first floor contained the dressing rooms of Paramount's biggest stars—Mae West, Bing Crosby, George Raft, Randolph Scott, Carole Lombard, Fred MacMurray, and W. C. Fields. The second floor was for the lesser stars, the third for the supporting players. I assumed that since I was going to be the star, my dressing room would be right down among the rest of the biggies. Wrong! Up the stairs I went (there was an elevator, but it never worked), to the second floor—and then to the third, and took a long walk to the end of the hall. A left turn would have taken me into the makeup department where Wally Westmore toiled to make us all gorgeous. I made a right turn instead to my dressing room—a dark, dingy little room with one chair and a small dressing table with a narrow, worn-out mirror. It reminded me of that room Mother and I shared at New York's Chesterfield Hotel, only worse.

After seeing my wardrobe test, someone in the front office decided that I had to fix my two front teeth. I refused to have them capped, and I was certainly too old for braces. Instead they sent me to Beverly Hills' top dentist. He decided to make me some temporary caps of extremely fragile, thin porcelain that I could slip on before going in front of the camera. He made up three sets of two teeth each—one set to cover my two front teeth, and then, to even up my bite, two more sets for the teeth on either side. They made me feel as though I had a mouthful of piano keys, but they did look good on screen—and that, I quickly learned, was all that counts. Still, I could hardly believe that I had $750 worth of porcelain in my mouth. The studio paid for the first three sets but stipulated that if I broke them, I had to pay for any replacements. Since my salary was still only $200 a week, you can imagine how careful I was!

I was very curious about my first leading man, whose name had been Reginald Truscott-Jones before he changed it to Ray Milland. According to publicity releases, he had been on his way to be interviewed for a job in a gasoline station when a casting director offered him a role in *Bolero* with George Raft and Carole Lombard. He had done several pictures since, but hadn't yet had a big hit. In his delightful book *Wide-Eyed in Babylon*, he credits me with helping him get the role in *The Jungle Princess*. I frankly don't remember, but if that's so, I'm glad.

He also relates the following:

> *In the film I was supposed to be a young aviator who crashed in the jungle. I was discovered by this young child of nature who was nursing me back to health. She lived all alone in a cave above a jungle pool, her only companion being this five-hundred-pound Bengal tiger. The scene in process was where I was supposed to be teaching her English while lying on a rock above the pool, wearing just some tattered shorts. We were doing that tired bit where I say, "Me Chris. You Ulah."*
>
> *She would reply, "Kees?"*
>
> *I'd say, "No, Chris."*
>
> *And again she would say, "Kees?" Then I would demonstrate the difference between Chris and kiss.*
>
> *When I kissed her, she sat back on her haunches as if she had just tasted her first banana split. Then a look of absolute joy came on her face as she leaped on top of me, wanting more. With that, I was supposed to struggle free and dive into the pool with her after me. She would emerge and we would go into an embrace with the water just up to her breastworks. An idyllic scene, wouldn't you say?*
>
> *On the morning we were to shoot this little vignette, scattered clouds caused some delay, sunlight being necessary for the entire scene. Everything was set. I was lying on the rock, Dorothy kneeling beside me, the cameraman watching the clouds through a smoked glass, and Attila the Hun [Ray's nickname for director William Thiele] pacing up and down, building a nice head of steam, ready to explode. Everybody was triggered to*

> *go as soon as the sun broke through, and then I felt the first twinge. I had to go to the bathroom. Oh, God, I thought, not now! It was at least fifty yards to the nearest cover, and if I departed and the sun came out, that Pomeranian pimp [Thiele again] would slaughter me. No, I had to stick it out somehow!*
>
> *I whispered Welsh prayers. I crossed and uncrossed my legs. But slowly and inexorably, the pressure built and panic came. Then someone shouted, "Here it comes! Get ready! Roll 'em!" By this time I was in extremis. How I got through the dialogue I'll never know. But by the time Dorothy started manhandling me, I knew I had to go. So I went, headfirst into the pool with Dorothy after me. As I came to my feet, the dear girl surfaced in front of me. And as she put her arms around my neck and started kissing me, the cold water of the pool did its work, and I let go. Ah, the sheer sensuous bliss of it—and all the time I was doing it, Dorothy and I were necking like teenagers in a hayloft.*

Ray was a genuinely unselfish actor—a rarity in the film business. One of the first scenes we did involved a big close-up of me, shot over Ray's shoulder. What did I know about camera angles? After all, other than my screen test and the family Brownie, this was my first experience in front of a camera. I kept turning my face away, but Ray would gently take me by my shoulders and adjust me so I was facing the lens. Sometimes Ray would even sacrifice his own scenes to get my face in the proper position. That's really something when a performer does that for a colleague! I think he taught me more about the technique of motion picture acting than anyone I knew.

The only contention I might have with Ray was that he offered me my first cigarette, insisting that it was the "social" thing to do. At first I refused; I didn't smoke and had no desire to learn. But then I, in turn, taught my mother. I still smoke too much to this day, but am trying to cut down.

As Ray so succinctly pointed out, our director was William Thiele from Germany's famous UFA Studios. He could speak English clearly, but not too well. For one shot, I was supposed to climb a cliff. After I got halfway up, he shouted, "Dorotay, come heah!" So back down I went to the camera. "Vy you heah?" he asked. "Ven I say 'Cum heah!' I mean go *der,*" pointing dramatically toward the cliff.

One Saturday morning I noticed Mr. Thiele and Harry Fischbeck, the cameraman, looking me over. Thiele was concerned about the dark circles under my eyes and told me that I really should stop keeping late hours, at least while working on the film. My feelings were terribly hurt since in those days I neither drank nor stayed out late. When I got home that night, I told Mother what Thiele had said. She pulled out a baby picture of me. At the age of six months I'd had huge circles under my eyes, and I certainly wasn't keeping late hours back then.

My other leading "man" was a chimpanzee called Gogo. Working with the chimp was a delight for me, but one day he got mad at two of the workmen on the set. Gogo scratched one man's back to ribbons, and he picked up the other and threw him 40 feet down into a rocky waterfall. That man was hospitalized, and some time later he died from the complications. The story was altered by the Publicity Department and released as "Chimp Attacks Lamour on Set of First Film." But fortunately, I had a good working relationship with the chimp—and also the leopard and the tiger.

In order to make the picture as authentic as possible, they sent us on location, way out in the San Fernando Valley to a place called Brent's Crags. They put up tents for all of us to live in: one served as a dining room and two others as the ladies' and men's showers. We had to wait in line for the shower, which consisted of a hose hung up on a rack with a spray attachment in place of the nozzle. For my role as Ulah, *The Jungle Princess*, I had to cover myself from head to toe with greasepaint body makeup which was a chore to wash off even under normal circumstances. In our makeshift shower it was darned near impossible. I soon developed skin poisoning on my face and had to be sent to a specialist highly recommended by my idol, Carole Lombard (more about her later). The dermatologist poked and pulled at my face, leaving a slight scar on my right cheek that's never been noticeable to anyone but me. But his treatment worked. After a weekends recuperation, I was back on my way to the jungles of San Fernando.

Because we couldn't get trucks through the densely overgrown brush, everything—even the heavy cameras and props—had to be carried by hand. We had to march for 45 minutes, and by the time we arrived at the location to start shooting, we felt as though we had already done a day's work.

Having none of the conveniences of home led to other problems, too. I had just finished doing one of my numerous swimming sequences and had to rush to get ready for the next scene. My hair was supposed to be dry and lovely, of course, instead of stringy and soaking wet. To wash it properly back in the tent shower would have taken me an hour and a half, round trip, so our hairdresser came up with a purportedly bright idea. Telling me to bend over, she poured liquid dry cleaner over my head. But some of it went into my eyes. The pain was so intense I panicked, screaming and running around blindly. Finally Ray seized me, slapped my face to stop my hysterics, and then dunked me under the waterfall to dilute the fluid. I was a mess, so they shot around me until I pulled myself together.

Ten days after we started shooting, Perry Bodkin—a musician I had met at the studio—came staggering onto the set, lugging his guitar. Practically exhausted after the long hike, Perry told me that the studio had taken another look at my first test and realized that I was a singer. (How flattering!) But since the *Jungle Princess* script didn't include a song, they commissioned Frederick Hollander and Leo Robin to write me one—which they did in a half hour. Perry had been sent out to teach it to me.

We shot the scene a half hour later. Off camera, Perry kept hitting one note on his guitar for every bar of music to keep me on key. Later, back at Paramount, they dubbed in the orchestra. That song was "Moonlight and Shadows," which went on to become Number One on the "Hit Parade" radio show, and is now regarded as a standard. I still use that 40-year-old song in my nightclub act.

I was still self-conscious about my feet, which I felt were very unattractive. To humor me, the studio had them cast in plaster of Paris and constructed a pair of pretty rubber feet for me to wear. I first tried them out in a scene in which Ray was shaving at the top of the waterfall. Since Ulah is very inquisitive, I was to climb up to see what was going on. It was a very hot day, as Valley days tend to be. As I made my climb, I was perspiring so much that one rubber foot slipped off, and I tumbled back down. That was the end of that! I was doing too many potentially dangerous action scenes to mess with rubber feet, so I learned to live with my "ugly" ones.

We sometimes worked a very hard sixteen to eighteen hour day, six days a week. (Of course, that was B.U.—Before Unions.) Each Saturday night, the cast and crew would drive back into town to spend the "weekend"—just Sunday—at home. First, though, we would stop by the studio to view the rushes. (Later on the director and the film editor would put the finishing film together. I entered the projection room for the first time with great glee, looking forward to seeing all the footage shot during the week before—but I hated everything I saw, and I left wanting to die! Mother consoled me as usual, but I never overcame that dislike of seeing myself in rushes. The same thing goes for listening to my own recordings; I guess I'm my own most severe critic.

Finally we finished location shooting and returned to the studio to wrap up the picture. Since I was still a third-floor actress, I didn't have permission to park on the lot and had to leave my Ford at the gas station a block away. After working very late one night, I walked to the station to find my car had been stolen! I had to make out a report at the Hollywood police station. Three days later they found it, all smashed up. Since repairing it would take quite some time, the studio sent a car each morning to pick me up. At long last I was sitting in the back seat of a limousine, driving down Gower and right onto the studio lot!

On one of my few days off I had to do a picture layout for a fan magazine. The publicity man assigned to me showed up at our La Belle Tour apartment with a photographer, an armful of tropical fruits, and a small monkey. So far I had worked with a tiger and a leopard, and had learned that unless monkeys like you immediately, they can be far more dangerous than any animal. And this was my first meeting with the little darling!

The publicity man told Mother to set up the fruit on our breakfast table so that the photographer could snap me in a sarong having breakfast with the monkey—as if this was an everyday occurrence! Then he excused himself to go to his car "to get something he had forgotten."

Ten minutes later there was a knock at the door. Mother opened it, assuming it was the publicity man back again. Instead if was a policeman! An unidentified phone caller had complained that there was a half-naked woman and a monkey running around the halls of the La Belle Tour!

This was my first experience with an overimaginative publicist. *He* was the unidentified caller! Leaving our apartment, he had gone to the nearest phone and called not only the police, but every newspaper in town. The incident was reported over all the wire services and made a big splash in all the papers. I was so shocked and embarrassed that I felt I couldn't face a soul at the studio the next day. But everyone at Paramount thought it was a real hoot and congratulated me on all the coverage I received.

Well, *almost* everyone! The following Sunday Mother and I went to church as usual. The clergyman must have seen the story and the pictures of me in my sarong that Paramount was releasing. When he spotted me sitting in his congregation, he dropped his regular sermon and started to attack "nudity" in films and half-naked women cavorting with animals." I was so humiliated that I never returned to that particular church again. I often wonder what that minister would say about today's movies, which often make my sarong look like long johns!

Still a dedicated movie fan, I used to ogle the big stars who worked around the studio. My most frequented spot was near the first-floor dressing rooms where I could glimpse my favorite actress, Carole Lombard. She must have heard I was the "new girl" on the lot, so one day she smiled and said hello. The next time I saw her, she stopped to chat for awhile. As far as I was concerned, I had now arrived.

A couple of weeks later Paramount informed me that as soon as we finished *The Jungle Princess,* I would be going directly into a new film called *Swing High, Swing Low.* The stars of the film were to be Fred MacMurray—and Carole Lombard!

5. Swinging Into a Hurricane

Not only a great star, Carole was a beautiful woman inside and out and a great humanitarian. She did more for people in need than anyone I ever met in Hollywood—and she did it quietly. From the lowest to the highest paid, everybody at Paramount loved her, and I was absolutely thrilled to be in the same picture. Since I was still working on *The Jungle Princess*, Mr. Thiele had to reschedule my scenes so I could do wardrobe, hair, and makeup tests for *Swing High, Swing Low*. It was very hard work, but I thrived on it.

Finally we wrapped up the last of *Princess.* The very next day I started *Swing High,* which was the second film version of the Broadway hit, *Burlesque.* (*The Dance of Life* with Nancy Carroll was the first. Several years later it was filmed yet again as

With Gilbert Roland and Anthony Quinn (top) in Last Train From Madrid

When My Baby Smiles at Me with Betty Grable, Dan Dailey, and Jack Oakie; Dailey was nominated for an Oscar for best actor.) Gary Cooper and Irene Dunne had originally had been set to do *Swing High*. It was common practice for stars to be announced for films far in advance, but when shooting actually started, it was often with a whole new cast. (Paramount once announced that I would co-star with Ida Lupino and George Raft in *Argentine Love*. It sounded like fun, but I never even saw a script.)

Carole and Fred had worked so successfully in *Hands Across the Table* that Paramount wanted this to be a repeat hit; therefore we had the best of everything, including the great director, Mitch Leisen, whom Carole called "Popsie." On my first day, I was nervous at having to record a song with Carole on the music sound stage, but she immediately made me feel at ease. Within minutes, I felt like I was working with a good friend instead of a big star. The next day we did a scene in a nightclub involving about 150 extras. I was standing in the middle of that crowd, waiting for my cue, when Carole took Popsie aside. She told him that my makeup was not "natural" enough and asked that Wally Westmore, one of the top makeup men on the lot, be brought in to fix me up. Carole had a wonderful way of asking for something, and Wally worked on me until Carole thought I looked better.

Again I became nervous during the first close scene I had to do with Carole, but she deliberately kept "blowing her lines" until I settled down. (I never forgot that, and I in turn tried to help any newcomer who worked on my films.) Once in a while she would invite me to her dressing room to indulge in girl talk, and one day I admitted I would love a dressing room like hers, so elegant and roomy when compared to mine. Carole left Paramount shortly after that; the studio brought me down from the third floor and gave me her dressing room, which I kept until I left the studio myself.

In the middle of shooting *Swing High,* I was called back to do retakes on *The Jungle Princess.* The studio already had set up my third film, *High, Wide and Handsome* with Randolph Scott and Irene Dunne. Whenever I had a breather, they arranged for more interviews and picture layouts for fan magazines.

Working on *High, Wide and Handsome* wasn't as pleasant as my first two films, in several ways. First, Mother took ill and had to have a hysterectomy—back then, a more serious operation than it is today. We were both upset about it, but she came through with no complications. Then it so happened that one of the stars of the film had her day off when the cameraman had to photograph me in an extremely tight close-up. That's the shot when an actor's whole face fills the silver screen, and one that most of us actors like the best. But not every actress is a Carole Lombard. Petty jealousy is a gremlin in some actors' lives, and when this particular star saw the rushes, she was furious. From what I heard, she had the cameraman fired.

But everything became a little brighter when I got to know Randolph Scott, one of the finest men in Hollywood. Gossip columnists kept trying to build up a romance between us, but we were really just good friends. He escorted me to several Hollywood functions—with Herbie's permission, I might add. (Critics never gave him raves, but he did many films and saved his money. Now a retired millionaire, he's still as handsome as he was in 1937, totally charming and loads of fun.)

Every Sunday I used to go out to a beach house in Santa Monica that Randy shared with Cary Grant, right next door to another friend of mine, Townsend ("T") Netcher, whose family owned the Boston Store in Chicago. I used to tease him about owing me money: Back when I worked for Marshall Fields, I once went out to the Boston Store on my lunch hour to demonstrate a rowing machine, for which I was to get paid $45 for the week. But the man promoting the machine up and left at the end of the week, without paying me a cent, and try as I might, I could never cajole "T" into paying it either.

I vividly recall one Sunday dinner at the beach house with eight other guests. After the main course had been served, I remarked how tasty the chicken had been. Cary looked at me and said, "Dottie, that wasn't chicken, it was rabbit." When I imagined the darling little rabbits that had become our supper, I had all I could do to keep from excusing myself from the table.

My next film was *The Last Train from Madrid*, touted as the first picture to deal with the Spanish Civil War. As with today's "disaster" epics, *Last Train* featured several "names," all thrown together in tragedy and turmoil: Lew Ayres, Gilbert Roland, Karen Morley, Lee Bowman, Robert Cummings, Helen Mack, and another newcomer—Anthony Quinn. He and I had a few scenes together. I didn't think Tony was handsome, but I couldn't dispute his magnetism and talent. (I was to bump into him in several other films later on.) During filming, the makeup men and hairdressers went on strike, and we actors were informed that we'd have to fend for ourselves. I thought I could handle my own makeup, but I was never good at doing my own hair. We finished the picture on schedule, but after doing it all myself, I had new respect for those artists who never appear on camera and whose work comes off with cold cream at the end of the day.

I was then rushed into *Thrill of a Lifetime* starring Judy Canova, Ben Blue, Johnny Downs, Leif Erikson, Larry Crabbe, and my old buddies, The Yacht Club Boys. We had a brief but fun reunion. Paramount put me in this picture simply to keep me on screen so they could continue their publicity buildup. Rather than take a major role, I played myself in a cameo spot and sang only the title song. But working on this film I began my lifelong friendship with one of the sweetest women in the world. Betty Grable had played a couple of featured roles and still hadn't reached her peak. But I knew that with the proper exploitation by a big studio, she could become a top star. She was another of those blessed people whom everyone loved, and her much-too-early passing left a terrible void in many lives. But back in 1937 Betty and I were just a blonde and a brunette who were chosen by Wally Westmore who needed a blonde and a brunette so he could test some new makeup for something called television. They put a very vivid blue on me; Betty looked very Irish in a bright Kelly green. It was fortunate that they perfected the television cameras only later, because even in black and white we really looked like two ladies from outer space.

Not long after, the front office at Paramount called me in; Sam Goldwyn had seen *The Jungle Princess* and wanted to meet with me and the great John Ford, who had already directed *Arrowsmith, The Informer, Mary of Scotland*, and *Wee Willie Winkle*, just to mention a few of his pictures. By the way the front office was acting, I could tell this would be an important meeting. I had heard of Sam Goldwyn, of course, but still being rather new in town, I didn't have the faintest idea who Ford was.

I was driven over to Goldwyn's office and introduced to the two gentlemen. Mr. Ford did most of the talking, asking me some of the silliest questions I'd ever heard. In reality, it was my first taste of his dry sense of humor. "Dorothy," he asked me, "how long will it take you to get a tan?" I told him that if I spent ten days on the beach, I would get a great tan. Then he asked, "Dorothy, do you like *my* suntan?"

He was as white as a sheet, but being raised to be polite, I replied, "Yes, Mr. Ford. Where did you get it?"

"In Honolulu," he said without cracking a smile, "they have beautiful sunlamps in the bars there." (Later he told me that he had the kind of skin that couldn't take much sun, and that even on his gorgeous yacht the *Araner*, he had to keep himself covered up.)

I left Mr. Goldwyn's office still not sure just why I had been invited there. But, Paramount informed me that I was being loaned to Sam Goldwyn for his new production, *The Hurricane*, which Ford was directing. It seems that they had already shot some background footage with doubles on some faraway island in the Pacific, and were now shooting the rest of the film at Goldwyn Studios. Even though another actress had already begun work as Marama, Goldwyn screened *The Jungle Princess* and decided that I was perfect for the part. He had to pay off the other girl and, in order to get me from Paramount, loan them Joel McCrea for *Union Pacific.*

It was very flattering to hear that they wanted me badly enough to trade me for McCrea, an extremely popular and handsome actor whom Goldwyn had under exclusive contract. Up to this point, I only *thought* I'd been working hard. This picture would be great for my career, but hard on my physical being!

The Hurricane had an incredible cast: Raymond Massey, a terrible "heavy" on screen and a charming pussycat off; C. Aubrey Smith with his delightful British sense of humor and insistence that we have a "tea break" every day; the warm, wonderful, roguish Thomas Mitchell; expert-at-evil John Carradine; the fine character actor Jerome Cowan; and the talented star with the most incredible facial features—Mary Astor.

The lead role of Terang went to a very handsome young man who had made a few films as Charles Hall Locher (his real name) and a couple as Lloyd Crane. He changed his name the third time for this film, and thus Jon Hall was born. (Coincidentally, his uncle was James Norman Hall, who with Charles Nordhoff had written the original book *The Hurricane*, as well as *Mutiny on the Bounty*.)

John Ford, who loved the South Sea islands, was determined to make this film as authentic as possible. While filming the big luau wedding scene, he had truckloads of real gardenias, ginger, and every conceivable Hawaiian flower delivered to the set each morning. All of the 200 or more extras wore gardenia leis around their necks, and every woman had flowers in her hair. This scene took weeks to shoot, and the beautiful scent floated through the air for blocks around the Goldywyn Studios.

It was during this, the most pleasant part of the filming, that I first became an adopted Hawaiian. There were a lot of native Hawaiians working on the film, and I soon discovered their happy-go-lucky attitude was contagious. But these happy days were merely the lull before the "storm." Soon the technical geniuses at Goldwyn went to work: the rains fell, the wind blew, and the actual shooting of the hurricane began.

To make the great winds, the special effects department rigged up half a dozen airplane engines with huge propellers. Then to make the wind whistle, they mixed a concoction of dried leaves and yellow sulphur, which photograghed like dust, and flung it in front of the propellers. Each night after work, I was covered from head to foot with small nicks from the gale-swept leaves, and the sulphur didn't have the greatest effect on my eyes and throat. However, thanks to my youth and the expertise of the makeup artist, I always looked fresh the next morning. Cinematographer Bert Glennon did a terrific job of photographing the whole shebang.

First the long shots of the hurricane were filmed on a huge set consisting of grass houses, stores, and a church. The next set, on which we spent a least four months, was smaller than the first, but there was more of everything—more wind machines more dried leaves, more sulphur. And on either side of the set were two huge tanks holding about 2,000 gallons of water each. When the wind machines were started, the water was released to create truly enormous waves. Smack in the middle of the set was a huge tree, specially constructed by the special effects crew so that it would collapse, limb by limb, at the proper time.

This set was so tricky for both cast and crew that a doctor and a nurse were present at all times in case of emergency. Since Jon's dressing room was closest to the set, the doctor asked if he could set up his instruments inside. Jon was really a nice guy, but since our dressing rooms were the collapsible type, only six feet by six, I can't blame him for saying no. Still, when I heard him refuse, the Girl Scout in me came out and I offered the doctor my dressing room. After all, what did I need it for? Except for a white Tahitian wedding dress in one scene, all I ever wore was my sarong, and a lot of leaves and sulphur.

One day a heavy light fell from a catwalk above the set and struck one of the crew. Since my car was parked nearby, the doctor and I drove the injured man to the hospital. Fortunately, it wasn't too serious, but because Jon had refused the doctor his dressing room, the rest of the crew decided to pay him back.

In the big scene involving that huge tree, the script called for Jon to lash Mary Astor, our daughter Tita (Kuulei De Cleag), and me to the trunk. When the hurricane hit us, the branches were intended to break away on cue, letting us float "out to sea," away from all danger. Jon had already tied up Kuulei and me, and was getting ready to tie the last knot on Mary, when the crew "accidentally" let the water out a mite too early. The tidal wave nearly swept Jon into the wall of the set. He wasn't really hurt, just scared silly. We started the scene over again, and this time it went beautifully—the crew had made their point.

Sam Goldwyn was famous for his "Goldwynisms,"

twisting around the English language, and creating strange lapses of logic. Once he strode over to me on the set and said, "Dorothy, your hair looks like a cheap wig! Why do you wear it?" I tried to hide my indignation. My hair was my very own, and each night I spent hours washing and braiding it so that the next morning it would look as natural as any island girl's. I was greatly relieved when "Pappy" Ford came over and gruffly told Sam that my hair was just right and it was not going to be cut or "coiffed." As usual, when Pappy's wild Irish came up, Sam just meekly walked away, muttering to himself.

The next time Sam Goldwyn came on the set, he brought along two songwriters, Frank Loesser and Alfred Newman, to play "The Moon of Manakoora," which they had written for the movie. (Manakoora, of course, was the name of the island where we all lived.) Since my part wasn't really all that big, I was very pleased that they were adding a song for me. Then Sam told me that they were going to road-show the picture—that is, screen it only once a night, just like a stage play. They planned to play my song only during the intermission. To this day, film buffs will swear that I sang "The Moon of Manakoora" in *The Hurricane*, but I did not sing the song *in* the film.

Just before we finished shooting, I had my own turn with the doctor. Jon, Kuulei, and I were in a boat making our escape—actually in a studio tank with a huge screen behind us on which was projected an ocean view. "When the wind machine starts," Pappy told Jon, "hold up your arm so Dorothy doesn't get hit in the face with the boom." No sooner did the wind machines go on than poor, dear Jon forgot. Fragile little me got hit right in the kisser and had a beautiful shiner for a couple of days during which they had to shoot around me.

In my opinion, the finished product was a masterpiece of movie technology. Proof of the pudding was that *The Hurricane* won two Oscars in 1937—for Sound Recording and for Special Effects. (Thomas Mitchell was nominated for Best Supporting Actor but lost to Joseph Schildkraut in *The Life of Emile Zola*; and Alfred Newman's magnificent score lost to Charles Previn's music for *One Hundred Men and a Girl*, a Deanna Durbin-Leopold

Stokowski film.) Looking at the film today, I'm still amazed at how well it holds up. The storm sequence need not take a back seat to any of the modern "disaster" films.

A couple of months before his death, Pappy called me to tell me that he had seen *The Hurricane* on Channel 5, where it pops up at least every other month. "Toujie," he said, using his nickname for me (shortened from the expression, *toujours l'amour*), "you did a beautiful job in *The Hurricane*. I saw it on television this afternoon."

I thanked him, of course, but asked why it had taken him over 30 years to say so!

"I never did see that darned film," he replied. "I was feuding with Sam Goldwyn so much over the cutting of the film that I never saw the finished print." I knew that the two of them had battled a bit during the course of the filming, but had no idea that the rift had been that deep. It was the on-screen storm that had commanded most of my attention.

While we were shooting the tree sequence, I had begun to have a pain in my right side. Thinking it was only exhaustion and hard work, I finished the picture and went on to NBC to rehearse my songs for the "Chase and Sanborn Show," which I had been broadcasting all during the filming.

We rehearsed the radio show every Saturday and usually had one hour off for dinner. Even during my breaks I had to do some business, and now I was asked to dine with a very big motion picture distributor and theater owner from Malaya named Joe Fisher—better known as "Singapore Joe"—who had buried a print of *The Jungle Princess* in the forecourt of his newest theater in Singapore. He had arrived in Hollywood with many greetings from the Sultan of Jahore, who had once written to Paramount asking for my hand in marriage, stating that he ran *The Jungle Princess* in his palace at least once a night. Told that I was still very much married to Herbie Kay, the Sultan wrote Herbie, offering a bucket of rubies and diamonds if he would grant me a divorce. (I've always wondered if Herbie ever regretted turning down that offer.)

Singapore Joe and I were discussing the Sultan over dinner at Lucey's, a restaurant near Paramount where all the stars ate, when the pains in my side became worse. I called Dr. William Branch, who immediately ordered me to get to Hollywood's Cedars of Lebanon Hospital. That night he performed an emergency operation and found my appendix nearly about to burst. It was a very close call from possibly fatal peritonitis.

The studio gave my illness so much publicity that my hospital room was crammed with flowers, and the corridors outside crowded with people wanting my autograph. "This girl is sick," thundered Dr. Branch, "She is not a monkey in a cage!" and shooed all the fans away. When I heard him, I started to laugh and nearly broke all the stitches in my incision (which, incidentally, was almost seven inches long because my appendix had actually shifted from one position to another). I figured that I would have a nice leisurely hospital stay, but was told to report back to Paramount as soon as I could for a new picture. So much for rest and recuperation!

6. On Location

I now found myself making films at Paramount six days a week, rehearsing for Chase and Sanborn on Saturday nights and Sunday afternoon, and then broadcasting live that evening. A heck of a schedule, but I was having such a good time that I didn't mind. Funny thing about the Chase and Sanborn people: When I was singing with Rudy Vallee's band in New York, Rudy had taken me to see John Reber, the head of the J. Walter Thompson Advertising Agency; he was totally unimpressed and turned me down. In May 1937, Mr. Reber and Danny Danker, the head of JWT's West Coast offices, came on the set to talk to me about doing a radio show for "a coffee company," and for very good money. Mr. Reber had obviously changed his mind. We all went around the corner to Dema Harshbarger's NBC office to set the deal.

To warm myself in that cold NBC studio, I bought my first mink coat

I sang one or two songs each week and appeared in some of the skits, but the best part was the company I would be keeping: Edgar Bergen, W. C. Fields, Nelson Eddy, and Don Ameche were the regulars. W. C. Fields was forever teasing Bergen about his reputed stinginess. One night about twenty of Bergen's friends got together to wish him a happy birthday. Fields ordered spotlights put in front of Edgar's house and had a sandwich board painted with the words "After much delay, Bergen finally came thru with a party." Fields then proceeded to "picket" up and down in front of the house to let everyone know that Bergen was spending some money.

One week our special guest star was Mae West who was to play Eve to Don Ameche's Adam in a takeoff on the Bible story. Mae always had it in her contract that she would write her own lines and, as usual, she had inserted some bawdy West-isms. The minute the censors read the script, blue pencils appeared like magic. Mae innocently agreed to all the changes. Then she went on the air and read her script exactly as she had written it, word for word. Right in the middle of the skit, we were cut off the air. The repercussions were incredible. Church groups were outraged and the mail came pouring in. I can't even remember what she said that was so terrible, but I'm sure it was mild by today's standards.

The show was a big smash, and with my success on radio, Paramount was eager to get started on my next film, *The Big Broadcast of 1938*, the latest in a series. In 1932 the first *Big Broadcast* film—utilizing radio performers Bing Crosby, Kate Smith, the Boswell Sisters, the Mills Brothers, Burns and Allen, and Arthur Tracy (the Street Singer)—had been a huge box office success. Jack Oakie, Ethel Merman, and Burns and Allen did the '36 *Broadcast*; the '37 version starred Jack Benny, Burns and Allen, Bob Burns, Martha Raye, Shirley Ross, Raymond Milland (how formal!), and Benny Goodman and His Orchestra. Since the "Chase and Sanborn Show" was so popular, they put W. C. Fields and me in this one along with Martha Raye, Leif Erikson, Lynne Overman, Ben Blue, Kirsten Flagstad (making her film debut), Grace Bradley (Bill Boyd's wife), and Tito Guizar.

Jack Benny turned it down. Still needing another comedian, they went through their contract players. A young man, fresh from Broadway triumphs in *Roberta; Say When* with Harry Richman; *Ziegfeld Follies* with Fanny Brice, Josephine Baker, and Gertrude Niesen (in which he sang "I Can't Get Started With You" to a showgirl named Eve Arden); and *Red, Hot and Blue* with Ethel Merman and Jimmy Durante, had just been signed to a seven-year contract. He hadn't done a film yet, and still wasn't known to the national audiences. But I knew that if they gave him the proper buildup, Bob Hope was going to be one of the biggest in Hollywood.

It was really great to see Bob again and reminisce about the "good old days" in New York. I had always liked him, and I was surprised to hear that the front office thought Bob was too much like Jack Benny; they might not pick up his next option. I told them if they would *please* take up his option and put him into a few pictures—the *right* ones—they would have another big star who someday would be an institution. (I didn't realize that institution would be a bank).

I got so carried away that I even offered to let them cut my salary in half and give it to Bob. Now that was really brave, because I was earning peanuts by Hollywood standards. A thousand dollars a week wasn't much for someone starring in one picture after another. Naturally, they didn't deduct any money from my salary, but Hope was assigned several films in a row, and we all know where he is today.

Mitch Leisen, that fabulous director from *Swing High, Swing Low,* was now a good friend of mine, but he was quite a taskmaster. We had a scene to do on the deck of the ocean liner. Mitch told me to walk to the rail of the ship, take off my scarf, twist it around my right wrist, then turn and say my lines. "Popsie," I asked, using Carole Lombard's nickname for him, "do I have to do all of those things at one time?" He told me that I definitely had to do them all—and to get going. (Many years later I acknowledged his presence in the audience at one of my performances in *Hello, Dolly*. When you play Dolly Levi, you have to do a great many things at one time, so I said to him, "See, Popsie? I can do much more than four things at one time now, and I owe it all to you!" He laughed, but it was true—he taught me a lot about acting.)

Leo Robin and Ralph Rainger wrote a lovely song, "You Took the Words Right Out of My Heart" for me to sing to Leif Erikson. The setting was perfect: a moonlit night on a ship. Leif is a tall guy, and since his feet weren't in the shot, he kicked off his shoes to get more comfortable. My feet weren't in the shot, either so, copycat that I am, I pulled off my tight shoes too. So the sighing in that scene wasn't really all passion; some of it was just comfort.

I wouldn't say that the storyline of *Big Broadcast of 1938* was hard to follow, but Hope once cracked that *Variety* was offering a $10,000 reward to anyone who could tell him the plot of the film after seeing it. But it did bring Mr. Hope stardom and a theme song. Mitch valued my intuition, so he asked me to meet him in the music department to hear some of the songs written for the film. After hearing the whole score, I told him it was very good—and that in one song, "Thanks for the Memory," he had a major hit. He explained that it had been written for Bob Hope and Shirley Ross, but he would fix it if I really liked it. But I argued that would involve some rewriting of the script, and besides, I wanted Bob to sing it. Mitch teased me for years about that: "Toujie, you really goofed when you turned that song down." I'm glad, because I could never have done as much for that tune as Bob did. The Academy agreed and awarded "Thanks for the Memory" the Oscar for Best Song of 1938.

Seeing the huge box office grosses from Sam Goldwyn's *The Hurricane*, Paramount decided it was time for me to swing back into the jungle in a reasonable facsimile of *The Jungle Princess*, called *Her Jungle Love*. Again Ray Milland crashed on a tropical island and found love with a young native girl. Lynne Overman, a very funny character, was added for comic relief; J. Carrol Naish played the native chief.

To authenticate the "jungle," we went on location to an Indian reservation near Palm Springs. Since there were many tourists in the area, we posted a "Completely Closed Set" sign, meaning that no visitors were allowed without special permission, and absolutely no cameras at any time. A very nice young girl who worked at our hotel kept after me to let her visit the set, so one day I invited her out—but warned her in advance about the no-camera rule and, even more important, about Jiggs, the chimp. Chimpanzees can be a lot of fun, but only if they know you.

I was shooting a scene at the time so I didn't see her arrive on the set—but I soon heard her. She had immediately begun snapping photos, and then went over to make friends with Jiggs. He didn't like her advances, so he sank his teeth in her behind, right through her western jeans. We got the doctor for her, and since her wound wasn't too serious, all was forgotten, or so we thought. One Sunday night after the "Chase and Sanborn Show" I was handed a subpoena in the NBC parking lot. The girl was suing Paramount, a long list of John and Jane Does, and me! She lost the case, naturally, because there was ample proof that she had been forewarned.

Despite all those wild stories that one hears, no liquor was allowed on a movie set until the last day, when we usually had a wrap party. But since we were on an Indian reservation, "firewater" was outlawed. I had a terrible cold and a temperature of 102 degrees, but just couldn't see taking time off, because I was needed in almost every scene. My absence would only run the budget sky-high.

I was just finishing one of those swimming scenes. On screen, the water looked like a tropical lagoon, but it was actually ice cold. I wasn't a pretty sight: my hair was soaking wet, I looked like a drowned rat, and one of the crew was standing by with a warm blanket to throw around me. Then I started sneezing my head off. Another crew member rushed to his prop box and poured me a stiff whiskey to ward off pneumonia. Just as I took a sip, one of our friendly visitors whipped out a camera and took a picture of me.

A couple of days later, as I was walking down the main street in Palm Springs, there it was! A giant blow-up of me getting out of the pool dripping wet and belting down a drink. They were selling 8-by-10 copies for five dollars! For a little more, you could own an 11-by-14. I called Paramount immediately. They must have had a little talk with the owners of that shop, because a few days later the photographs disappeared from the window.

When we had "lost the light" (when the sun went

behind a mountain) and had to stop shooting, we would all pile into the studio cars and return to our respective hotels, clean off our makeup, and go out for an early dinner, after which we'd usually go to the local bowling alley, make up our own teams, and bowl until 9:30 or 10:00 P.M.. One night Adolph Zukor, the head of the studio, came to visit us. Although a giant in the motion picture industry, he stood only about five foot, three. It was a particularly hot night, and naturally the air conditioning wasn't working, so most of the fellows had taken their coats off. Mr. Zukor did the same. We had a lot of laughs and soon Mr. Zukor got up to leave and reached for the nearest coat. When he put it on, the sleeves hung far below his hands; by mistake, he had picked up the jacket of six-foot-two Ray Milland! We all howled, Mr. Zukor the loudest.

Although I had been in films only two years, Paramount informed me my fan mail had reached the proportions of Gary Cooper's, Claudette Colbert's, and Carole Lombard's. A newspaper poll placed me in a list of the fifteen Greatest Discoveries of that year:

1. Don Ameche
2. Charlie McCarthy
3. Wayne Morris
4. Andrea Leeds
5. Phyllis Kennedy
6. Annabella
7. Me
8. Kenny Baker
9. Judy Garland
10. Deanna Durbin
11. George Murphy
12. Alan Curtis
13. Rose Stradner
14. Allyn Joslyn
15. Fernand Franet

In the paper appeared a funny release that said Herbie Kay was elected Prez of the Society for the Protection of Bandleaders with Hollywood Wives. The roster included Ozzie Nelson (wife: Harriet Hilliard), Roger Pryor (wife: Ann Sothern), Johnny Green (wife: Betty Furness), and Harmon Nelson (wife: Bette Davis). The rules were simple: the wives had to make at least one weekly phone call to their "one-nighting" husbands—with reverse charging privileges—and the husbands had to dedicate one or more songs annually to their wives. Herbie and I both laughed at the story, but we knew that the humor arose from the strain in this type of marriage.

As it turned out, Ozzie and Harriet were the only ones who were able to survive it. We were beginning to have problems, but we were both determined to make it work. I had to be seen around town, so I began to "date" friends like Randy Scott, but always with Herbie's blessing. They were not "romantic" dates, merely business.

Six days a week I was toiling on the film and commuting to Hollywood each Saturday night to rehearse the "Chase and Sanborn Show." As soon as I could get away, I'd rush to the hotel, take a quick shower and wash my hair, then wrap my head in a big bath towel and jump into one of the studio limousines. In those days before freeways, it took a couple of hours to drive in from Palm Springs, so I would sit in the back seat with my hairdresser brushing my hair dry. She would then braid it and wrap the braids around my head. As we neared Hollywood, I would put on my regular street makeup and emerge from the limo in the NBC parking lot "all done up."

After rehearsal with the cast and orchestra, I sometimes stayed over to go through the songs again with Merle Alderman, the show pianist. Merle was going with Ruth Etting, who was legally separated from Marty Snyder, best known as "The Gimp." Her matrimonial battles with Snyder were well known. She seemed very happy to come to the rehearsals, sit in the back row, and wait for Merle. This triangle was filmed by MGM in 1955 as *Love Me or Leave Me* with Doris Day as Ruth, James Cagney as "The Gimp," and Cameron Mitchell as Merle.

One particular night, I had dashed over from Paramount to the rehearsal without stopping to eat. Merle asked me if I would like to go over to Nickodell's, a restaurant next door to NBC where studio people still go for a bite to eat. Later he offered to drive me home, but my car was next door in Paramount's lot. I thanked him, drove home, and went straight to bed.

The next day the papers were filled with the news that Merle had been shot. Driven by jealousy, "The Gimp" had waited for Merle in the NBC parking lot! Fortunately, he hadn't killed him.

Monday morning I left to make a personal appearance at New York's Paramount Theater with Jack Benny. I used to make no bones about hating Jack's cigars. To get back at me, he would get the chewed end really sloppy wet and, when I wasn't looking, try to shove it in my mouth. I never dreamed that he would try that gag in front of the Paramount audience, but he did—and, of course, he got a big laugh.

Mother and I were staying in a suite on the eighteenth floor of the Sherry Netherland Hotel overlooking Central Park. Early one morning the doorbell rang. I thought it was room service with our breakfast, but when I opened the door, a man I had never seen before told me he was a friend of George Raft's, that George had sent him there to see if I needed any help in the "Gimp" affair. The hotel had been under strict orders not to disclose my room number, so I asked how he found me. Mysteriously, he replied, "I got ways." The elevator operators always asked people where they were going, but he told me that he had fooled them by walking up to the eighteenth floor. I wasn't quite sure what he was talking about, but I thanked him graciously and told him I would be sure to get in touch if I needed any help—and I got him to leave. (Whether George really sent him I'll never know, because I never remembered to ask.)

When our breakfast finally arrived, I picked up the newspaper, and suddenly it became clear why I'd had my "visitor." "Dorothy Lamour Named By Merle Alderman As Secret Sweetheart," the headlines read, "Not Ruth Etting." Soon the phone began to ring like crazy. The only call I took was from Paramount advising me to talk to no one. I was to pack my bags. If anyone asked where I was going, it was back to Hollywood for retakes on *Her Jungle Love.*

Paramount was taking every precaution to keep me from being served with a summons to appear in court when Snyder was tried. I was sneaked out the back door, and whisked off to the airport. Arriving in Los Angeles, the plane stopped in midfield, where a car stood waiting to take me directly to the studio. Actually I *wanted* to testify under oath to clear my name, but the studio wouldn't hear of it. They must have used their clout, because everything soon simmered down. Merle eventually married Ruth, they went to live in Florida, and I never got my day in court.

Quite a few years later, after I was married to Bill Howard, I was doing a Bob Hope radio show when a page came to my dressing room to say a gentleman named Merle Alderman wanted to see me. I almost went into shock—and then began to get angry. I hadn't seen or heard from Merle since that trial, and he had never even given me any explanation. He came in, meek as a lamb, and tried to apologize for dragging me into that mess. At that point, my temper almost got the best of me, but I kept my ladylike demeanor and allowed him to explain. It was difficult, but he seemed so sincere. Finally I looked at Merle and we both laughed. I told him to forget it; it was all water under the bridge.

Meanwhile, Paramount informed me that my next three pictures would be set in Mexico, London, and Alaska. At last, I began to look forward to travel, all expenses paid.

7. "Red Lips, White Arms, Black Pearls"

But in those days, to make a film set in Mexico, London, or Alaska, you didn't go to those locales, you simply sauntered over to the back lot at Paramount. When I did *St. Louis Blues* later in 1938, I didn't even get to go to St. Louis. (I was glad I *didn't* have to go on location for *Journey to Mars*. I was slated to do it with Randolph Scott, but the studio never got around to it.)

Studios loved to create screen teams because audiences would flock to see them. Ray Milland and I had filmed *The Jungle Princes* and *Her Jungle Love* with good results, and Martha Raye and Bob Burns had audiences laughing with *Rhythm on the Range* and *Waikiki Wedding*. So Paramount put all four of us in *Ensenada*. (Later, when the studio decided not to take me out of the jungle entirely, the title was changed to *Tropic Holiday*.)

With Jack Benny in Man About Town

While working on this film, Maggie Raye and I became pretty good friends. She has always been a bundle of energy, and it took a lot to keep up with her. One night after work, she invited me up for dinner to her beautiful white house at the top of Laurel Canyon and Mulholland Drive. At that time she was engaged to David Rose (who later married Judy Garland). After dinner Maggie suggested we all go out to Rudy Vallee's nightclub.

We both had to work the next day, and I was exhausted, but Maggie's energy was so infectious that I said yes. Well, before I knew it, it was three o'clock in the morning, and Maggie still wanted to sing and dance. Finally I sneaked out the back door and had her chauffeur drive me home. The next morning I was dragging around the set, but she was as bright and chipper as ever.

For a bullfight sequence, director Teddy Reed needed a bull with enough courage to tackle Maggie; but to make sure the bull wouldn't hurt her, the "prop" man took off for Mexico to find the right toro—or rather, toros. They figured they'd need more than one because after a certain amount of takes any single bull would get savvy and might be likely to cause trouble, even without an agent representing him. So they brought back *six* bulls to fight Martha Raye.

Edith Head, who was again making my clothes, had been raised on an Indian reservation in Southern Mexico, so she knew the proper motif—coarse linens, sheer voiles and batistes, square necklines, and full skirts with unpressed pleating. Augustin Lara, known as the Irving Berlin of Latin America, wrote six exciting numbers for the film. Dance director LeRoy Prinz sent for José Fernandez, one of the foremost exponents of Latin dance, and together they created some native dances with an added modern flavor—all without leaving Hollywood.

Next stop, Alaska! This time we did leave the studio for Big Bear, a resort area near San Bernardino with all the snow we could ask for. Cary Grant, Randolph Scott, and Carole Lombard had originally been set for this film, *Spawn of the North*, but the roles were taken over by Henry Fonda, George Raft, and me. I was thrilled at the chance to work with Henry Hathaway, one of Hollywood's most brilliant directors, and with John Barrymore, who was also cast in the film.

Long before it was fashionable, Hathaway came up with the idea of putting me in a sweater without a bra, and his mostly profile shots of me, caused a small rage with the press. A few months later Lana Turner did the same thing in *They Won't Forget*, caused a mammoth storm, and became a star. "Well, kid," Henry always said to me, "we did it first!"

Our location was only a few miles from Lake Arrowhead, where my father's plane had crashed. In a way I don't know how to describe, I felt very close to my father, as if he were there watching over me. Big Bear may not have been Alaska, but it certainly was cold. I had to do a scene in which Raft pulled me into the water. So that I wouldn't catch pneumonia, I had to wear a specially constructed rubber suit under my regular clothes. Later, the script called for me to become so distraught that I break a shot glass in my hand. Again I discovered the special effects department's ingenuity—they made the shot glass out of thin rock candy.

John Barrymore was one of the most charming of men, but he loved to shock people. One day the set was visited by a group of schoolteachers. John went over and introduced himself in his most suave manner. He even kissed the hands of some of the ladies, who tittered nervously. And once he had them in the palm of his hand, he regaled them with one of the most off-color stories I'd ever heard. But he'd so totally flustered them all that they could only continue tittering.

One of my most literally pungent memories of *Spawn of the North* is of the scene I had to do with a seal. Trained seals are as cute as children; they applaud, roll over, and do many tricks. But they have an odor all their own, and it isn't Chanel. To get rid of it, I'd sometimes have to scrub myself raw. And then to add to the olfactory overkill, Henry Hathaway brought up his dog for a visit, and the hound promptly got into a furious fight with a skunk!

After *Spawn* I went into *St. Louis Blues*, my first picture with Lloyd Nolan (in later years we did *Johnny Apollo* and *Wild*

Harvest). *Blues* wasn't one of the best films ever, but it was a pleasure to work with a fine actor like Lloyd. I played a Broadway musical comedy star who, tired of playing sarong roles, takes off to the wilds of the U.S.A. I meet a showboat skipper (Lloyd) who offers me a role in his new revue. As we did each scene, director Raoul Walsh used to sit right under the camera and mouth the lines to all the parts. Every once in a while he'd get carried away and you could actually hear him on the rushes.

After the film was finished, Lloyd told me, he went on a junket for *Union Pacific*, starring Joel McCrea and Barbara Stanwyck. He went to a town in Nebraska called Aksarben (Nebraska spelled backwards), where they claimed to serve 10,000 meals a day—and they did. While George Raft was performing one of his dance specialties, Lloyd was sitting next to Mrs. J. C. Penney who leaned over to him and said, "Who is that young man?"

He was astounded, because George was one of the most popular actors of the period. She apologized, saying she didn't go to films very often. "As a matter of fact," she went on, "my kids dragged me to one called *St. Louis Blues* that I thought was just terrible." He told her that he agreed with her: "I should know, I played the leading man!"

I was scheduled for a break between films, but when my pal Betty Grable had an emergency appendectomy, I had to be rushed in to take her place in *Man About Town*. (Later on, Betty rejoined the company for a specialty number.) This film also featured Jack Benny, Edward Arnold, Binnie Barnes, Eddie "Rochester" Anderson, and Monty Woolley; I got to sing a duet with Phil Harris called "That Sentimental Sandwich."

Just a few months before his death Jack Benny told me: "I made twenty-two pictures that nobody remembers. They always think I just made that one lousy one, *The Horn Blows at Midnight* because I joke about it so much. Out of the twenty-two, I think that four were pretty good. *To Be or Not to Be, George Washington Slept Here, Man About Town,* and *Buck Benny Rides Again* are all considered good pictures. One with Fred Allen called *It's in the Bag* made a lot of money simply because of our celebrated radio "feud," but it really wasn't that good, and I enjoyed doing *Charley's Aunt*. But I must say, truthfully, *Man About Town* was one of the most fun pictures that I ever made. When you can go through an entire film without any problems, then you've already got something going for you. And when you work with Grable, Harris, Lamour, Barnes, Arnold and Woolley, you really can't miss."

Jack also reminded me of one of my hangups during the filming: "Dottie, you were always concerned that your behind was too big. You used to say to me, 'Jack, when we walk into the shot, please walk directly behind me so they can't see my rear.' You actually had a lovely shape, but I humored you!"

I had given out an interview of my own, saying that I was planning to retire from films for a year so that I could have a baby. The story went around the world. Paramount loved the publicity, but weren't too happy about losing the money my pictures were making. Actually I'd made that statement in a last ditch effort to save my marriage; I thought a child might bring us back together.

Herbie was in Hollywood, playing at the famous Cocoanut Grove in the Ambassador Hotel. So each night I would get all dressed up, and run into town to see him. We both really wanted to ease the strain on our long-distance marriage, but we seemed to be becoming more friends than lovers.

As I look back on it now, I realize that Herbie was a sweet, wonderful man, but we were never really close, so in April 1939 we decided to call a halt to our "long-distance" marriage. It was mutually agreed that I would sue for divorce in California, which in those days required a year before the final decree. That was all right with me, since I had no romantic entanglements and was in no hurry to end our marriage. You can imagine my surprise when a couple of days later a Paramount publicist came tearing into my dressing room. The news had just come over the wire that Herbie was suing me for divorce in Chicago, where a divorce took only a short time to become final, and that the grounds were desertion. The press was already converging on the studio for the "real story," and Paramount wanted me to disappear for a few days until the headlines died down.

I couldn't believe the coverage our divorce got. You would have thought the Roosevelts had separated. A very short time after the divorce became final, Herbie married a lady from Texas, whom we both knew. I certainly didn't know that he had already picked out his next wife. But we had decided we could remain good friends, and I'll always be grateful to him for having the faith in me and giving me a start. I took it in stride and wished him well.

Mother also remarried about this time. O. L. Castleberry, an insurance agent she had met back in New Orleans had been seeing her for years. She said that she didn't want to give me another stepfather, but I gave her my blessing. I asked only that they come to live with me, which they did.

I had become used to going out with friends on a friendly basis and found it very strange to be suddenly "free" and available for serious dating. I decided to throw a "coming-out" party at my home and invited every big name in town, including many eligible bachelors like my good friend Cesar Romero. I even invited top Hollywood columnists Hedda Hopper and Louella Parsons. I had always been fair to each of them, and though professional rivals, they even managed to say a cool hello to each other.

The party was a huge success except for a couple of gate crashers, one of them was a well-known actor. He and his date had both downed a few drinks before crashing the party, and they spent most of the evening thereafter at my bar. Among the guests was the great blind pianist Alec Templeton, who graciously consented to play a few numbers for us. As he went to sit down on a small antique piano stool, the two intruders thinking it would be funny, pulled the stool out from under him. I couldn't imagine anyone being so insensitive, and I immediately told them to leave, which they did—indignantly. On the way down my very steep driveway, the "lady" fell, and later tried to sue me for damages. When my lawyer informed their lawyer that I was about to sue *them* for trespassing, the suit was immediately dropped.

I was involved in a different kind of triangle in my next film—*Disputed Passage*, based on the novel by Lloyd C. Douglas. (Douglas had written *The Magnificent Obsession*, which in 1935 had been made into a smash movie with Irene Dunne and Robert

Taylor.) In *Passage*, John Howard played a young medical student who studies with the greatest of all living neurological surgeons, played by Akim Tamiroff. Akim's favorite principle is that most doctors lack sufficient devotion to their work and as a result, commit terrible atrocities on their helpless patients. He tells his students that they must ban everything from their lives—friends, pleasure, love—except pure science.

Howard goes along with that advice and, four years later, is asked to be the great doctor's assistant. Then I come into the picture, as an American raised by Chinese foster parents. And that's where "the strangest triangle ever brought to the screen" begins, as the ads proclaimed it. John was portrayed in the middle, and under his picture was the question, "Must a man shut love out . . . close his heart to all personal emotions . . . when he consecrates his life to science?" Akim was on one side of him, with the words, " 'Give me your brain,' the world's greatest surgeon demanded, 'Forget love . . . forget life itself . . . and I will make your career rich in accomplishment. There is no place in science for emotion.' " On the other side of the ad was me: " 'Give me your heart,' the only woman in the world pleaded, 'leave me and you will blast two lives . . . to gain emptiness! All your skill and learning will be useless if you kill your soul . . . for life without feeling is death!' " Pretty heavy, but you don't need to be Confucius to know that all ended well.

In those days publicists used to love to matchmake the stars, and start new "romances" with each new movie. (Strangely enough, these romances would quickly fizzle as soon as the film was released!) Since I had been married, I had been relatively exempt, but now the rumor mills started to work in high gear. My next leading man was Robert Preston, and the film—originally titled *South of Samoa*—was soon changed to *Typhoon*. The ads didn't miss anything: "Red Lips . . . White Arms . . . Black Pearls! . . . Tidal Wave . . . Forest Fire . . . a Tornado of Tropic Love!" And the gossips thought it was real.

At first Bob and I laughed off the romance rumors, but pretty soon we became genuinely attracted to each other and began to date seriously. He was a wonderful man and we considered marriage several times, but it never seemed to work out. The press had us breaking up and making up for most of the time we were together—and that was true. He wasn't quite *The Music Man* then, but we did make beautiful music together and I have fond memories of our relationship.

Someone else in *Typhoon* also became very attached to me: Coco the chimp. Jealous, he would slap anyone who touched me, even my hairdresser, and his long hands could really leave an impression. We were on location at the isthmus at one end of Catalina to shoot the sequence in which Bob—playing a heavy drinker—finds a case of booze in a sunken ship. He gets loaded and falls asleep. Even in my "primitive" mind, I know that the booze is bad for him, so Coco and I begin to break the remaining bottles.

When Bob got up to stop me, Coco was supposed to jump onto a branch and make a lot of noise. But in the confusion, perhaps thinking that I was being hurt, he missed the branch, and landed, all 50 pounds of him, on my back, and started pounding on me "protectively." They finally got him off, but the pain was so excruciating that I can remember only getting up from the ground, clapping the dust off my palms, then walking away from the scene and collapsing.

They took me back to my dressing room. I insisted that I could return to the set, but when Lloyd Pantages, a friend of mine who had dropped by, saw my obvious pain, he bundled me up and took me back to Hollywood Presbyterian Hospital aboard his yacht. I kept insisting that I had to get back to work, but doctors told me to forget it and proceeded to tape me.

The next day Paramount sent the studio car to bring me to the front office. It seems they had heard from the assistant director (who was not my biggest fan) that I wasn't hurt that badly. After all, I had gone off on a yacht with two men (Lloyd and his friend). When Paramount saw how trussed up I was and noted my obvious discomfort, they became appropriately contrite!

On the lighter side, a Bali-Javanese dancer told the press that "Dorothy Lamour is not wearing a sarong." This controversial news hit all the papers. W. E. Oliver, a writer from the Los Angeles *Herald-Express*, interviewed an expert named Dr.

E. F. Winckel and wrote, "According to Holland-born Dr. Winckel, for 26 years a resident of the islands, Dorothy Lamour does, indeed, wear a sarong but if she had stopped at that, the Hays office [the censors] would need a double sedative to quiet their nerves. The garment that clings cosily below her waist is a sarong. But the cloth wound around her upper part is called a 'slendang.' So Dorothy Lamour is really a 'slendang-sarong' girl."

8.

"A Grand New, Brand-New Screen Team"

Amidst rumblings of another world war, audiences wanted to be entertained when they paid their money at the box office. There were the screwball comedies starring Carole Lombard, David Niven, Katharine Hepburn, Cary Grant, Jean Arthur, Loretta Young, Claudette Colbert, Irene Dunne, Melvyn Douglas, Rosalind Russell, and Madeleine Carroll. The "ghost–mystery" comedies like *The Thin Man* with Myrna Loy and Bill Powell and *Topper* with Roland Young, and the social-comment comedies of Frank Capra (with Gary Cooper in *Mr. Deeds Goes to Town* and Jimmy Stewart in *Mr. Smith Goes to Washington*) were all big hits, but Paramount wanted a new idea.

By this time I had reached "stardom" singing beautiful songs in my sarong. I had made fifteen films in less than three

As Lucky Dubarry in Johnny Apollo

years, and I, too, wanted to do something different. We both got our wishes.

There have been as many different accounts of how the "Road" films were born as there were people involved. According to one version, the "Roads" were planned for George Burns and Gracie Allen. Another rumor has it that *Road to Singapore* was originally earmarked for Jack Oakie and Fred MacMurray and that only when they were "unavailable" did Hope and Crosby come into the picture. Except that neither Oakie nor MacMurray recalls that story.

I remember I had just finished lunch with Pauline Kessinger in the Paramount commissary, and on the way out stopped at a table where Bob and Bing were carrying on so that I nearly choked from laughing. Leaving the commissary, I was still laughing when I bumped into two writer friends. "What's so funny?" they asked. I told them that I had just been joking with Hope and Crosby, and that if they could only come up with a story involving two crazy guys and a "gal in the middle," I would love to play her.

Those two writers have forgotten our brief conversation that day, but soon after, the first "Road" story was turned in to the front office and I got my wish—Hope, Crosby, and I were set to star in it.

Bing commented in an interview: "I was intrigued with the idea of working with Bob and Dottie because it seemed to me that it would be a winning combination. A foreign land . . . the natives . . . the music . . . Dottie in a sarong . . . Bob being the clown, and me singing the ballads—it was one helluva format for a series." However, I must admit that none of us ever thought the picture would be that successful, it just seemed like a good idea.

I had always been very strict with myself about learning my lines. The night before we started *Road to Singapore*, I naively studied my script like crazy. That was my first mistake. When I arrived on the set, director Victor Schertzinger was already shooting a scene with the two fellows alone. As I sat and watched, I realized that *nothing* in their dialogue sounded familiar, not even vaguely like the script I'd read. Perhaps there had been some rewrites?

At last it was time for my first scene, a three-shot with me standing between Bob and Bing. As soon as the assistant director called "Action!" ad-libs started flying every which way. I kept waiting for a cue that never seemed to come, so finally in exasperation, I asked, "Please, guys, when can I get my line in?" They stopped dead, broke up, and laughed for ten minutes.

"We all hit it off beautifully," Bob told a columnist. "I, of course, had known Dottie since the old days at Number One Fifth Avenue in New York, and Bing had met her when she was singing with Herbie Kay. But this was the first time we were all working together. We used to rib her mercilessly. It used to get so crazy that it was like a tennis game with Dottie in the middle watching. Fortunately, she had a great sense of humor; most dames would have walked off in a huff. Bing would yell, "If you find an opening, Dottie, just throw something in.' "

It wasn't that easy to find the openings but I learned fast—even though it used to drive the writers crazy. More than once, Don Hartman and Frank Butler came on the set to see their "baby" being filmed, only to stalk off in a rage when they heard lines being altered or left out completely. I think oh-so-patient Victor Schertzinger, who also directed our next picture, *Road to Zanzibar*, put up with all that nonsense because he knew that it would pay off in the end. A very talented songwriter, he wrote many excellent songs for me, the first being "The Moon and the Willow Tree" for *Road to Singapore*.

After the first few days, I decided that it was ridiculous to waste time learning the script. I would read over the next day's work only to get the idea of what was happening. What I really needed was a good night's sleep to be in shape for the next morning's ad-libs. This method provided some very interesting results on the screen. In fact, I used to ask to see the finished rushes just to see what the movie was all about.

The plot of *Singapore* was simple, but funny. Bob is running away from an old flame whose Daddy has sent out some gangster types to bring him back for a hurried wedding. Bing is on the lam from his dad (Charles Coburn), who wants him to marry snooty Judith Barrett (whose idea of a honeymoon cottage is fifteen rooms) and take over the family steamship line. The boys pair up, demolish Bing's engagement party, and end up in Kaigoon, where they meet Mima (that's me), a dancer whose partner, Anthony Quinn, is a real cad—with a whip, yet!

Quinn received the "patty-cake" routine that became a staple in future "Road" pictures. Remember that? Whenever a bad guy (in this case, Tony) threatens the boys, they stop, bend their knees, and start playing patty-cake. The villain is usually so dumbfounded that he stops to watch them, whereupon they flatten him and run. Also in *Road to Singapore* was one of my favorite pith-helmeted zanies, Professor Jerry Colonna. He and I had been friends ever since we did a recording session together and Jerry was on trombone. I made a mistake in the lyrics of "I'm Getting Sentimental Over You." To cover it, Jerry burst into a trombone solo, then finished up the song in his inimitable voice. That wasn't the version that was released, naturally, but I still have a copy of it.

In the script, I end up moving in with the boys as their housekeeper. That was a little racy for those days, but the censors made sure that everything in that little cottage was on the up-and-up. One of the funniest scenes in the movie is when, broke and hungry, the boys make sarongs out of my window curtains, darken their skins, and off we go to crash a native wedding feast.

In another scene I was washing their clothes in an old-fashioned washtub. Regular soapsuds would have melted under those big lights, so the special effects department made me some special suds. When we were given a lunch break, Bob began throwing the soapsuds at Bing and me. Then Bing got into it and they both began throwing them at me, so that I ended up with a face full of suds. As they ran across the sound stage, I grabbed a huge can of suds and ran right after them. In the commissary, which was packed at that time of day, I caught up and dumped the whole can over their heads. It provided a lot of amusement from the other actors and executives who were having lunch, but the director wasn't too thrilled. It meant that our hair, along with all our clothes, had to be dried again, and that took time—which is money to the studio.

All good things must come to an end, and we all felt bad when the shooting was over. Certainly we all had fun, but we didn't know that *Road to Singapore* would be the first of a series that created one of the most successful screen teams in movie history.

There was one absolutely gorgeous man in Hollywood I had admired from afar for several years. When I saw him in a nightclub or at a motion picture function, I would just stare. And when I was told that Twentieth Century Fox wanted to borrow me for a film with this dream man, I nearly fainted. At last I was going to work with—and more than likely, be kissed by—Tyrone Power. One of my favorite directors, Henry Hathaway, was to direct. Originally *Dance with the Devil*, the title was later changed to *Johnny Apollo*.

Of course I tried to be very sophisticated, but privately, on the inside, I was very excited. As I began to know Ty, I decided the word "devil" certainly suited him. Not only was he more handsome off screen than on (and that took some doing), but he was one of the funniest men I ever met.

Henry Hathaway decided to put me back into a sweater without benefit of bra, shorts, and boy's cap, in a production number called "Dancing for Nickels and Dimes." When Henry insisted I wear my hair in bangs to boot, I really blew my top. Like it or not, of course, I agreed. Ty thought it was very funny; I definitely did not. I wouldn't even go into the commissary to eat with that outfit on and hate it even now when I see it on "The Late Show."

The production number took place in a nightclub, and at the end of the song thousands of balloons came floating down from the ceiling. We rehearsed the number, then shot it. It went very well, but when I looked at the clock, I saw we were running a bit late. I had to do a live radio show that evening, and Hathaway and the producer, Darryl F. Zanuck, had agreed to let me leave early. I didn't even have time to take off my ugly costume. But when I rushed out to my car, I almost fell over laughing. Ty had tied balloons to the bumpers, windshield wipers, and door handles of my La Salle convertible. I didn't have time to take them off, so all the way to the studio, I'm sure the bystanders thought I had flipped. I didn't even have the time to brake and shout, "Blame it on Ty Power!"

Another time during the shooting Ty came into my portable dressing room to ask for a cigarette. I was fixing my makeup, so I absently handed him the pack. He held it in his hands for a few seconds until someone called him for his close-up, whereupon he left the cigarettes behind on my dressing room table.

One loose cigarette was lying beside the pack, so I picked it up and lit it. It gave off a terrible odor, and my dressing room began to roll and pitch as if floating out to sea. I thought I was in an earthquake, or had lit a reefer by mistake. But it was just my friend Ty. He had put a trick sliver of wood in my cigarette to cause that awful smell and had some of the crew outside to shake my dressing room back and forth. Had anyone else done that, I might have shot him, but Ty's devilish grin always won me over.

The final joke he played on me was during a torrid love scene that opened with us standing by a long sofa. He tells me how much he loves me, but has to go to prison to pay for his crimes. He puts his arms around me, kisses me, and slowly pulls me down to the sofa. Then, as he gently moves me into a supine position, the scene fades to black. (In those days we didn't show everything that happened. Frankly I think leaving it to your imagination is much sexier.)

The rehearsal went smoothly, and we all went to our respective corners to ready for the actual take. The cameras started rolling. Ty told me he loved me, kissed me, and slowly pulled me down. When I sat down, the sofa emitted the kind of noise you make by putting your tongue between your teeth and blowing loudly. Ty, it seems, had sneaked a rubber whoopie cushion under the sofa.

We finished the film the middle of January, just in time for me to accept a White House invitation to come celebrate President Franklin D. Roosevelt's 58th birthday. The Hollywood stars invited included Mickey Rooney, Brenda Joyce, Pat O'Brien, James Cagney, Gene Autry, Bill Boyd, Red Skelton, Edward Everett Horton, Edward G. Robinson, Elsa Lanchester, Olivia de Havilland, Ona Munson, Kay Kyser, Gloria Jean, and Tyrone

Power. Six different balls were held at the Mayflower, Raleigh, Wardman Park, Shoreham, Hamilton, and Washington hotels, with the proceeds going to the March of Dimes.

I wore one of my favorite dresses—"Eleanor Blue" (a subtle compliment to our First Lady), with a fitted, molded bodice and flaring skirt covered with tiny coque feathers of the same shade. There were floating panels from each shoulder covered at the ends with the feathers and draped gracefully around my shoulders. We met at a noon reception in the office of the District of Columbia commissioners. From there, we went to a luncheon at the White House, followed by a tour hosted by Mrs. Roosevelt.

As she escorted us through the White House rooms, Ty stayed right behind me. Every time Mrs. Roosevelt stopped to make a comment, he'd whisper some shockingly funny aside in my ear. When I looked him in the eyes, his face always bore the most innocent expression, and I'd start to laugh. Mrs. Roosevelt must have thought I was a little daft.

Then it was on to dinner and another reception at the Hotel Willard. We then were whisked to each hotel to make an appearance and also to three theaters where people had gathered. At 2:00 A.M., we ended up at a gold-plate breakfast that cost $25 a plate. I danced with the President's son, Franklin Jr. *Life* magazine took a picture of us and printed it with the intimation that we were having a romance, which was ridiculous because he was a happily married man.

Like millions of other women, my hairdresser Elaine Ramsey, was madly in love with Ty, so at the end of the evening I asked him to take me upstairs to my suite at the Shoreham. Together we sneaked into Elaine's room, where she was fast asleep, her hair up in curlers. Ty leaned over and kissed her gently. When Elaine opened her eyes and saw who it was, the trip to Washington became a big moment for her too.

When the *Harvard Lampoon* announced their "worsts" for 1939, I was given the dubious honor of being mentioned twice. Their "Ten worst pictures" were *The Rains Came, Hollywood Cavalcade, Winter Carnival, St. Louis Blues* (their first swipe at me),

Five Little Peppers, Bad Little Angel, The Fighting 69th, Idiot's Delight, 20,000 Men a Year, and *The Man in the Iron Mask.* "Most consistently bad performances" went to Don Ameche and me. Ann Sheridan and Richard Greene were cited as "least likely to succeed" and *The Wizard of Oz* was designated as the "most colossal flop." Just goes to show that Harvard men don't know everything.

Paramount publicity had a field day with my next film, *Moon Over Burma.* The ads read, "The Glamorous New Lamour in Her Most Exciting Tropic Tale of Jungle Love." In reality, the "glamorous new Lamour" nearly came about over Paramount's dead body. Wally Westmore and everyone at the studio—with the exception of the front office—had been after me to cut my hair. I heartily agreed: the girl in *Moon Over Burma* was too modern to have such long hair, and besides, the longer it grew, the more work it was to take care of. The front office, of course, argued that my jungle films had earned the studio over ten million dollars, and they might decide to make more—therefore, my hair must stay long! Wally even assured them that my hair grew so quickly I could sport another jungle coiffure within a few months. But no dice—or rather, no haircut. Finally I rebelled. Before starting *Moon Over Burma,* after finishing all the retakes on *Johnny Apollo,* I made an appointment to meet Wally in his makeup department.

Wally was waiting with a tall Scotch and soda to give me the courage I needed. Holding the glass in one hand and the shears in the other, he couldn't wait to start snipping. He was halfway around my head when I jumped up and, loyal to the end, screamed, "My God, Wally. I have to get permission from Mr. Frank Freeman. He'll never forgive me if I don't tell him."

I grabbed the phone on Wally's makeup table and dialed the studio head's office. Fortunately Mr. Freeman had a late meeting and was still there. "Mr. Freeman," I meekly said, "I've been thinking about something for a long time and would like to get your permission to do it."

In his gentle Southern accent, Mr. Freeman asked, "What is it, Dorothy?"

In sheer terror, I looked at myself in the huge makeup

mirror. Half of my hair still hung down to my waist, the other half to my shoulder. I swallowed another large gulp of Scotch and soda. "Mr. Freeman, I want to cut my hair."

"Well, Dorothy," Freeman replied, "I suppose you are going to be like Mary Martin who called me to ask if she could get married *after* she got married. You're probably asking me if you can cut your hair *after* you've cut it."

I mumbled something about his being only half right. "If that's what you really want," he told me, "go right ahead." A photographer was immediately sent over to record the historic trim, which Paramount dutifully called the "$10 Million Dollar Haircut," and it received columns of publicity. Harry Ray, my personal makeup man, took me out to dinner to celebrate, and I almost ran through the parking lot of the Beachcomber, shaking my head, deliriously happy with my new comfort.

Burma kept me out of the sarong, but not out of cheesecake entirely. Paramount chose a very revealing white sharkskin sunsuit for me to parade in. The studio's foreign department loudly complained that in Burma, sunsuits were frowned on by the better people. Director Louis King solved the dilemma by keeping me in the sunsuit, but having the natives register appropriate shock when I wore it.

Robert Preston, now married to Catherine Craig, and Preston Foster were assigned as my two leading men.

I played Alta, a Brooklyn-born entertainer who is stranded in Rangoon and is posing as a Spanish singer. That gave me an opportunity to do a snappy novelty number called "Mexican Magic." I ran into Bob and Pres, who own a teak lumber camp in partnership with blind Albert Basserman. Bob gets into a brawl with the owner of the cafe where I'm working, and I lose my job. I end up returning to their camp with them. Sound familiar? Of course, I constantly get into mischief in the all-male camp—first with the sunsuit, then by getting stuck in a huge water jar I'm trying to bathe in. Again, I was the "gal in the middle," but at the end I went off into the sunset with Preston Foster.

There was some confusion with the names Robert Preston and Preston Foster. Whenever anyone yelled "Hey,

Pres," they both answered. Some wag put out a phony memo on Paramount stationery announcing that "Paramount is going into production with a new film starring Robert Preston, Preston Foster, and Susanna Foster to be written and directed by Preston Sturges, with additional dialogue by Lewis Foster and music by Stephen C. Foster."

Until *Burma,* I had never worked with any real snakes, and this was, of all things, a king cobra. Grace Wiley, a famous herpetologist, had trained the cobra, but I was terrified nevertheless. In the first shot we took, the snake began shedding its old skin and emerging in a shiny new black coat. It was probably the only strip act that could get past the censors in those days, but we still couldn't use it in the film. In another crazy scene, to help rescue my two boyfriends I had to ride an elephant through the jungle. Believe me, elephant is not my favorite mode of transportation. Pachyderm buffs will be interested to know that since the male elephants are too tough to handle, the movies use only female elephants.

During the filming of *Burma,* someone sent me a card filled out by a Chicago radio station when I did my first audition back in the early 1930's. It read:

> *Name: Lambour, Mary Leta*
> *Description: Brunette, slender, fairly good looking.*
> *Talent: Auditioned as a singer.*
> *Remarks: Not recommended. Bad style as a singer. Didn't even try as an actress. Doubtful prospect.*

I was happy I hadn't read that until I was making my *seventeenth* picture.

Twentieth Century Fox, pleased with my work in *Johnny Apollo,* asked to borrow me again to co-star with Henry Fonda and Linda Darnell in *Chad Hanna,* based on Walter D. Edmond's very popular novel. Mary Beth Hughes had been assigned my role originally and Anne Baxter was to do Linda's, but since neither were yet too well known, Fox decided to go with better-known names on the marquee. (In early 1960 Linda Darnell and I were both working New Orleans nightclubs, she at the Roosevelt and I at the Monteleone. We had different nights off, so we would visit each other's shows. We became close friends, and her tragic death by fire in 1965 was a great loss to those who knew her.)

Chad Hanna follows a traveling circus as it troupes through upstate New York in 1841. I played Albany Yates, a circus bareback rider. Hank falls in love with me and decides to run away from home to join the circus I'm with. Linda, who is in love with Hank, joins the circus too, thus making Hank "the guy in the middle." Receiving a better offer with a bigger circus, I leave, and Hank finally marries Linda. Later, thinking that he made a big mistake, he comes to me. Virtuously, I send him back to his wife. Fade out—the end.

Hank's only memory of that particular film is the scene in which he lies asleep in the barn, and is awakened by the playful pachyderm I need to save my show. Hank has memories of lying there perfectly still, take after take, while that elephant slobbered over him. But *I* enjoyed making *Chad Hanna,* not knowing it was only a rehearsal for a much bigger circus picture coming up twelve years later.

Tickled to pieces about the receipts that *Road to Singapore* had brought into their box offices, Paramount came up with a sequel called *Road to Zanzibar*. They wisely stuck close to the winning formula. We had the same director, Victor Schertzinger; the same writers, Don Hartman and Frank Butler, and only slightly changed the *Singapore* storyline.

This time around, Una Merkel and I played performers stranded in the wilds of Africa trying to get some money to get back to civilization. I was Donna Latour (now where did they get that name?) and the boys were stuntmen, barnstorming Africa in hopes of also getting home. Bing gambles the money they've saved on a phony diamond mine, but Bob manages to get it back, only to be conned by Una into saving me from "white slavery." As Una and I have done several times before, we work out a deal with the slave auctioneer, who splits the money with us. The boys take us with them on a cross-Africa safari, and both fall in love with me.

Bob said: "Dottie knew that in dialogue and laughs, she was doomed to come in a distant third. Of course, she was always dressed in a costume that made the eyes of the audience wind up on her, so she was patient with us."

He was right. In keeping with the studio's slogan, "show as much of Lamour as the censors will permit—with or without the sarong," the script had me take a bath in the nude (actually wearing a flesh-colored bathing suit). Two leopards steal my clothes, so I cover up with whatever's near at hand. On May 7, 1941, the Hollywood cameramen voted me one of the "Ten Best Undressed Women" for my appearance "clad only in a handful of ferns . . . in Paramount's *Road to Zanzibar.*" Naturally, the ads featured pictures of me in fernwear along with the line, "Bob and Bing take a tour with Lamour through brightest Africa . . . and it's touriffic!"

This picture poked a lot of fun at the movie industry. When Bob and Bing revive their patty-cake routine, it backfires. Bob, sprawled out on the floor, looks up and says, "They must have seen the first picture." In a takeoff on romantic songs, Bing and I sing a love ballad, frantically searching for the source of all that beautiful music coming from the middle of the jungle.

Later, I was sitting on a rock, singing "You're Dangerous" to Hope, who was sitting at my feet. He looked just like a little teddy bear Mother had given me when I was six months old and that I had kept for years. Whenever I pulled the eyes off, Mother would replace them with some of the buttons off my Mary Jane shoes. For some reason, I just kept seeing my teddy bear with the "Shoe Button Eyes" in Bob's face, and I got a severe case of the giggles—at first a snicker, then I laughed out loud.

You know how it is when you can't stop laughing and people keep asking you what the heck is the matter? Even Victor, who has the patience of a saint, began to get annoyed with my inability to explain what was so funny. Finally I pulled myself together and got through the song, but Hope, who was supposed to get up and walk away, just stayed on his knees and walked on them. Then I really started howling!

The set was as crazy as ever, with wisecracks and adlibs still flowing like water, but every once in a while I got revenge. During one rehearsal I remained very tight-lipped while Bob and Bing bantered back and forth. The scene ended with them both turning to me and saying, "How about it?" I smiled demurely and they fell on their faces. Makeup man Harry Ray had blacked out two of my front teeth.

When a flu epidemic hit, even that turned into a laughing matter. We had a sign made up with Schertzinger, Merkel, Crosby, Lamour, and Hope on it. Beside each name was our current temperature, and the one with the lowest had to buy lunch. Hope lost, and we took a picture to prove it.

As Bill Holden remembers, "I had a split contract with Columbia and Paramount, so I bicycled back and forth a lot. Whenever I did work at the Marathon lot and Lamour, Hope, and Crosby were making a "Road" picture, I always hung around their sets to watch those three work. My director would literally have to come and grab me by the collar and drag me back to my own set. There was so much warmth in their teasing of her. One scene had them sitting on a big log to figure a way out of some crazy situation. They came in, sat down, and Dottie jumped back up. Hope yelled, 'Cut! Get me a barber!' Crosby said, 'Why cut? Why a barber?' Hope explained, 'We need a barber to shave this log. Miss Lamour's sitter is much too sensitive to sit on this rough log.'

"Let's say that Lamour, Hope, and Crosby had gotten together for a new "Road" film. You could have called it *Road to Santa Monica,* or any city. Give them the script, then have a hidden camera film the shenanigans during the filming. File away the *Road to Santa Monica* picture, and just release the on-set, off-camera scenes. That would have made the funniest motion picture you've ever seen."

On this film Barney Dean, a gag man, would watch the rehearsals and then come to each one of us privately before the take. "Now Bing, when Bob says this, you say that." Then he'd go to Bob, "Now when Bing says this, you say that" and back to me. In other words, there would be three new lines that none of us had ever heard before. Sometimes this technique produced a whole new line of comedy.

One afternoon, Crosby had quite a few visitors—children, brothers cousins—and spent a lot of time talking to them. Waiting and waiting, Hope finally whispered to the assistant director, who announced "Quiet! Mr. Hope is all ready to work as soon as he can find a certain untalented millionaire." Bing started to chase Hope, calling after him, "Come back, you son of riches!"

I had met a young actress named Patti McCarthy and to help her out I gave her a job answering fan mail. Bing said that I was always taking in strays, so both he and Bob began calling me "Mother" or "Mommie." Everyone picked up on it. Harry Ray started to call me "Mah," which I thought was very funny until he informed me that *Mah* spelled backwards was *Ham.*

In my next Paramount film, Bob Hope was to play a big movie actor who definitely didn't want to be *Caught in the Draft.* (Strange that Bob had that type of role, considering that in real life he has done more for the Armed Services than any other entertainer.) I played Colonel Clarence Kolb's daughter. In an effort to impress me, Bob fakes his enlistment with a phony recruiter. It doesn't work; he is really drafted. One of the biggest laughs came when Bob, doing K.P., extracts a small object from the belly of a fish he's cleaning, holds up a "Wendell Willkie for President" button, and mutters, "I wondered what happened to those things."

For *Draft,* Edith Head designed me 22 gorgeous outfits, and not a sarong in sight. "Dorothy was always easy to dress," Edith has said, "She had a marvelous figure and complete trust in me. Motion picture designers have a particular job of trying to make an actress look as attractive as possible on the screen, rather than follow the latest style innovations. I always designed for the character, not the actress, and Dorothy was one of the few who understood that. Since she was a colonel's daughter and not a movie star in *Caught in the Draft,* I kept the wardrobe simple and confined it largely to smart-looking black and white."

Harry Ray, my makeup man, had become a very close friend, and as close friends have a tendency to do, we argued—a lot. I had just bought a brand-new Cadillac convertible and used to drive myself up to the location at the Paramount Ranch, about 30 miles from town. Harry would usually drive with me to keep me company.

For the life of me, I can't remember what we were arguing about this particular morning, but finally I slammed on the brakes and shouted, "Get out!"

He looked at me. "You must be kidding!"

"No," I yelled back, "I mean it. Just take your makeup kit and get out!"

He got out of the car and slammed the door. I'm sure he thought I'd never leave him there, four miles away from the location, but I just took off, thinking I'd teach him a lesson. When I arrived, I asked David Butler, the director, "Where's Harry?"

"I don't know," he replied. "I thought he was with you."

Forty-five minutes later Harry came straggling in, looking like he had been on a four-day toot.

David and Harry had been buddies since the Keystone Kops days, but David yelled at him, "Where the hell have you been? Do you think you own Paramount? Why weren't you here to do Dottie's makeup?"

"But David," Harry kept trying to say, "I was with Dottie and she threw me out of the car. I had to walk all the way here."

Everyone turned and looked at me. Looking very innocent, I said sweetly, "Why, Harry, I don't know what you're talking about. I haven't seen you since yesterday."

Since Harry had to make up all the principals, he didn't have time to argue, but boy did I get it while he was making me up! I asked him if he wanted a ride home, but he turned me down. I wonder why?

Paramount decided to premiere the film at Fort Ord, a large Army installation in Monterey, California. The soldiers got a full-dress view of Hollywood on parade as stars like Bing Crosby, Madeleine Carroll, Pat O'Brien, Ellen Drew, Frances Farmer, Paulette Goddard, Joel McCrea, Patricia Morison, Melvyn Douglas, Betty Field, and Susanna Foster joined Bob and me for the festivities. They responded in kind by demonstrating the latest military equipment, staging boxing matches, and fêting us at a gala dinner in the mess hall. And no, Bob didn't have to do K.P.!

9.

Hello to Hawaii

In 1940 I began two important love affairs—one with a man and the other with an island.

Now that I was divorced, it was very flattering that my phone was constantly ringing, but five A.M. does come early! I still took my work very seriously and did not go out when I had to work the following day.

One very attractive and eligible bachelor in town was an up-and-coming young attorney by the name of Greg Bautzer. All the girls were crazy about him, but he was very much involved with an actress under contract to MGM—Lana Turner. I didn't know either of them personally, but used to run into them at the local watering holes like Mocambo's or Ciro's. Greg was a real Beau Brummel and an incorrigible flirt. I remember

Arriving in Honolulu, still swaddled in leis given to me by the welcoming crowd (Mid-Pacific News Bureau)

him dancing with Lana and smiling at me over her shoulder. But knowing of his reputation, I didn't give his come-on a second thought.

A week or so later I was driving down to Del Mar, a fashionable weekend hangout for a lot of motion picture people, with my good friend and stand-in, Laura LaMarr. (A strange coincidence I know, but that was really her name.) About halfway there, we saw a man standing by his car, which had evidently been in some type of accident. As we slowed, I recognized Greg—and for some reason I refused to stop.

A few nights later my agent, Wynn Rocamora, took me to Ciro's. Greg stopped by the table, ostensibly to say hello to Wynn. The huge plaster cast on his leg didn't stop him from asking me to dance. Greg was a very determined gentleman. We not only danced, we did a rhumba. He told me that he had broken up with Lana and asked me to dinner the next night. From that night on we began one of Hollywood's "hottest romances."

My other big love affair arose because of my teeth. I mentioned before that when I finally had the money to afford braces, orthodontists told me I was too old. But when I met a dentist who swore he could straighten my teeth in six weeks' time, I asked Paramount's top brass for the time off, stating that I had been working continuously for three years and really needed a good long rest. They reluctantly agreed, so I had the braces put on.

Now what to do while I was waiting? I decided to make a trip to Honolulu with Mother to see what a real South Sea island looked like. We booked passage on the Matson Lines' *S. S. Lurline* for a five-day voyage. We boarded in San Pedro, sailed up the coast to San Francisco, where we stayed for the day, and then headed west for Hawaii. On the way over we played shuffleboard, swam in the ship's pool, had dinner at the Captain's Table a couple of times, and learned to dance the hula. It brought back memories of my New Orleans childhood, when a song called "My Little Grass Shack" had come out and I created my own interpretation of the hula to the record.

With Edith Head's help I had designed a striking

floor-length evening gown based on my now world-famous sarongs. I wore it one night for dinner with the Captain, not knowing that there was a famous New York designer on board. Obviously she liked the gown, because a short time later she put a copy of that dress on the market without my permission or Edith's. They sold millions of gowns, and she became a very wealthy woman on *our* idea.

The day we were to dock in Honolulu everyone got up very early because the *Lurline* was sailing along the coastline of Oahu, offering us the most beautiful vista I had ever seen. Although our nurserymen at Paramount had tried to duplicate this tropical splendor, nothing could match the majesty of the sunrise over Diamond Head, the beautiful Royal Hawaiian Hotel, sandy beaches, palm trees—Mother Nature at her most lavish.

Even before we docked, they began putting leis of *real* flowers around our necks. At the quai we were greeted by a Hawaiian band playing native music, and a chorus of singers with high, heartfelt voices. We all threw pennies and nickels for the boys and girls swimming alongside the ship to dive for.

Everyone, including the crew, was wondering why there was such an enormous crowd at the dock. There were always a few people on hand to welcome a ship, but never a turnout like this. Well, a Paramount representative was among the first to greet me. The studio publicity department had figured out an angle to get some mileage out of my free vacation time and had neglected to inform me that they had put a print of *The Hurricane* aboard ship, to be premiered in Honolulu. Almost every child on the island, as well as some of their teachers, played hooky to be there. Leis of gardenias, pikakes, and carnations hung from my nose to my ankles. With the help of the police, we fought our way through the crowds and were whisked off for an official welcome at the Governor's mansion, then to the Royal Hawaiian Hotel. One of the assistant managers was Bob Jallow, now one of the top men in the hotel and a very good friend. (After all these years, I love Hawaii as much today as when I first saw her, even though both of us have matured a bit.)

Not until Mother and I were settled in the hotel did I

remember the braces on my teeth! To think of all those photographs of my arrival with a big smile on my face! Needless to say, the pictures were sent all over the world, and I do think it probably helped a lot of mothers talk their children into orthodontics. After all, if I could do it at my age, why couldn't they?

In Hawaii I met George and Lucille Vanderbilt, who had a home in Kahala, a kind of suburb of Honolulu. To celebrate the arrival of the entire United States fleet in Honolulu that week, the Vanderbilts held a *real* Hawaiian luau; with a pig cooked in hot rocks, poi, and all the trimmings. A huge but very low table was set up in their lavish garden so that everyone had to sit on the heavy, carefully mown grass. Music came from a three-piece group: two Hawaiian guitars and a bass, all painted white to match the all-white clothes of the native Hawaiian performers.

This was the first time I had heard "The Hawaiian Wedding Song." Picture, if you can, those immaculate beautiful gardens, a full moon, and a high male voice from one end of the garden beginning the song. A high female voice joined in from the other end. The music swelled as they slowly walked toward each other through the moonlight until they met and concluded the song. Just after that, the fleet arrived in the bay, and the ships began flashing their searchlights. I don't know how many there were, but it was a truly impressive sight.

The next night Mother and I were invited to a big Navy ball at the Royal Hawaiian and had the pleasure of sitting at Admiral William "Bull" Halsey's table. It is an old Hawaiian custom to take off one's shoes when dancing, but it was funny to see all the top brass of the Navy, Army, and Air Corps waltzing around in their socks. I remember when I was 12, I had teased my mother, saying that she was "too old to be dancing about." But now I spotted her whirling around the dance floor with Admiral Halsey, no less.

Rather early the following morning I went out to the beach. The sand was already crowded with the sailors from the fleet, and naturally they recognized me—braces and all. I decided the only way to get a bit of privacy was to go out on a Hawaiian war canoe (better known as an outrigger) with a couple of beach boys from the hotel. While you're waiting for a wave that's big enough to ride in, an outrigger often "swamps"—a wave comes in over the gunwale—and you bail the water out with a large can. Well, the enlisted men on the beach were watching us through binoculars, and when they saw us all beginning to bail, they thought I was going to drown. A good twenty or more swam out to rescue me, and the force of all my gallant rescuers *did* capsize the outrigger! I kept hollering that I knew how to swim, and finally did—back to the shore. Of course, any available camera was shooting away. Eventually I saw one of the "home movies," which showed my bathing cap twisted around the back of my head, my long hair sticking out from all corners, and my braces blazing in the bright Hawaiian sun.

After the Governor invited me to the Lei Day ceremonies on May 1 (as the Hawaiians say, "Lei Day is May Day"), his office kept checking to make sure I'd be there. Now one of my personal rules is never to promise anything I can't do. But even so, I couldn't figure why the office was so persistent—until I got there. At the end of the ceremony they brought me up on the stage and announced that I had been unanimously voted to be crowned an authentic Hawaiian Princess. They named me Ke Aloha Lani ("heavenly flower") and my title was officially registered in the Archives of Hawaii. After another tour of all the historic sights, they made me a complete hula skirt and bra made not of grass, but gardenias. When I sat down, there must have been hundreds of the sweet-smelling blossoms spread around me.

Robert Preston had a friend who had a short-wave set, and he called me a couple of times. The press got hold of the news and, since Paramount had once tried to promote a big romance between us, were making a big thing of it. I also met two terrific guys, Ralph Rudy and Bill Flood, both captains in the Air Corps, who were kind enough to escort Mother and me occasionally. The Hawaiian press kept asking if I was in love with either of them, even though Ralph was in love with a girl back home. One night Ralph and I were in a devilish mood. We told the reporters that we were very serious, and for the cameras he gave me his Air Force wings as an "engagement gift." That story—and picture—broke in every newspaper in the world, we hoped Ralph's girl thought it was as funny as we did.

Ralph and Bill also came to see us off on the *Lurline.* Naturally all of the passengers were on the upper decks to take their last took at Hawaii. As we sailed past the Royal Hawaiian, we threw our leis in the ocean. It is an old belief that if you throw a lei into the ocean and it floats back to shore, you will return to the islands in a short time. *I* knew I'd definitely be back (though it took me a year to return).

Back in Hollywood, I was needed for retakes on *Caught in the Draft.* Then Paramount caught *Jungle Fever* again and decided that a re-pairing of Jon Hall and me would be very profitable. *Aloma of the South Seas* had been a silent hit starring Warner Baxter and that shimmy Gilda Gray, so it was dusted off for us. The script put me back into a sarong and into the arms of Jon—otherwise known as Casanova, a nickname he had acquired because he was known to disappear from the set for a romantic fling with any lovely girl who came along.

The film also featured handsome Philip Reed, with whom I went out occasionally, mainly to make Greg Bautzer jealous. Greg had dated practically every actress registered in the Screen Actors Guild. I had dated very little since my divorce from Herbie and was determined not to become just another statistic in Greg's little black book. However, Phil and I were really just good friends.

Even before shooting *Aloma,* the studio began to pour on the publicity. The final scene, a big volcanic explosion, was to be bigger and better than the climactic moments of *The Hurricane,* and the studio invited the top press to watch it being filmed. In order to escape the burning lava, Jon and I were to swing on a vine over a 40-foot chasm between two mountains. Jon held onto the vine with one hand and was supposed to put his other on my waist. I, of course, used both hands to grip the vine.

"Action!" called the assistant director, and across the gap we went. Jon let go of the vine and landed on the other side but I, hanging on for dear life, didn't let go in time. There I was, swinging back and forth over a 40-foot drop, when I realized that my sarong was slowly slipping down to my waist, with the whole darned Hollywood press corps for an audience. "I don't care," I kept yelling, "I'm not going to let go!" Finally I was pulled in by a hook, and some kind soul handed me a robe. Better late than never.

I was hoping to keep out of the jungle for a while, but Paramount knew where the gold was and put me in another picture with young Richard Denning, who had done small parts in a couple of my films—as an officer in *The Big Broadcast of 1938* and a pilot in *Her Jungle Love.* The studio had been keeping its eyes on him and had now decided to make him a major star. (For you trivia collectors, Barbara Britton played Pamela, a small role in the film. Years later, she and Richard Denning would have a hit in the television series "Mr. and Mrs. North" and she would again play a woman named Pamela. Denning later became the governor of Hawaii—in the television series "Hawaii Five-O"—and moved to Hawaii with his wife, Evelyn Ankers, who used to be known as the Queen of the Screamers when she starred in those fabulous Universal horror films in the Forties.)

This film was originally called *The King and Queen of the Jungle*; then it was switched to *Her Jungle Mate,* then to *Malaya.* By the time shooting was finished, the Japanese had taken over Malaya, so the title wound up as *Beyond the Blue Horizon.* The elephants we used in this film were so old and feeble they could barely walk. For one big chase sequence in which we were supposed to be running for our lives from a herd of pachyderms, we had to run practically in slow motion, and the cameras had to be undercranked so that the elephants would seem to move on the finished film.

In his syndicated column on April 25, 1942, Erskine Johnson wrote: "Paramount changes name of chimpanzee in new Dot Lamour pic, *Beyond the Blue Horizon* from Muk to Gogo. I don't know why either." *I* know why. Everyone connected with the film had taken to calling the chimp by a well-known Yiddish slang word that rhymes with Muk—and the front office hadn't found it as funny as we did.

That chimp certainly caused a lot of trouble. In one scene, he was supposed to throw a banana to me as I stood talking to Walter Abel. We started the scene and, on cue, I looked up at the chimp and smiled. The trainer whispered "Give the lady fruit!" Muk started to jump up and down and began to get very excited . . . very *sexually* excited. Alfred Santell, the director, yelled, "Cut!"

We waited a few moments for Muk to calm down, then started the scene over again. "Give the lady fruit!" the trainer repeated. Again Muk got carried away.

The director called for makeup and young Westmore came running over. This was his first picture, and he thought I needed some fixing up. Instead the director told him to cover up Muk's privates with some black shoe polish so he wouldn't look so exposed. After Frank found—and applied—some shoe polish, we started the scene again. But Alfred's bright idea dimmed as Muk's enthusiasm was still evident.

Finally I said, "Why not call Al Teitelbaum [a well-known Beverly Hills furrier] and have him make a pair of fur panties."

It seemed like a good idea. We shut down shooting, and the next day Al brought in a pair of monkey-fur shorts. It had taken us two days to get this important shot, and now it looked like we had it made. I looked up at the chimp, resplendent in his fur shorts and smiled. Muk looked at me, then down at the pants, ripped them off and flung them right in my face. Never much of a gentleman, he was replaced the next day by a gentle female chimpanzee, and we finally got the shot.

Pleased with the remake of *Aloma,* the front office dusted off another oldie, *The Fleet's In*—which calls for a flashback. One Saturday afternoon in New Orleans, I went to the Saenger Theatre on Canal Street to see Clara Bow and Jack Oakie in *The Fleet's In.* I loved it so much that I just had to see it again the following Tuesday. I had never played hooky in my whole life; but now, instead of going to the Beauregard Elementary School, I walked to the theater—which was some distance—paid my fifteen cents, and sat there all day until it was time for me to arrive home. But instead of avoiding the school on my way home, I walked right past the front door. When the principal spotted me talking with some boys in my class, he immediately suspended me from school and called my mother to inform her of my truancy, adding that I had been running around all day with boys.

Now years later, I was so eager to see the original Bow/Oakie version again that I fibbed and told the studio I'd never seen it before. For one solid week I had them screen it for me whenever I had a free moment. Over and over I made them run that one courtroom scene where Clara wears a black satin dress with a feather boa and chews gum like mad. The story was changed somewhat in the remake, but I made up my mind that that was how I'd do it, too.

I was very pleased that Bill Holden was assigned to be my leading man in *The Fleet's In.* Bill is not only charming, talented, and handsome, but also has a great sense of humor. Nobody knew how much he was going to need it; at the beginning everything went so well that none of us could have imagined all the troubles that were to follow.

One of the first sequences involved Betty Hutton, Eddie Bracken, Bill, and myself. Betty and I share a house with about one hundred steps leading up to the front porch, and in an effort to impress us the boys decide to carry us up those stairs. "Just before the picture started," Bill recalls, "I had had an emergency appendectomy. Today, with the modern surgical separation of the muscle tissue, you're up and walking around the day after the operation, and four days later you're out of the hospital and home. But in those days, with the McMerny incision where they cut *through* the muscles, the recovery period was much longer. You stayed in bed for a week and then—very slowly and very carefully—put one leg over the edge of the mattress to get up. My doctor, Dr. Neal, told me not to strain myself or else I'd pop open.

"I took one long look at those steps and another look at Dorothy. 'Well,' I thought, 'she doesn't weigh much, so what the hell?' I picked her up and climbed up seven steps before I felt the strain. Without thinking, I asked, 'How the hell much do you weigh?'

" 'Cut!' the director called. 'You are aware, Mr. Holden, that we recorded that.' Dottie only weighed about 125, and she looked a little put out until I explained that they had almost filmed their leading man's collapse. We ended up doing the scene in bits and pieces, and when they got to the long shots, doubles were called in."

Bill also used to make up his own lyrics to the picture's title song. As written, the lyrics went like this: "Hey, Rookie, you'd better hide your cookie, cause the fleet's in." Various Holden versions included "Hey, mister, you'd better hide your sister," or "Hey, brother, you'd better hide your mother," or "Hey, rookie, you'd better hide your nookie"—and those were just the printable ones. No matter where I'd run into Bill, I'd hear those lyrics, and I seemed to run into Mr. Holden in some pretty unusual places.

One night Greg took me out for dinner. No sooner had we sat down than in walked Bill with my makeup man, Harry Ray. Harry was one of my dearest friends, and madly protective of me. When he had a few drinks in him, he'd get the idea that Greg was no good for me and that he would only mishandle my affairs. This particular night Harry had talked Bill into following us.

They made their presence very well known, so Greg and I got up and drove out to a restaurant in the valley to be alone. They came in after us, and Harry bribed the headwaiter to put them right next to our table. After a few remarks, I got up and stormed over. "Now listen, Harry, let's get one thing straight; I don't want your advice, and I don't want to see you unless it's at the studio in the morning!" Then I turned to Bill. "And you, Bill Holden, you ought to know better. Now take him home; he's had too much to drink."

"Harry doesn't want to bother you," Bill meekly tried to explain, "he's just terribly concerned."

"I've known Harry a lot longer than you have," I emphatically replied. "And I am not particularly interested in his concern."

"Now just a minute," Harry piped up.

"*You* wait a minute," I stopped him. "And stop following me!"

With that, Greg and I left once again. The next day Bill came over and apologized, but I just laughed it off, because this had been going on for years. Harry would take one drink too many and become my agent, my business manager, and my father. But he was always my dear friend, and he meant well.

The Fleet's In was Betty Hutton's first picture. Remembering how Ray Milland had come to my aid when we were shooting *The Jungle Princess,* I decided to help Betty with camera angles and all the other little things that are hard the first time around. Whenever she stepped out of camera range, I gently pulled her back. A bouncy and very talented lady, she certainly did learn fast.

It was Cass Daley's first picture too. A few weeks before her tragic death, she told me, "I was pretty leery of you when I first met you, but I soon found you were a good Joe. I don't know if you ever knew it, but you and I might have worked together a lot more if Victor Schertzinger had lived. One day he came to me and said he felt that since you and I got along so well, we could be very successful in a series of films like the Thelma Todd-Patsy Kelly series. Vic was going to go to the front office when we finished *The Fleet's In*."

If Victor Schertzinger had lived . . . One Sunday morning I was getting ready to go to a brunch at his home when his daughter called to tell me that he had died in his sleep. It was a shock because he hadn't even been ill. His assistant, Hal Walker, was given the directorial reins, and after a couple of days off we had to continue the film.

When a good friend like Vic goes, it is awfully hard to try to play comedy. Our first shot was of me singing "I Remember You," a song to which Victor had written the lyrics. I had already pre-recorded it, so I only had to lip-synch. Pretty heavy stuff to sing after you've lost a good friend, but I really thought I could do it.

We used to shoot each scene three times—a close-up, a medium shot, and a long shot. After I finished the first shot, Hal Walker yelled "Cut," but the tape kept on running. Then over the sound system came Victor's voice, *"That was wonderful, Dorothy. You're just beautiful."* That was his comment when I had pre-recorded the song.

The shock waves could be felt around the set. My eyes

filled with tears, and I ran to my dressing room. Hal was furious with the sound man, but he honestly hadn't known that Schertzinger's voice was on the track.

After a short break, I composed myself for the medium shot. But at the end of the song, Victor's voice once again came through the speakers. *"That was wonderful, Dorothy. You're just beautiful."* The sound man was sick about it; he had tried to stop the tape, but for some strange reason he couldn't. I broke down for the second time, and finally we had to do the long shot in bits and pieces so that the track wouldn't run to the end. Later, as I thought about it, I came to the conclusion that perhaps Victor *wanted* to reassure me. It was fate that his voice came back from the grave twice that day. We threw ourselves into making a picture that we hoped would have made him proud, and I think we succeeded.

10. Hollywood Goes to War

The Japanese attack on Hawaii left me in a state of shock. My birthday was December 10, and to get my mind off Pearl Harbor for a while, Greg had arranged a small dinner party for me. He sent over a lovely corsage of white orchids, and just as I pinned them on, a blackout was declared all over Los Angeles. As I sat there in the dark, waiting for him to pick me up, I got so angry at what the Japanese had done to my friends in Hawaii that I started to cry. Then I realized tears weren't the answer. I had to *do* something—but what? My mind wandered back to the time during World War I when I was very small: Mother dressed me up like a Red Cross nurse and I went out and sold thrift stamps.

I began to smile, and common sense took over. Could I use my name to sell War Bonds? I had been to the White House

A triumphant return to Hollywood after a Bond Tour. The roses and the soldiers caused my mascara to run

on several occasions and had met President Roosevelt, who had jokingly invited me to make a South Seas Islands picture in his summer white house in Warm Springs, Georgia. He told me that one night his family was screening *The Hurricane* in the downstairs White House theater, and the sound during the hurricane sequence was so loud that it nearly knocked him out of bed on the floor above. But I couldn't just approach F.D.R. on such a trivial matter.

Bright and early the next morning I called Paramount boss Y. Frank Freeman for his advice, but was told he had a cold and was going to stay home for the day. "Home" to Mr. Freeman was a house connected to the Beverly Hills Hotel. I called him there, and he told me to come on over, though the rain was coming down in torrents. I wrapped myself up, drove over, and explained my need to do something for my country by selling War Bonds. "But I don't know who to contact."

"How would Henry Morgenthau, the Secretary of the Treasury, do for starters? He's an old friend of mine."

Within minutes I was on the phone with Mr. Morgenthau, who loved the idea and told me to start packing. I had to do some publicity and a few retakes for *The Fleet's In*, but before I knew it, I was on my way to my first stop on my first War Bond tour . . . New York City.

Because of the rain, I started sneezing, so to make sure I was all right—and not wanting to spread my bug all over the country—the doctor gave me a new sulpha drug, which unfortunately gave me the first allergic reaction I ever had. I broke out along my arms, back, legs, and over most of my body, but thank heavens, my face was all right. For my first meeting, with a group of bankers at one of the top banks in the world, I picked out a ladylike, long-sleeved black dress with high neckline, a very conservative hat, and gloves.

One very old, dignified gentleman rose to his feet and said, "Miss Lamour, I cannot tell you how happy I am to see you dressed that way. We were afraid that you might not remember that you are now working for the United States of America and that you might be wearing one of those . . . sarongs!"

Dying to scratch, just once, I assured him that I had

every intention of behaving like the lady that my Mother had raised me to be. They informed me that one of President Roosevelt's speechwriters had written an address for me to read on tour. I politely told them that I'd prefer to write my own speeches. "But if President Roosevelt can read this kind of speech," they asked me, "why can't you?" and I backed down.

At New York City College—my first top—I walked out on stage, and began to read my speech. Although well written, it just wasn't me, and the kids—who are always alert to insincerity—picked up on it immediately. I had finished only the first two sentences when from the back of the auditorium came, "Hey, Dottie, take it off."

Determined to be the lady the bankers wanted me to be, I just ignored that remark, but soon it began to echo from all sides of the room. So I laughed, put down the speech, and just talked from my heart. The audience was largely composed of college kids who didn't have that much money, but I sold $10,000 worth of savings stamps in one afternoon.

I was then assigned to tour New England and was given a special railroad car with comfortable and elegant berths, dining room, and showers. Being from the South, I imagined New Englanders to be very staid, with no sense of humor, and absolutely boring. How wrong I was! They were wonderful people whom I loved meeting. Traveling with me were some of the top Boston press, including a young reporter named Elliot Norton, who later became a famous drama critic.

Some days we would make appearances in as many as ten or twelve towns, and I think I really surprised those hard-bitten newsmen. "Hey, Dottie, we're tired. Can't we stop for awhile?" they would moan, only half in jest. But the War Bond sales were going so great that I just couldn't let up. In most places there were as many as twelve to fifteen thousand people lined up on the streets. I had a table set up where I would sell the bonds and had someone with me to count the money. I had made a deal with the Treasury Department: I would not take pledges, only cash. That way I got the money before they got the autograph. I was extremely proud that in the first four days I brought in $30 million.

Later, my New England friends sent me a wonderful memento that I've kept to this day—a mammoth mounted photo-montage arranged around an outline map of New England with a huge V in the center. Newspaper clippings documented my whole last bond tour in which I traveled 1,500 miles in nine days, visited 25 cities, and sold $31,439,515 worth of bonds.

As soon as I finished my first bond tour, I was back on the "Road" again, this time on the *Road to Morocco.* Paramount pulled out all the stops to make it escapism fare. I played a Moroccan princess named Shalmar, and Edith Head went wild with exotic fashions. But the wardrobe department felt the wartime shortages. A lot of Edith's extravagant designs called for full net skirts trimmed with cloth of gold, or pantaloons made of silk chiffon. Since silk was needed for the war effort, she substituted cotton with trimming of gold-painted kid. With Hollywood's magic touch, however, they looked like the real thing on film.

Hope had a ball in this film. In one scene he reclines on a velvet couch that is heaped with satin pillows. Dona Drake and seven other beauties surround him, all wearing filmy harem trousers and a few strategic veils. One paints his toenails while another applies lacquer to his fingernails; still another sprays perfume in his direction, and a fourth pops grapes into his mouth.

Anthony Quinn played the villain. Old-time actor Monte Blue, who was also in the film, walked over to him one day and told him, "It's remarkable you look so much like Rudy Valentino. I've never seen such a likeness, and I should know—I worked with him." The writers obviously agreed, because they wrote one scene in which Tony kidnaps me and gallops away over the sand dunes, very much like Valentino and Agnes Ayres in *The Sheik.*

One funny moment comes when the boys are in a desert jail and I send them a magic ring to give them three wishes. Not believing in such tomfoolery, Bob starts to wish for a cool Scotch and soda to ward off the desert heat. Lo and behold, a frosted glass appears in his hand. He is so shocked that he says, "I'll be a monkey's uncle" and, of course, turns into a monkey; it takes the third wish to bring him back. While setting up the shot, the director, David Butler, told Bing he had to stand perfectly still so they could match the shot of Bob and Bing with the next shot of Bing and the monkey.

"Don't worry, Dave," said Crosby. "You're making a monkey out of Ski Nose and you think I won't stand still for that? Try me, brother, I'll be a real statue."

When Bob had to wear some fancy Moroccan-type sashes, turban, and robes, Bing lost no time in accusing him of gaining weight. "After this picture," he told Bob, "you're going to be known as the man with the balloons fore and aft."

"Well," replied Bob, "you've always been best known as the little fat man who sings."

"Maybe," laughed Bing, "but right now you look like a pile of old, tired laundry."

Quick as a bullet, Bob replied, "And you look like the bag for it."

For this film the publicity department thought up some interesting gimmicks. One was a series of cards attached to the drinking fountains all around a town in which the film was playing. It read: "Thirsty for Entertainment? See what happens when Bob Hope chases Bing Crosby and Dottie Lamour to a desert oasis on the *Road to Morocco.*"

Since Bob buys me in a slave auction, Paramount arranged to auction off eligible males as escorts for the opening night of the film in each city. Bids were taken in the form of Savings Bonds, so it helped the cause too.

Greg and I had lots of fun, some serious moments too, and of course, a great deal of intrigue. We would break up for a couple of days, make up again, then break up a couple of weeks later. Greg even gave me his mother's twin solitaire diamond ring. Deep down, though, I knew that Greg was not a one-woman man, but that I was definitely a one-man woman. We eventually broke off, but did remain good friends.

As soon as the film was completed, I was off on another bond tour to Philadelphia, where I met an astrologist who insisted on doing my chart. "Toward the end of the year," he told me, "you'll meet a man from the South, but you won't meet him in the East. You'll meet him in California, and he'll be in uniform." And then came the topper: "You will marry him within six months of the time you meet him." I laughed very hard, saying I would *never* get married again.

Sam Goldwyn borrowed Bob Hope and me for his newest picture, *They Got Me Covered.* This time Sam didn't want me in a sarong. In this one I was "legit," playing secretary to Bob's Pulitzer Prize-winning war correspondent. The first day, Bob came through the gate on a pogo stick. As he came hopping up to the sound stage, I lifted my skirt and held up my thumb, à la Claudette Colbert in *It Happened One Night.* But he just hopped along without stopping.

In one scene, we are trapped in an office and spies are trying to bump us off. The office is pitch black, and Bob flicks on a cigarette lighter. Shots come through the window, shattering it and a water cooler. Of course the first take wasn't right, so director Dave Butler said, "All right. Let's do it again."

We sat there as the technicians fixed up the set. A rifle was set on a rigid stand and aimed so the shot would whiz right by me. Another was pointed alongside Bob to smash the water cooler.

I began to get a little nervous. "Is there any chance—." I started to ask.

"No, no." replied Dave. "Just air rifles, that's all they are."

"I'm surprised at you," Hope told me, "being afraid after all the jungle pictures you've been in." He turned to the crew: "You've got to forgive Dottie, boys. She's been making so many jungle films she's only used to talking to apes and chimps. In fact, she's done so many jungle films that she makes me rehearse my lines with her . . . in a tree."

One day comedienne Vera Vague called to ask me to a club that she was organizing, called Hollywood's Own. Rita Hayworth, Hedy Lamarr, Pat Morison, Frances Gifford, Jean Parker, Martha O'Driscoll, Vera, and I were the charter members. We each pledged to write one letter a month to actors now in uniform, like Jimmy Stewart and Gene Raymond, and also to former studio office workers, cutters, stand-ins, grips, technicians, and cameramen who were now serving their country.

Just about this time, producer William Perlberg was assigned to produce *The Song of Bernadette* for Twentieth Century Fox. He had some difficulty in casting the leading role and gave out this interview to Louella Parsons:

> *Dorothy Lamour and Gene Tierney would not be suitable because they could not be convincing in a religious role after having worn such scanty South Sea Island attire. Irene Dunne, whose life off the screen has always been above reproach and who is a devout Catholic, has appeared in too many sophisticated comedies and matrimonial satires. A young Irene yet to be discovered would be perfect. I've considered Teresa Wright, but she is a married woman and I am not sure that we wouldn't be criticized if a married woman played St. Bernadette. Anne Baxter is a top choice, but I still think we should use a total unknown."*

It wasn't too long after that Phyllis Isley, a young actress who had done a few things at Republic, got the job. They changed her name to Jennifer Jones, and another star was born.

This was when the studios began putting together all-star extravaganzas wrapped around a slim storyline concerning a serviceman. United Artists released one called *Stage Door Canteen* a tribute to the American Theater Wing, which had founded and operated the Stage Door Canteen to entertain servicemen coming through New York. Making appearances were Tallulah Bankhead, Ralph Bellamy, Ray Bolger, Helen Broderick (Broderick Crawford's mother), Katharine Cornell, Jane Darwell, Virginia Field, Gracie Fields, Alfred Lunt, Lynn Fontanne, Helen Hayes, Katharine Hepburn, George Jessel, Otto Kruger, Gypsy Rose Lee, Aline MacMahon, Elsa Maxwell, Ed Wynn, Ethel Merman, Paul Muni, Merle Oberon, Selena Royle, Martha Scott, Cornelia Otis Skinner, Ethel Waters, Dame May Whitty, and the bands of Xavier Cugat, Benny Goodman, Kay Kyser, Guy Lombardo, and Freddy Martin.

Warner Brothers produced two such pictures: first

Thank Your Lucky Stars, featuring Eddie Cantor in a dual role as himself and as a Hollywood tour bus driver trying to help Dennis Morgan and Joan Leslie get into a charity show. Such Warner heavyweights as Humphrey Bogart, Bette Davis, Olivia de Havilland, Errol Flynn, John Garfield, Ida Lupino, Ann Sheridan, Dinah Shore, Alexis Smith, Jack Carson, and Hattie McDaniel sang and danced. One standout in my mind was Bette Davis singing "They're Either Too Young or Too Old." Second was *Hollywood Canteen*, about the servicemen's center in Hollywood where a lot of us spent many hours during the war. The Andrews Sisters, Jack Benny, Joe E. Brown, Joan Crawford, Faye Emerson, Sydney Greenstreet, Paul Henreid, Peter Lorre, Janis Paige, Eleanor Parker, Roy Rogers and Trigger, Zachary Scott, Barbara Stanwyck, Craig Stevens, and Jane Wyman, frolicked in this one along with most of the stars in the first picture.

MGM had *As Thousands Cheer,* which featured Gene Kelly, Kathryn Grayson, José Iturbi (his acting debut), Judy Garland, Mickey Rooney, Red Skelton, Eleanor Powell, Ann Sothern, Lucille Ball, Lena Horne (who sang a wicked "Honeysuckle Rose"), Margaret O'Brien, June Allyson, Gloria De Haven, Virginia O'Brien, Marilyn Maxwell, and Donna Reed.

Paramount's contribution was *Star Spangled Rhythm.* Fred MacMurray, Franchot Tone, Ray Milland, and Lynne Overman did a hysterical George S. Kaufman number: "If men played cards as women do." Walter Catlett, Arthur Treacher, and Sterling Holloway came out in drag as Paulette Goddard, myself, and Veronica Lake. They sang "A Sweater, A Sarong, and A Peek-a-Boo Bang," which poked fun at us. Then we came out and sang the song ourselves. (I understand the title is a big favorite among charade players today.) Bing, Bob Hope, Victor Moore, Vera Zorina, Mary Martin, Dick Powell, Betty Hutton, Eddie Bracken, Alan Ladd, Susan Hayward, and Rochester also appeared. This all-star vehicle was an easy job—you just came in, did your cameo, and left.

Then a real-life extravaganza began called "Stars Over America." A group of actors banded together to boost War Bond sales to the billion-dollar mark. Among those who enlisted for this tour were Walter Abel, Edward Arnold, Wallace Beery,

Joan Bennett, James Cagney, Leo Carrillo, Claudette Colbert, Ronald Colman, Joan Crawford, Bette Davis, Laraine Day, Andy Devine, Irene Dunne, Nelson Eddy, Alice Faye, Henry Fonda, Greer Garson, Janet Gaynor, Paulette Goddard, Miriam Hopkins, Hedy Lamarr, Charles Laughton, Joan Leslie, Herbert Marshall, Dennis Morgan, Thomas Mitchell, Walter Pidgeon, Norma Shearer, Alexis Smith, Margaret Sullavan, Gene Tierney, Franchot Tone, Jane Wyman, Robert Young, and Vera Zorina. A lot of things have been said about Hollywood actors, but when it counts, most of them come through.

Soon after I went to Washington where Secretary Morgenthau asked me if I would be the "guinea pig" for a new idea called The War Bonds Savings Plan. I was to go into the war plants and ask the workers to invest 10 percent of their gross salaries in Savings Bonds. It sounded workable, so I immediately agreed. But Mother, who had traveled back East with me, had been having a lot of difficulty with her back. Several months before, the doctors in California had put her in plaster of Paris (which was like cement) from under her breasts to below her waist, and the cast was becoming most uncomfortable. So I decided to see if Johns Hopkins Hospital in Baltimore could help her.

The doctors admitted Mother for a series of tests. When I returned to the Belvedere Hotel, there was a telegram from Paramount head Y. Frank Freeman, asking me to call him immediately.

"Would you do me a big favor?" he asked. "Bing Crosby is slipping at the box office, and since you're in the top ten this year, I'd like you to do a film with Bing as soon as you get back." Paramount had signed a huge contract with Bing and wanted my help to get him back where he belonged. So I agreed to *Dixie,* but first I wanted three days' vacation. One of the favorite places of Hollywood folk was the Arrowhead Springs Hotel, right outside San Bernardino, a spa of natural steambaths with the steam coming right out of the mountains. I still drink Arrowhead Springs water at home in memory of my good memories there.

I said good-bye to Mother and boarded the train for

California. But in Chicago, there was a call waiting from Dr. Walter Dandy at Johns Hopkins. Mother had to have a serious operation, and they thought I should be there. I caught the next train back to Baltimore.

On the train I panicked, remembering that Dr. Dandy was a renowned brain surgeon. When I arrived there, they explained that Dr. Dandy had also been the first to perform a delicate operation for spinal disc problems. By this time, Mother was in such pain that she agreed to be the third patient to undergo Dr. Dandy's operation.

It was a success, but she had to recuperate in the hospital for three more weeks. Personally, I couldn't wait to get out of Baltimore. Because of the wartime gas shortage, we had to share cabs all the time, and the weather was horrible—nothing but rain, rain, and more rain. Since mother was doing so well, the doctors gave me their OK to return to Hollywood and fulfill my commitment to *Dixie.*

11. My Man, Bill

As soon as I got home, I found out that I had a couple of days off before shooting began. So I repacked and drove off with Laura LaMarr, for Arrowhead Springs.

Because of the war, we had the hotel pretty much to ourselves. We took the hot spring baths, were massaged, and generally relaxed. One evening after finishing all our "treatments," we stopped in the rather elegant little hotel bar for a cocktail before dinner. As we entered, a man yelled, "Dottie!" and came running over.

Oh, no! I thought, there goes my peace and quiet. But then I started to laugh. It was Charlie Boettcher, whose family had owned the Brown Palace Hotel, the newspapers, the railroad, and practically everything else in Denver. I had met him there

Bill Howard and I had many pictures taken, but this is one of my very favorites

when I was singing with Herbie Kay's orchestra. (Charlie later was kidnapped for $100,000 ransom, which his father paid; fortunately, he lived to talk about it.) He was now a lieutenant in the Air Corps, stationed at the San Bernardino Air Force Base, only 15 miles from the hotel.

Charlie asked us to join him for dinner. As Laura and I sat down in the main dining room, more and more servicemen appeared. Instead of just the three of us at the table, we soon became about twelve. In the middle of dinner, up came a lieutenant in the Air Corps, ostensibly to say hello to Charlie.

I looked up.

There stood the most beautiful man I had ever seen, in or out of motion pictures.

I kept talking to the other fellows, but even though my voice was coming out of my mouth, my thoughts never left the handsome lieutenant. Charlie made no effort to introduce him, however, and so he went over to a small table and sat down by himself.

"Charlie," I asked, "Where are your manners? Why don't you invite that poor lonely soldier over to dine with us?"

"Not on your life." Charlie replied. "Not that wolf Howard. I've waited much too long to get a date with you!"

I immediately turned and waved for the young wolf to come over and join us. He didn't need a second invitation, and pulled up a chair right next to me. I told him I had just returned from Baltimore and commented on just how much I hated that city: "All I ever saw was the hospital, the rain, and some damned man on a horse in a park.

He listened patiently, and then said, "Baltimore is my home town. That 'damn man on the horse' is my great-great grandfather, General John Eager Howard. He was the fifth governor of Maryland, one of the first members of the Continental Congress. George Washington offered him the position of Secretary of War in the first cabinet, but he turned it down."

My face turned crimson red. I was probably more embarrassed because he didn't seem to be bragging, just *telling* me about his forebears with his nice smile and twinkling brown eyes. He told me his full name was William Ross Howard III.

After dinner we all decided to go to the movie that was playing in the hotel. Don't ask me the name of the film; by then I was much too involved. Bill sat on the aisle, me in the middle (as usual), and Charlie on my left; Laura and the other guys sat behind us. Seeing that Charlie was holding my left hand, Bill excused himself and went out to the gift shop in the lobby. Coming back, he placed a little stuffed animal in my left hand—and then took my right hand. He was a sly one, but frankly I loved it.

Lieutenant Howard, the perfect Southern gentleman, asked both Laura and me to lunch at the Air Corps base the next day. After lunch I mentioned that I'd never had a ride in a jeep. Of course, Bill immediately commandeered one, and we all went for a ride up the side of the mountain, through streams. I held on so tight that I pulled off the door handle. Bill laughed his head off. But I didn't think it was very funny, and started to get really angry until I looked into those brown eyes. He had a way about him that made you forgive him almost anything, and he never lost that quality, either.

We went out for dinner that night. It was Halloween of 1942, but neither of us needed a mask. We didn't even question our falling in love; it seemed the most natural thing in the world.

I was so smitten that I didn't even balk at the script of *Dixie.* My role was quite a departure for me, but then I've never been one not to take a chance. I didn't get to sing one song (except in the finale, when we *all* sang "Dixie"), and even though it was my own idea, I lost Crosby to Marjorie Reynolds. Marjorie, you see, becomes crippled, and I just have to make things right.

The period dresses of *Dixie* and those awful hoop skirts were bothersome to wear. On the set one afternoon, the leg of a heavy metal stand supporting an arc light slid off the edge of its platform. Fortunately, it toppled onto the hoops of my skirt, crushing them but not me!

Naturally, I thought Harry Ray was just kidding when he came over and said that he wanted to join the Navy. He told me he needed me to go with him—so I did. When the two of us walked in, the recruiting officer was a bit stunned, but he signed

Harry up. Harry's only stipulation was that he be allowed to finish doing *Dixie* with me before reporting for duty. Harry wasn't the only one from the Paramount lot who joined up: A hairdresser got so fed up with one of Paramount's biggest stars that she joined the WAVES just to get away from the temperamental lady.

Seeing Bill meant more and more to me, but it wasn't always easy. Actors and actresses still worked six days a week, and with the gas rationing, I had to borrow coupons and spare gallons from a lot of friends whom Bill and I referred to as "assistant cupids." Without freeways, it took me about three hours to drive to San Bernardino, the Arrowhead Springs Hotel, and Bill.

Instead of living on the base, he had rented a cottage on the hotel grounds and I always took a room in the hotel. (We also moved a little slower in those days.) One evening we stopped in the bar for an after-dinner drink. There was literally no one in the place except Bill, me, and the piano player. Bill ordered a stinger. I've never been a heavy drinker, and then I hardly drank at all. But not wanting to seem square, I ordered one, too. It tasted very good, so I had another.

When the pianist asked me to sing something, I went right into the medley I used to sing with Herbie's band: "Bill," "My Man" and then back to "Bill." We all liked the medley so much that we celebrated by having another stinger. Now I was really feeling great! When Bill asked me if I wanted to go to his cottage for a while, I couldn't have thought of a nicer idea.

It was a gorgeous night, with moonlight spilling down on the bridges spanning the hot, steamy springs. But the air was a bit chilly, so it was really nice when we walked into Bill's cottage, where there was a cozy fire burning. I later wondered if Bill had tipped a bellhop to fix the fire before we arrived. But how could he have known that I would say yes?

I couldn't have written a more perfect script. We sat down by the roaring fire, soft music in the background (for a change, it wasn't Crosby!), and began to talk. Naturally, we started to get a bit romantic when all of a sudden, the big movie star got so sick to her stomach that I had to dash to the bathroom.

When I returned, romance was out of the question. Bill, ever the Southern gentleman, walked me back to my hotel room and said he would wait on the balcony until I was undressed and in bed.

Still a little tipsy, I *thought* I knew what was on his mind. So I pulled out the most unglamorous Grannie nightgown I owned. Hurriedly I put gobs of cold cream on my face, then jumped into bed and demurely called to Bill that I was ready.

He entered and kissed my forehead. "Honey," he said, "if you need me for anything, call me. If I'm not here, the operator will know where to find me on the base. Good night!" And he left.

Was I furious! How dare he treat me so casually!

I had always made a rule not to go out in the evenings before working, but sometimes Bill would wangle a pass to come into town. Staff Sergeant McCarthy would drop him off, and then we would go out and often stay up talking most of the night. Bill would leave just in time to make it back to the base for duty, and I would have two hours' sleep. "What a damn fool you are," I would say to myself, "to stay up all hours and then face the camera!" But I was stuck on the guy, and I knew I'd do it every time he came in.

In a very dramatic scene one morning in *Dixie,* I was to cry very hard. I tried desperately, but not a tear would come. The assistant director dropped glycerin in my eyes, which usually does it; no luck. They even used the old "peeling the onions" routine, and still no tears. I lost count, but the takes took all afternoon. By then I was so tired that when I finally started to cry, nobody could stop me.

Again my birthday came around. I was madly in love, but having been burned once, I knew I didn't want to get hurt again. I thought I was playing it cool, but I guess everyone in town knew. My agent, Wynn Rocamora, decided to throw me a big birthday party, and Bill managed to get leave to come in for it.

When we made our entrance, one of the first guests I saw was Eddie Albert, very dashing in his Navy uniform. I told some friends that Bill was "a soldier that I picked up on my way here." Everyone laughed, but I guess Eddie believed my hitchhiking story. A little later on, when Bill put his arm around me, Eddie said, "Listen you! This is a nice, decent girl—one of the few left in the town. And if you make any false moves with her, you'll have to answer to me."

Before I knew it, he and Bill were asking each other out in the alley for a fist fight. "Eddie," I finally said, "I was only kidding about picking up Bill, and besides, I happen to be in love with him."

Bill just looked at me, his beautiful brown eyes twinkling; then he took my hand, and we walked out of the party. Neither one of us said a word as we left the house and drove over Wilshire, up Whittier to Sunset, toward my house on Coldwater Canyon.

All of a sudden he stopped the car and turned to me. "Did you mean what you said back there?"

I looked at him, and all my reserve just blew away. I told him I loved him dearly but had been trying not to let it show.

"Dottie." He took my hand. "I love you very much." What an incredible birthday present!

By now mother was home from Baltimore and fully recovered. She and my stepfather "Cass" lived with me in the Coldwater Canyon house and we always had a nice Christmas together. This year I decided that Christmas Eve was going to be very special.

One of my guests was Billy De Wolfe, a crazy, wonderful man who had become a good friend from the instant I met him. *Dixie* was only his first movie, but he was terrific in it. That Christmas Eve he had made up his mind to enlist in the Navy, but he was sure he'd be killed were he sent overseas. The more he thought about it, the more nervous he became, so he had taken a few nips of Scotch. Seeing columnist Louella Parsons making an entrance, I told Billy to behave himself. "Louella, may I introduce my new and good friend, Mr. Billy De Wolfe?"

In his best New England accent, Billy said, "I don't think I care to know you"—and walked off.

The look on Louella's face was not to be believed, but

I managed to minimize the incident with a few cornball remarks. (Apparently to good effect—eventually she and Billy became good friends.) It turned into a delightful party, and I noticed every woman there was giving my Bill the eye. More than once, Lana Turna has remarked to me, "Dottie, I could have really gone for Bill, if only you and I hadn't been such good friends."

Bright and early Christmas morning I woke up and smelled breakfast cooking. The maid was spending the holiday with her family, so I couldn't imagine who was in the kitchen. Bill had slept in the maid's room, and when we came downstairs, there he was cooking breakfast for all of us, wearing her cap and uniform over his uniform.

Then Bill received the news that the troops he'd been training were ready to go overseas—and that he'd be going with them. He had tried to prepare me for this moment, but I was still heartsick. When they sent him to Camp Tanroran, near San Francisco, I went along, and Laura joined me for company.

We spent New Year's Eve at San Francisco's Mark Hopkins Hotel. The last time I had been there, I'd been singing with Herbie's band. As we were leaving the hotel. Bill sneezed and said he felt a cold coming on.

From the camp's lack of heat and the terrible sleeping condition, his cold developed into pneumonia. His commanding officer teased him that it was only "Lamouritis," but Bill was crushed not to be able to accompany his troops overseas. They insisted that he had to be sent back to San Bernardino to recuperate, so off he went. He caught pneumonia three times in a row and ended with a "bug," later diagnosed as emphysema, that would plague him the rest of his life.

Paramount assigned me my first western musical, *Riding High*, with a fabulous cast. Dick Powell had done a couple of straight movies, in an attempt to break his image as a song and dance man. (His shattering performance in *Murder, My Sweet* would come within the next year and a half.) But for the time being the public kept insisting that Dick do a musical, so he agreed to be my leading man. Rounding out the all-pro cast were that very funny lady Cass Daley, comedian Victor Moore, Gil Lamb, Bill Goodwin, Rod Cameron, and Glenn Langan.

I played an ex-burlesque queen who returns to

Arizona to see my father, who supposedly strikes silver. It doesn't work out, so I get a job at a dude ranch owned by Cass. I didn't wear denims and plaid shirts all the time because I had two big production numbers, even though I had never really danced on screen before. The costume I wore for "Injun Girl, Heap Hep" looked scanty, but weighed a ton, with a headdress made up of three-foot white ostrich plumes. I don't know how the Ziegfeld girls managed their headdresses, but each time I started to dance I did a bit of praying. The other number—"I'm the Secretary to the Sultan," I sang in an abbreviated version of a *Road to Morocco* outfit.

When Bing heard that Cass and I had a duet called "Whistling in the Light," he offered his assistance in "tutoring you in the art of imitating the birdies." I told him I had become familiar with his fabulous whistling technique after working with him so much on screen and off, but that I'd learned to whistle in New Orleans at the tender age of five.

George Marshall, who had directed many westerns (among them the classic *Destry Rides Again* with Marlene Dietrich and James Stewart), was our director. "One thing you've got to admit about horse operas," he once said, "It's the only heavy industry still doing business unchanged after about forty years. Back in 1903, nickleodeon patrons were wowed by the first real western, *The Great Train Robbery,* and fans have been going for them ever since. The only fly in the ointment is when they started with the singing cowboys," he opined. "When the average cowpoke found he had to hire a music teacher to teach him to sing or take a mail-order course in the steel guitar, he went back to the range. We lost a pack of good cowboy actors that way."

One day Cass Daley told me how, at 14, she had quit school and gone to work. Her boss caught her imitating him and she was fired, but her co-workers' laughter spurred her on. She got a "combination" job in a cheap nightclub, running the hat check concession, selling smokes, and working the spotlight for other acts. Finally she got a chance to sing. Cass had a heck of a voice, but she also had buck teeth, and much as she wanted to sing straight, she couldn't help making faces. The audiences roared. Instead of being discouraged, Cass played it smart and parlayed those buck teeth into big bucks.

A few months before she passed away, I showed her a photograph of the two of us in *Riding High,* perched on a wagon that's supposed to be running away. In the still, Cass has a particularly tense look on her face. "Were you frightened of doing that bit?" I asked her.

"Heck, no," she laughed, "I looked that way because it took almost half a day to get that shot right, and they wouldn't let me get down off the wagon to go to the ladies' room."

Edith Head was always trying to stay well within the government-fixed limitations on screen clothes while still giving the audience an eyeful when they went to the movies. The government had imposed restrictions on the use of copper rollers, and printed textiles were in short supply—so to get a similar effect, Edith had us wear unusual combinations of solid colors. Because of the dye shortage, the government was pushing pastel shades, so she whipped up two lovely evening gowns, one of pastel pink and the other pastel blue.

On a lovely March weekend after wrapping "Riding High," Laura and I again drove to San Bernardino. By now I was really hooked on Bill. His mother had come out from Baltimore to visit him, and this was their last weekend together before she went back East. Bill's sister Polly (who lived in Long Beach with her husband, a Philadelphia stockbroker named John C. "Jack" Bogan, Jr.) was going to accompany Mrs. Howard on her trip home.

The first time I met Polly I had been in Long Beach for a bond rally, and Bill had asked me to stop by to see his sister. I was very nervous about meeting Polly. She was feeling the same way, meeting her brother's Movie Star girl for the first time and she wanted to impress me just as much as I wanted to impress her. I was all dressed up for the rally, of course, and that meant my best mink; a chauffeured limousine brought me to the Bogan house—but a bit too early. Polly was up on the roof taking down her laundry, and trying to make dinner at the same time.

Her husband Jack answered the door. When Polly

finally came running out from the kitchen, she took my coat, then dropped it on the floor as she realized that the onions were starting to burn. They say that a bad beginning is a good ending, and we ended up becoming very close. In fact, Polly is more like a sister than a sister-in-law.

Now on that March weekend in San Bernardino, Laura had gone out with a fellow officer of Bill's. Mrs. Howard had retired early, and there we were, just the two of us, alone at last. A perfect setting, complete with a romantic fire (no stingers, this time, thank you). Bill started to propose when the phone rang. It was the husband of a close friend, advising us that she was in labor and needed me. I wanted to hear what Bill was about to say, but said, "I'll be right there."

Tracking down Laura, I told her we had to get back to Los Angeles immediately. "Don't forget what you were about to say," I shouted to Bill. "I've got to run into town, but we'll be right back!"

Laura and I drove to town and had our baby boy—it took only a couple of hours. When we arrived back in San Bernardino, the whole Howard family was heading for the train station, so I went along. When Polly leaned over to kiss me goodbye, I whispered that I thought Bill was about to propose. "Welcome to the family, little sister," she smiled.

"Not yet," I said, "not until we finish our serious discussion."

I whispered to Laura to get lost for a couple of hours, and Bill and I discussed the fact that we'd both been married before. His small son, William Ross Howard IV, was already nine years old. Bill's first marriage wasn't a happy one and he was afraid of repeating himself; I felt the same way. But after talking it over thoroughly and sensibly, we decided to give it a good, hard try.

I mentioned that maybe I should give up my career. "No, honey," Bill said very firmly. "Twenty years from now you might resent that decision and never forgive me. Let's let it go for a couple of years and see what happens." And as it turned out, he was right. A lot of actresses refuse to admit that although husband, children, and family always come first, our careers *are* important as well.

Mother and I

Graduation Day from elementary school—which turned out to be my last graduation

The "American Beauties" as toured by Fanchon and Marco. Dorothy Dell is at top center, and I'm second from the right (Gunnel & Robb Studio, Salem, Oregon)

Later in 1938, I sang with Rudy Vallee, who had helped me out when I first reached New York

Leonore Sabin, head of Paramount's hairdressing department, measuring my hair, which at 30 inches were, the studio claimed, "the longest tresses in the film colony"

Mother and I loved lunching at the Brown Derby where we could watch the other stars.

Rouben Mamoulian directing me singing "The Things I Want" in High, Wide, and Handsome

Following the wedding scene in The Hurricane

My husband, Herbie Kay, visited me on The Hurricane *set and signed autographs for the fans*

Dancing with Randolph Scott, while Herbie Kay conducts

A publicity still from Spawn of the North. *If you had smelled that seal, you wouldn't look too happy either*

With Robert Preston in Typhoon

Dining out with Liz Whitney, Tyrone Power, and Franklin D. Roosevelt, Jr.

Road to Zanzibar'*s celebrated fern sequence with Bing and Bob*

(Left to right) Hope, me, Bing, Una Merkel and director Victor Schertzinger. The person with the lowest temperature had to buy lunch (Acme Photo)

Mother and I, being entertained by members of the U.S. Navy

William Holden kissing me, and Eddie Bracken bussing Betty Hutton in The Fleet's In *(Note poster with Bob Hope in the background)*

Signing up defense workers for War Bonds. Scenes like this occurred across the country; everyone wanted to do his part (Ellis Sweatte)

Bing and Bob in full Islamic regalia for Road to Morocco

Director Eddie Sutherland and cinematographer William C. Mellor help celebrate my birthday on the Dixie *set (Paramount photo by Talmage Morrison)*

The Indian outfit in Riding High
(Paramount Photo by Jack Koffman)

Bill visited me on the And the Angels Sing *set, just before we decided to marry*

It took hours of greasepaint and eyebrow pencil each morning to age me for the last scene of Road to Utopia *(Paramount Photo by Jack Koffman)*

Singing Christmas carols with Virginia O'Brien, Frances Langford, Judy Garland, Ginny Simms, and Dinah Shore (Photo by Bill Dudas)

High-stepping with Billy Daniels in Masquerade in Mexico. *My favorite director and good friend Mitch Leisen, designed the gown*

"Baby" Hope was wheeled in as a surprise guest at the baby shower given by the studio workers in the Paramount commissary

Charles Laughton, Martin and Lewis, and I horsing around before going on the air (NBC Photo by Elmer W. Holloway)

Lionel Barrymore may have seemed grouchy to movie audiences, but he was a teddy bear when he sang for us on radio (Photo by Lee Weber)

Joan Crawford talks to Ridge at his birthday party (Floyd J. Hopkins)

No Special Effects: to play the Girl with the Iron Jaw took several weeks of training for The Greatest Show on Earth

Our "Misto Cristofo Colombo" number in Here Comes the Groom *(Paramount Pictures)*

Off camera with Jane Russell, who did a cameo role at the end of Road to Bali

Robert Alda wheels his co-star through the Lakes Region Playhouse

In This is Your Life, *I was crying so hard I could hardly hear what Ralph Edwards was saying. Seated beside me are Ridge, Tommy, and Mother. (Standing, left to right) Edwards, Paramount talent scout Jack Votion, Harry Ray (who in the the excitement put makeup on everyone but himself), Bill, and behind him, Bill Jr.; Paramount's Y. Frank Freeman, my hairdresser Elaine Ramsey, Dorothy Gulman, Bill Meiklejohn, Mary Utzinger (who taught me to run an elevator), and Jeanne Deshotels*

With Lee Marvin in Donovan's Reef *(Paramount Pictures)*

Director John Ford's wife Mary loaned me the muumuu I wore for Donovan's Reef *(Associated Press)*

With Ridge and Bill at Guantanamo Naval Base (Official Photograph U.S. Navy)

One of the funniest drunk scenes I've ever done: in Noel Coward's Fallen Angels, *Judith Jett and I are served champagne by Anne Haney*

A cast party in which a ship—or at least a life preserver—was named after me

That Monday we went in to see Mr. Freeman, who liked Bill and was pleased about our good news. We decided to get married on April 7, 1943.

I used to feel that Bill reminded me of someone, but who would dare say to her fiancé, "Gee, your face is so familiar"? One day when Hank Fonda was a guest on my radio show, the three of us went over to the Brown Derby for lunch. Sitting between them, I looked from Hank to Bill, and it suddenly hit me just how much they looked alike. The only difference was that Bill had brown eyes and Hank's are blue. They had met each other many years before when Hank (along with Margaret Sullavan and Jimmy Stewart) had been with the University Players in Baltimore, Bill's hometown.

On April 4 we went to City Hall to get our marriage license. Murphy McHenry, a press representative from Paramount, went with us, and there were photographers all over the place. The next morning's papers—local, national, and international—carried a headline, "Dorothy Lamour to Wed Captain," at the top of the front page in huge black letters. In smaller letters underneath was the information, "Rommel Retreats."

My mother and stepfather accompanied us back to San Bernardino for our blood tests. Later I went into the bar at the Arrowhead Springs Hotel. Just after I'd met Bill, Mike the bartender had bet me that I'd marry Bill within six months. I had taken the bet; now I wanted to pay up.

Mike looked up and smiled. "Thanks, Dottie. You know, I did better than I expected with this romance. The first night you met Bill, he bet me a hundred dollars that he'd walk out the door with you before the evening was over, and even though I lost, I got my money back by betting with you."

I became properly indignant. To think of how I had felt so sorry for the poor serviceman, sitting all by himself! But then I started to laugh—it really was funny!!

12. April 7, 1943

That morning, the weather was perfect, and just as in the movies, everyone was singing—the birds, Mother, my friends. Bill had come into town the night before with Sergeants Mick, Trotti, and McCarthy plus Elmer I. (Mike) Carriker, the chaplain who was to marry us. Bill's brother-in-law was to be the best man, and Laura was my maid of honor. When Bill went to get into his trousers that morning, he slipped and split the seat of his pants. Not having time to get them sewed, he merely covered up the rip with his jacket.

Edith Head had designed my wedding dress in my favorite color, light blue. The dress was short and very simple, with matching blue shoes and a small blue hat covered with

Captain and Mrs. Howard. We vowed to love each other until death parted us, and we kept our word

flowers. I carried a bouquet of white lilies of the valley mixed with other flowers. Just before the ceremony, while Edith Head and Nellie Manley (head of the Paramount hairdressing department) were giving me last-minute touches, the phone rang. It was Greg Bautzer calling from South America, where he was stationed in the Navy. He just wanted to ask me if I was sure of what I was doing. I assured him that I was *very* sure and very happy, so he wished me luck.

At the wedding there were only about 35 guests, including Bill's commanding officers, Colonel Louis Merilat and General Lucas V. Beau and their wives; a few of my bosses from Paramount, such as Mr. and Mrs. Y. Frank Freeman, Mr. and Mrs. Jack Karp. Bill's mother couldn't return to California for the wedding, so my mother called her and left the phone off the hook so she could listen to the entire ceremony. We talked to her right afterward.

The living room mantle, which Nelson Eddy had given me when I built the house, was covered with flowers. My guests waited for me at the end of a spiral staircase also decked with flowers. In the dining room next to the staircase was a string quartette that Paramount had supplied to play the proper songs.

As the music began, I started down the staircase on my stepfather's arm. I was so nervous that I missed the first step and nearly fell downstairs, but I regained my composure and just kept smiling. As soon as the ceremony was over, Mr. Freeman came over and joked that I'd been so anxious to get Bill that I nearly ran down the stairs.

After one glass of champagne apiece, we all jumped into cars and drove over to the reception in the Crystal Room of the Beverly Hills Hotel. Most of the top stars were there, from Marlene Dietrich to Bob Hope (Crosby wouldn't come because he hated weddings, bar mitzvahs, and funerals). So were the top press, Louella and Hedda, and members of the film crews I had worked with, like the little wardrobe lady who had made my first sarong. It was really a celebration for everyone I liked or loved—about 500 people from all walks of life. It's a tradition that the bride and groom leave early, so Bill and I made our farewell speeches. Well, the morning had certainly been beautiful, but while we were inside celebrating, it had begun raining cats and dogs.

Driving down Sunset Boulevard, we decided to stop at the Mocambo, which had been a favorite nightclub of ours. All eyes were on us when we made our entrance. I guess they were wondering, "Why in the world are those two here when they were just married a few hours ago?" But we didn't care what anyone thought; we wanted to dance one dance at the Mocambo as Mr. and Mrs. William Ross Howard III.

We then drove through the rain to Bill's cottage at the Arrowhead Springs Hotel. I had spent a lot of time and money on my trousseau, including a really pretty nightgown, a negligee, and satin mules. But it was late when we finally arrived at the hotel, and there were no bellboys on duty. Neither of us felt like dragging our bags through the rain, so I ended up sleeping in Bill's pajama tops.

Bill's cottage was surrounded by gardens on one side and a swimming pool on the other, just far enough away from the main part of the hotel that we weren't bothered by anyone. Always the domestic sort, I decided to make one of two bedrooms into a kitchen-type of room. I say "type" because the hotel rules didn't really allow a kitchen. But to create the next best thing, we put some unfinished shelves into the clothes closet to hold canned goods, pots, and pans. Bill bought a two-burner hot plate from the PX, and we rented a refrigerator from a small local furniture store called McMahon's (today they have a chain of stores in California). We used one of the bathrooms for dishwashing: I washed dishes in the basin, rinsed them in the tub, and made a sign for the door stating, "No Admittance . . . Except for Dishwashing!" From Maryland, Bill would get Smithfield hams that had to be soaked for 24 hours—so of course we used our "kitchen" tub.

The Arrowhead Springs Hotel was one of the more popular places, so we had lots of company to enjoy—top executives from Joe Schenck on down to fellow actors and Bill's Air Force buddies. Bill would make mint juleps and chill the glasses in the ice cream freezer (we had no real freezers back then), and we would all party on the lawn.

One black cat in the neighborhood got wind of the garbage and came around each night to knock over the cans and generally make a nusiance of himself. One night he made such a racket that Bill decided to get up and chase off that cat once and for all. I heard Bill go outside, kick the garbage can, and then . . . "Oh, my God!"

Into the cottage came the most horrible smell imaginable. As I ran around closing our windows and doors, I heard all the other windows in the hotel closing in unison. No, it wasn't a black cat, it was a skunk! He wasn't partial to being kicked in the can, as it were, and he really let Bill have it.

Poor Bill kept yelling for me to let him in, which I most certainly would not. I told him to take off all his clothes (it was still dark outside) and wash himself off completely with the garden hose. I filled the tub with hot water, poured in lots of my gardenia bath oil, and made him soak for an hour. The combination of gardenia and skunk was still too much for me, however, so that night I slept on the living room sofa.

Well, you know how show business news travels. The next day the story was on the front pages. Dorothy Gulman sent me the front page of a Chicago paper. On the left was a very glamorous picture of me, on the right was one of Bill in his uniform, and there between us, a photo of a skunk.

I was happy to be assigned to work with George Marshall again in *And the Angels Sing.* Betty Hutton, Diana Lynn, newcomer Mimi Chandler, and I played the Angel Sisters, a musical act. Raymond Walburn, who had played my father in *Dixie,* was cast as our father. "Don't exert yourself striking matches," he'd say. "Someone will always do it for you. If there's no one around, don't smoke." Then he'd tell Fred MacMurray, "Never wear a hat. If you do, etiquette demands that you tip it when meeting a lady. This always results in sore muscles." To Eddie Foy, Jr., Ray advised, "If you must mingle in athletics, be an armchair athlete and let the other fellow sweat. To Mimi, Ray proclaimed, "As an actress, always be on the lookout for those choice roles which permit spending long days on the set reclining on a soft, comfortable sofa."

The daughter of Kentucky's Senator "Happy Chandler, Mimi had done only one movie, *Henry Aldrich Swings It* with

Jimmy Lydon, Paramount's answer to MGM's Andy Hardy series. Joe Lilly, my pal from One Fifth Avenue days, worked with us on the musical numbers: Mimi sang harmony, Betty Hutton and Julie Gibson (who sang for Diana Lynn) sang the other parts, and I did the leads. Mimi told me that she can still sing the harmony for "For the First Hundred Years."

This was my second film with Fred MacMurray (the first being *Swing High, Swing Low*), and in both he played a bandleader. Fred came from a musical family. His father being a concert violinist, Fred found a fiddle under his chin at the tender age of five. But classical music wasn't his thing; years later, he was the sax player and vocalist for the California Collegians; when they landed in Hollywood, he stayed on and took some extra roles in films. He was discovered, put into *The Gilded Lily,* and the rest is history. To this day, Fred and his beautiful June are good friends of mine.

Also in *And the Angels Sing* was Jack Norton, the celebrated inebriate of films, the Foster Brooks of his day. You might not recognize Jack by name, but almost every film in the Forties that had a drunk in it hired Jack. In this film he played a lush who kept pestering the Angel Sisters—a big mistake. We pounced on him. I pulled his coat down in back, Betty hit him in the midriff with her music case, Mimi took off his hat, and Diana bopped him with a jar of cold cream. That would sober up anyone.

A lot of my friends had been telling me about a fabulous clairvoyant, and though I didn't hold much stock in that sort of thing, I decided to see what she was like. It would have made things too easy if she knew who I was, so I went in a sort of disguise and told her my name was Dorothy Howard. The first thing she told me was, "You are getting no place in your present work, and you should really seek other employment."

My next film, *Rainbow Island,* was an out-and-out spoof of my previous sarong pictures. My co-stars were Eddie Bracken, Gil Lamb, and Barry Sullivan. Playing my handmaidens were four young actresses (each of whom went on to her own stardom): Yvonne De Carlo, Noel Neill (Superman's Lois Lane on television), Olga San Juan, and Elena Verdugo.

The studio was touting Gil Lamb and Eddie Bracken

as a new comedy team. When Eddie reported to work, he was elated that his dressing room was freshly painted—*too* freshly painted however. The weather was very hot, and the smell outrageous. Everyone was giving Eddie advice when Gil Lamb piped up: "Get a large onion, Cut it in half and leave it in the room for ten minutes. The paint smell will disappear."

Bracken asked the prop man for an onion and started to halve it. "How will I get rid of the onion odor?" he asked.

"That's simple," Gil responded. "Repaint the dressing room."

With that, Gil ran down the street, and Eddie wound up and pitched the onion after him.

One day Gil and I got into a discussion about the names of movie characters. I had been known as Ulah, Marama, Tura, Dea, Aloma, Tama, and now Lona. In his first three pictures, he laughed, he'd had three dillies for nicknames—The Waladoo Bird, High Pockets, and White Mountain Canary. (*Rainbow Island* was nothing fancy; we all called him Stinky.)

My leading man, handsome Barry Sullivan, had just made a big hit in *Lady in the Dark* with Ginger Rogers. Several years before, he and Eddie Bracken had both been in a road company of *Brother Rat;* in fact, that's where Barry met his wife Marie.

The publicity department sent the critics very loud flowered ties, each with a note saying that the tie was made from one of my sarongs: "If you think this tie is brilliant, wait till you see the Rainbow Technicolor in *Rainbow Island.*" Another publicity gimmick was to have girls wearing sarongs act as doormen for the run of the film. Ever thoughtful, they suggested that if the weather prohibited a sarong, the girl should wear a fur coat with a sign reading, "I wish I were on *Rainbow Island*—there's no place on earth or in heaven like it!" Sounds like Utopia . . . which was a clue to my next picture.

Paramount's *Road to Utopia* took place in Alaska in the 1890's, and my costumes, although stunning, took a long time to put on. To sing the song "Personality" to Bing and Bob, I had to be corseted and poured into a particularly lovely black evening gown. The elaborate hairstyles and makeup also took about two hours, so that to be on the set by 9:00 A.M., I had to arrive at the studio by 6:00.

This particular morning I was on the set by 9:00, and on my leaning board (a kind of recliner for actresses whose extremely tight gowns prevented them from sitting down). Nine o'clock came and went, with no Bing nor Bob. Ten o'clock, eleven o'clock, then lunch. I had to sing them that darned song, and if they weren't there, the time was completely wasted. I went back to my dressing room to get out of that tight dress and had a light lunch. Reluctantly I put the dress back on and went back to the set where 50 extras sat waiting too. We tried to joke, but it started wearing thin.

Finally at 4:30 Gary Cooper ambled onto the set and asked what was going on. I recounted my tale of woe. "Dottie," he said, "you shouldn't let those guys take advantage of you. Why don't you just give them a taste of their own medicine? Go back to your dressing room, take off your costume and makeup, and go home."

I had never dreamed of doing anything like that, I told Gary; that wasn't my style. But the more I argued with him, the more sense it made. Why should I sit around like a fool when they didn't even have the decency to call in?

So I gathered my wardrobe mistress Ruth Davis Stella, my makeup man Harry Ray, my hairdresser Doris Harris Durkus—in fact, my whole entourage—and told the director I had waited long enough. Picking up the train on my gown, took Gary's arm, and swept off the set. When I faltered, Gary hissed, "No. You're getting the hell out of here!"

As soon as I had taken everything off, the phone rang. Bob and Bing had arrived, and the front office wanted to know why I wasn't on the set. I told them how I had waited for my costars all day and how long it would take me to get back into makeup and costume. They were quite nice about it and told me that Hope and Crosby had gone off to some charity golf game and forgot all about the scene they had to do.

The next day all was patched up. Of course, Bing and Bob took turns teasing the life out of me, calling me "that temperamental Lamour woman who stormed off the set." But they didn't pull another stunt like that ever again.

Hope's favorite line in *Road to Utopia* comes when he and Bing enter a rough saloon and order a drink. Since they're supposed to be two famous tough guys, Bing orders "a couple of fingers of rotgut" but Bob requests "a glass of lemonade." Douglas Dumbrille, who played the villain, does a double take, and Bob hastily adds, "in a dirty glass."

But *Utopia* had its hazardous moments too, when Bob and Bing had to climb a rope up the side of a glacier. They were using a fairly high wall, and mattresses were always put at the bottom of it, just in case. Unfortunately, when the rope *did* break, someone had moved the mattresses, and Bing really threw his back out when Bob landed on top of him. He always had trouble with it after that. In another scene they had to work with a tame bear. The boys didn't take too kindly to doing that scene nevertheless, but all went well—until the next day, when the bear went berserk and tore the arm off his trainer.

They had to fit a sarong into the film, of course, even though it's supposed to be 40 degrees below zero. Bob sees me coming through the snow, all wrapped up in a fur coat with a fur hat and muff. Then a new shot shows how he *imagines* me—in a sarong, still holding the muff. That scene wasn't easy because the set really was cold, and I was afraid the reviews would mention my goose bumps.

In this film Bob gets the gal for the first time. All three of us were trying to escape the bad guys when suddenly a crack widens in the ice. Bob and I are stuck on one side of the crevice; Bing is left on the other to face the villains. Even though I love Bing, Bob and I assume that he's been killed, so Bob and I get married.

For the final scene, we are all supposed to have aged about 30 years, but the makeup people had us looking at least 100—white hair, glasses, the whole bit. Bob and I are sitting by the fire when Bing suddenly reappears at our door with two lovely young girls. It seems he made his escape, then went on to make a fortune in gold. He seems pleased with our marriage and asks if there are any children. Just then, in walks our son, who looks just like Bing (it *was* him, of course, in a process shot). Bob shrugs his shoulders and says, "We adopted."

We finished shooting in March 1944, but *Road to Utopia*

wasn't released until September 1945 because so many films had been made during that period. Crosby was rumored to be headed for an Oscar nomination for *Going My Way,* so they could have delayed *Utopia* for that reason too. When it finally opened, *Road to Utopia* was called a nearly perfect comedy, combining wit and sophistication. Robert Benchley had a running bit: he would suddenly appear in the corner of the screen and comment on the art of film making. "Personality" became a standard and "Welcome to My Dream" was a hit, while "Put It There, Pal" became a Crosby-Hope theme song.

I was headed for my own kind of Utopia: a heavy dramatic role. No sarongs, no ad-libs, no songs—just *A Medal for Benny.*

13. Motherhood

A Medal for Benny was my first chance to do a straight dramatic role—but still as the girl in the middle. Benny, one of the guys I find myself "between," is never seen in the picture. I am engaged to him, but after he joins the Army, I find out that he's a rat, a heel, a ne'er do well. Disillusioned, I turn to Joe (played by Arturo de Cordova) and fall in love with him. Just as we are ready to tell everyone, bad old Benny wins a posthumous medal for killing 100 Japanese. How can we tell the town—and now the world—that a war hero's girl didn't love him? Things do come out all right, of course, but meanwhile the film offers a lot of dramatic moments.

To find a typical California-Mexican location for the film, they had searched as far north as Santa Rosa but finally

Richard Thomson Howard, at age three months

settled on Paduca Street in the Elysian Park district of Los Angeles. We shot much of the film there and used many of the neighbors as extras. We all played "paisanos," as Chicanos were then called.

J. Carrol Naish was absolutely wonderful as Benny's Mexican-American father. A master of dialects, he had portrayed more nationalities than any other actor in Hollywood. "Carrol," I once declared, "you're a regular one-man stock company."

"This is an easy accent for me," he laughed. "You should have seen me the time I had to do 21 different Chinese dialects." (It came in handy for him years later when he starred on television as Charlie Chan.) As Lolita Sierra, I too had to speak with a Mexican accent, and Jack Wagner, who had spent most of his school years in Mexico, coached me. I mastered the tricky rising inflection by making a series of records of my voice practicing and having Jack criticize them.

I was very proud of my work, and even some of my strongest critics liked my work in this picture. Lee Mortimer wrote in the *Daily Mirror*: " 'New' Lamour tops . . . Paramount's sleeper. Dotty plays the first straight meaty role they ever gave her and flashes the fire, artistry and understanding of the born actress. *A Medal for Benny* is a natural, the kind of picture that makes us proud of the industry. Told simply, straightforwardly, no spangles, bunk or hokum."

Even in the first days of shooting we had known that Carrol would be nominated for Best Supporting Actor. However, he lost to James Dunn for *A Tree Grows in Brooklyn*. Author John Steinbeck co-scripted *Benny* with Jack Wagner; they received a nomination for Best Original Story but lost out to *House on 92nd Street*.

That fall CBS taped a special radio program for the GI's, to be broadcast later around Christmas with Bob Hope, Jack Benny, Fred Allen, Jimmy Durante, and Spencer Tracy among the headliners. Kay Kyser led his band, and Judy Garland, Frances Langford, Virginia O'Brien, Dinah Shore, Ginny Simms, and I sang Christmas carols.

During the Thanksgiving holiday Bill and I went back east to visit his family. One night we all went out to the Belevedere Hotel for dinner. A young sailor walked over to our table and said, "Miss Lamour, I saw your last four pictures. They were terrible, and I want my dollar and sixty cents back."

I was too stunned to say anything, but recovering a bit, I reached into my purse and gave him two dollars. "I'd like my forty cents change, please."

He started to giggle, then gave me back my money and admitted he'd come over on a bet. "You see," he explained, "my buddy bet twenty bucks that I wouldn't have the nerve to come over and say that to you."

When Louella Parsons came back from a long vacation, Wynn Rocamora and I threw an intimate "Welcome Home" party for her. At least, it *started out* to be intimate. We held it at Wynn's beautiful terraced hillside home, with a rhumba band playing scintillating Latin American music all night. Among the hundreds who dropped by were Edward Arnold, Joan Bennett and Walter Wanger, Robert Young, Connie Moore, Bing Crosby, Zachary Scott, Dinah Shore and George Montgomery, Darryl Zanuck, Allan Jones, Bob Hope, Frank Freeman, Ray Milland, Fred MacMurray, Herbert Marshall, Randy Scott, George Burns and Gracie Allen, Susan Hayward and Jess Barker, Greer Garson, Edith Head, Ginny Simms, Diana Lynn, Martha O'Driscoll, Anita Colby, Lucille Ball, Frances Gifford, Mary Pickford, Harriet Parsons, Ida Lupino, Pola Negri, Jennifer Jones, Betty Hutton, Edgar Bergen, Helmut Dantine, Mervyn LeRoy, Walter Winchell, Sir Charles Mendl, Arturo de Cordova, and a host of others (thanks, Lolly!).

In order to translate "Duffy's Tavern," an extremely popular radio show, to the big screen, Paramount decided to make it an all-star revue. Bing Crosby, Betty Hutton, Paulette Goddard, Alan Ladd, Eddie Bracken, Brian Donlevy, Sonny Tufts, Veronica Lake, Arturo de Cordova, Cass Daley, Diana Lynn, Gary, Phillip, Dennis and Lin Crosby (Bing's boys), William Bendix, Joan Caulfield, and Barry Fitzgerald joined Ed Gardner as Archie and Ann Thomas as Miss Duffy. Shirley

Booth played Miss Duffy on radio but they didn't use her for the film.)

Bing led a group of us in singing a parody of "Swinging on a Star," written by Johnny Burke and Jimmy Van Heusen. We were all dressed as kids: Hutton looked like Shirley Temple, Sonny Tufts wore golf knickers with a green and yellow striped sweater, and I had a sailor middy with a big red ribbon in my hair. Crosby started crooning the regular lyrics; then Sonny Tufts joined in:

A ham is an actor who believes he's adored,
But missed the Academy Award
His head gets bigger and his smile does, too.
The only kind of acting he can do.
So if you don't mind the critics when they slam
You may grow up to be a ham.

Then we all sang the chorus, and it was my turn:

Lamour is an actress and she gets reimbursed
To let the director do his worst.
She lives on islands and she sings a song,
And gets pneumonia in an old sarong.

Then Bing jumped in:

If you don't care what the public must endure.
You may grow up to be Lamour.

Cass Daley kidded herself:

She looks like every night was Halloween.

Diana Lynn commented on her screen image:

She can be nasty with the sweeetest grin.

Then Bing took a swipe at Hope:

A snob is an actor who will tell you he's tops,
Why, he even brags about his flops.
When he plays golf he never counts his strokes,
And that's not all, he tells the stalest jokes.

So if you're like a friend of mine called Bob
You might grow up to be a snob.

And *everyone* took a swing at Hollywood:

All the monkeys aren't in the zoo
Everyday you see quite a few
Haven't we met you at someone's bar?
Boy, you were swinging on a star!

It's strange that as soon as you put actors in children's clothes, they all really let go and enjoy themselves.

Paramount announced that because it was becoming too difficult to arrange Bing's, Bob's, and my schedules, the still-not-released *Road to Utopia* would be the last of the "Road" pictures. The public didn't like that one bit, and Paramount was flooded with 75,000 letters of protest. Another announcement was quickly made that the studio *was* considering another "Road" film after all. This one would cast Hope and Crosby as a couple of GI Joes returning to the girl they left behind. Tentative title: *Road to Home.* But nothing ever came of it.

Each Christmas at the Hollywood Canteen stars would dress up as Santa Claus and pass out gifts to servicemen. Usually the male stars played Santa Claus, of course, but this year we planned a surprise. Along with Sydney Greenstreet, Eddie Cantor, and Kay Kyser all dressed as Santas, I put on the red suit, beard and a lot of padding. To my surprise, they didn't know it was me until I started to take it off.

To ring in 1945, Bill and I went to a New Year's Eve party up in Coldwater Canyon, We left the party rather late and Billy De Wolfe decided to follow us down the canyon. So about two miles from our host's home we ran out of gas. Billy stopped and began to tease us, and we all began to laugh.

Suddenly, from the upstairs window of a nearby house, a woman with the most saccharine voice called gently, "Happy New Year to you." Just as we were about to return her greeting, she screeched, "*and shut up!*"

On January 2, 1945, I reported to work on *Masquerade in Mexico.* When director Mitch Leisen had first sent me the script, I returned it with a note: "This can't be for me. It's too good a script, and besides, it has some dialogue."

It really *was* good, loosely based on *Midnight,* a 1939 major success that Mitch had originally directed with Claudette Colbert, Don Ameche, John Barrymore, Francis Lederer, Mary Astor, and Hedda Hopper.

"Mitch," I asked, "why do you want to do a remake?"

"Well, the studio wanted me to do a film with a certain blonde actress who has an outrageous reputation for being difficult, to put it mildly. I told them, 'Anything but her!' Then they mentioned that they were very happy with the reviews on *A Medal for Benny* and would like to pair De Cordova and you again. I immediately thought of *Midnight* with music, and they loved it."

Arturo took the Ameche role, Patric Knowles the Barrymore role, and Ann Dvorak the Astor role. Ann Dvorak had taken a leave from her career; during the blitz she went to England and spent three and half years driving an ambulance and serving with the famed Women's Land Army. This was her first picture since she returned. Ironically, a French actor named George Rigaud had originally been signed for the part that Francis Lederer later played in *Midnight,* but his accent was too heavy. Francis got the part, and George went back to France. Now he had just come back and Paramount signed him again—for the same part!

Arturo had a problem with English too. He could never say "ing," so Mitch had the sound department dig up some tracks of Arturo saying "ing, ing, ing" over and over, recorded when he did *Frenchman's Creek* two years before. The "ings" would later be dubbed into the sound track of the film where needed—a lot of extra work.

Mitch told David Chierchitti for his book *Hollywood Director* that "Dotty was very slim in that picture, and designing her clothes was very enjoyable because I could do whatever I wanted. Edith Head helped me and did some of the street clothes, but I did the gowns. We kept her in black most of the time. The dress she wore when she danced with Billy Daniels was yards and yards of folded jersey, and all around the bottom were black ostrich feathers. She handled it beautifully; it just floated through the air. There was nothing to keep the bodice up. That piece that went around her neck was no help at all. The whole thing was boned inside and we used rubber cement, tape and everything else we could think of to keep it up."

Up to this point I'd done a few steps in production numbers, but nothing like the Veloz and Yolanda routine that dance director Billy Daniels dreamed up for us. We did a beguine number, sort of a slow rhumba executed with more sensuous movements and primitive rhythms. We worked a long time rehearsing, and at first I was sore all over, but it was a great way to keep in shape.

Sometime afterward I was overjoyed to discover I was pregnant. The doctors had told me that I would never be able to have a baby on account of that accident with the chimp on *Typhoon.* Bill and I had even been talking about adopting a baby girl, but now I could have my own! Mitch always said having me do that dance must have tightened some muscles or something. The doctors disagreed with him, but I was much too happy to care. I couldn't wait to tell Mr. Freeman, the head of the studio. He was a teetotaler, but after hearing the news, he went over to the elegant cabinet in his office and pulled out a bottle of Scotch for me to take home to Bill.

I had some retakes to do on *Masquerade in Mexico* and then planned to take off work until my baby was born. Although there was a strike at the studio, the Screen Actors Guild had told me it was all right to drive into Paramount to do the retakes. But the men in the picket lines weren't from our studio, and the first day they started to throw mud at me and threatened to overturn my car.

One bright sunny morning in about the third month of my pregnancy, I received a call from Henry Ginsberg, the "money man" at Paramount who made all the deals. But rather than inquire about my health, Mr. Ginsberg informed me that my contract ran 40 weeks out of the 52. Since I was going to be "out of commission" for so long, I would have to either extend my contract and take *less* money or take a complete suspension during my pregnancy.

As the contract stood, I was getting far less than any

other star of my caliber, even though I was making the studio far more money than many others. So I got up my Scotch, Irish, and Spanish temper and after discussing it with Bill, told Paramount that I'd take the suspension.

Since we loved the country around San Bernardino, Bill and I decided to buy a thousand-acre ranch called Sunnybrook. We had white-faced cattle, alfalfa, hogs, and inherited a fun-loving German ranch-hand named Walter who liked to drink a bit. He was a very funny man, especially when he was drinking, and he loved to play practical jokes.

We had brought a wonderful black maid, Louise, from Maryland to stay with me during my confinement. She herself had been with Bill's family for years, and her family had worked for the Howards for generations. Louise became an instant "member of the family" and still is after some 30-odd years. We have been through laughter and tears together.

Louise has always been a very religious lady, but she was terrified of certain things—like the coyotes who used to roam around the ranch. Both she and Walter stayed in the three-bedroom guest house. One night when the moon was full she was coming back from the main house and waiting for her outside the guest house was Walter with a sheet over his head, howling like a coyote.

Louise let out such a whoop that I jumped up and grabbed Bill's gun. When I came out, I realized it was only crazy Walter, but decided to teach him a lesson. "Whoever it is," I yelled out, "drop the sheet or I'll shoot!" Walter took off, needless to say, dropping the sheet as he ran.

Most of my time I spent with Bill out at the San Bernardino ranch, but when I had to go into town to see the doctor, I'd sleep over at our Beverly Hills home. On one such night I received a phone call from Walter at 4:00 A.M. He was frantic. One of our hogs, Hedy, was getting ready to have a litter of piglets, and another sow, Eleanor was expecting the next day. We missed Hedy's *accouchement,* but did make it back in time for Eleanor's. I actually went out in the pens to help Walter with the delivery. Everyone laughed at me, but I told friends with seeing a litter of piggies delivered is a really beautiful sight. (We had named all of the sows after our friends—Hedy, Eleanor, Edith, and so on. We meant it as a compliment, but on thinking about it now, I hope everyone took it that way. After all, we named the boar Bill!)

My baby was due on January 11. It was nearly time for Bill to be discharged, so we moved back into town for the Christmas holidays. No matter where we drove, we kept a fully packed overnight case in the trunk, just in case. That New Year's Eve we went to a party at the Beverly Hills Club with a group of friends and bumped into Greg Bautzer, who was with my idol, Joan Crawford. Joan was wonderful to me that night (as she would always be), fussing over me just like a mother hen. When Greg asked me to dance with him, wouldn't you know it would be a rhumba? "I hope," Bill whispered to me, "that while you're dancing with that man, my son kicks him in the you-know-whats." That's exactly what happened: the baby began kicking like crazy, and I had to excuse myself and sit down.

Somebody must have told Bill that if the mother-to-be were in a horizontal position, it would delay the birth. For the next few days he kept calling me from the Separation Center, advising me to lie down and "keep your feet up" so he could be home as a civilian for the birth of our first child. It may have worked: Bill was released on January 6, 1946, and two days later, on January 8, John Ridgely Howard was born in the Good Samaritan Hospital—6 pounds, 8½ ounces.

The "John" was for my father and "Ridgely" for Bill's brother, but we decided to call him Ridge. He was the first Howard born outside of Maryland since the Civil War, so for his christening we decided to take him back to Baltimore, the Howard's traditional home. When we asked Mitch to stand as godfather, he went right out to research his duties. From an heirloom in his own family, he made Ridge a christening gown trimmed with ermine tails.

The first time Bob and Dolores Hope came by to see him, Dolores noted that he had a "Howard nose," which was similar to a "Hope nose." She began to count on her fingers:

"Hmmm, where was Bob about that time?" Soon after, Bob sent over a picture of himself that we'd taken at a baby shower when Bob had been wheeled into the room in a baby carriage wearing a baby's lacy hat and ruffled dress. Across the photo Bob had written, "Don't let this happen to you." He and Dolores also gave him a beautiful English-built perambulator, so we took a picture of Ridge dressed in Mitch's fancy christening outfit, lying in the pram, and sent it back to Bob, saying, "*Now* you tell me. . . ."

Bill insisted that I not go back to work for at least six months after the baby was born so Paramount planned my "comeback" film on that schedule. I was to co-star with Hope in a comedy-mystery called *My Favorite Brunette,* also co-starring Peter Lorre and Lon Chaney, Jr. The first day of shooting, Louise brought Ridge to the studio, and I played the proud Mama, holding him up and showing off to my pals on the set. Ridge was laughing, trying to hold everyone's finger, and doing all those things that babies do to make grown men love them. Lorre and Chaney both came over to play. Finally "Uncle Bob" walked over, and said, "Hi, little boy."

Ridge stopped laughing and began to scream his head off. "See," Bob cracked, "Lorre and Chaney don't scare the kid, but I sure can!"

Though *Brunette* was being made on the Paramount lot, this was Bob's first independent production. As the head of Hope Productions, he used to say that he carried two watches with him, one set to Paramount time and the other to his own. He kept comparing them in order to discover how much time he'd be wasting if he were working for Paramount. It was a joke, but we didn't mess around as much as usual. One day, he was complaining about not being able to find a foursome at the Lakeside Country Club. I said, "Naturally not. Haven't you spotted the new sign over the door of the Lakeside? It says, 'Abandon Hope, all ye who enter here!' "

Bob had a habit of chewing gum off camera. He told me it was very helpful before a performance because it lubricates the vocal cords, and so I began to chew gum too. Before one particular love scene with Bob, I chewed a huge piece of bubble gum to the right consistency. Just as we were about to kiss, I blew a very large bubble. I've never seen such a look of surprise on Bob's face. When the bubble hit the tip of Bob's nose, spreading gum all over our faces, we both had to have our makeup fixed.

Even then, Bob was always doing things for charity. He held a bazaar for the benefit of war orphans in Europe, and I was elected his star saleslady. Before long I'd sold everything in my booth except a Mexican basket full of little grass horses. Then I realized there was only one person who'd buy horses that wouldn't run—so I sold the basket to Bing, whom we were always teasing about his bad luck at the track. (He also bought four puppies for his four boys.)

Bob and I had cut our first single record together to give Bing some competition. It was Ray Evans and Jay Livingston's lovely "Beside You," from *My Favorite Brunette*, and on the flip side was "My Favorite Brunette," a new song not even in the film. Both songs were backed up by Paul Weston. "Beside You" was a mixture of singing and talking. During the cutting of it Hope commented that Harry Truman's new campaign slogan (now that both Margaret and he were becoming musically famous too) was "Loew's State in '48."

My Favorite Brunette opened with a gala premiere at the downtown Paramount benefiting the Damon Runyon Memorial Cancer Fund for Research. Art Linkletter was M.C. for radio KFWB in the lobby, and part of the show was televised over ABC's Pacific Coast network and shortwaves to troops around the world by the Armed Forces Radio.

Hope, of course, was the master of ceremonies for the show, which had Gene Kelly, Burns and Allen, the Andrews Sisters, Cary Grant, Edgar Bergen, Van Johnson, Frank Sinatra, Al Jolson, Jerry Colonna, Desi Arnaz, Betty Hutton, Dinah Shore, Jack Benny, Danny Kaye, Eddie Cantor, Jimmy Durante, Red Skelton, Benny Goodman and his sextette, and the Victor Young Orchestra. That was a lot of talent and glamour for a premiere, but it usually paid off. The fans loved it, and we raised a lot of money for charity.

In the opening sequence of *My Favorite Brunette,* Bing played an executioner; Alan Ladd is already in the gas chamber when a governor issues a stay of execution. Ironically, Alan and I were set to do a bit in *Variety Girl* where Alan had to sing like Bing and I think that Alan would rather have taken the gas!

14. Produced by Hope and Crosby

The Big Haircut was not a remake of *Samson and Delilah* (Lamarr and Mature did that much later), but Paramount's idea of love and life in the wheat fields. The title referred to harvesting. Alan Ladd and my old beau Robert Preston completed the triangle in this film, with Lloyd Nolan, Allen Jenkins, and Dick Erdman supporting.

Everyone involved in this picture was a real gin rummy nut. There were games going on constantly on location. "Excuse me, ladies and gentlemen," director Tay Garnett would have to say, "I do hate to break up the gin game, but we do have a picture to complete!" (In between acts of any show I do, you can still find me shuffling the cards. It's not true that you have to play gin rummy to get a job in my show, but it's not a bad idea.)

In Road to Rio *Hope played Hot Lips Barton; Bing was Scat Sweeney; I was Lucia Maria de Andrade, and Catherine Veil was played by Gail Sondergaard*

Alan had had the good fortune to marry a wonderful lady named Sue Carol, who gave up her rather successful career when she married Alan and became his manager, his confidante, and his best friend as well. Since Bill and I were also very happy, it was natural that all four of us became very close.

MCA (my agents at the time) wanted Alan as a client, and when they heard about our friendship, they asked me to speak to him. I mentioned it to Alan, but didn't push the idea. MCA kept pestering me, so finally I decided to throw a big party for the Ladds and make sure that all the top MCA brass were invited. We put up a tremendous tent on our tennis court and hired caterers; the guest list consisted of nearly every star and newsperson in town.

Shortly afterwards, Alan signed with MCA. Now wouldn't you think that MCA would say a simple "thank you" for a party that cost us several thousand pre-inflation dollars and that enabled them to connect with one of the hottest stars in town? But I have yet to hear it. And whenever I have asked a favor from Universal (which MCA now owns), they have politely but firmly refused.

Another strike hit Paramount, but the Screen Actors Guild had okayed our working as long as we didn't *leave* the studio! This necessitated a mass move-in by all concerned. Sue Ladd was pregnant and due any day, so to relieve Alan of worry, she moved into his Paramount dressing room.

In spite of his "tough guy" image, Alan Ladd was just like any other new father, constantly dashing off to check up on his wife. I've never seen anyone so nervous, so to ease the tension, I threw a baby shower for the two of them, right there on the set. Because Sue was absolutely positive that she was going to have a baby girl, I served the drinks in baby bottles with pink ribbons tied on them.

But naturally, Sue bore a fine healthy boy, whom they named David. (He grew up to be a good juvenile actor in such films as *The Proud Rebel, The Big Land,* and *A Dog of Flanders.* David's wife Cheryl has reached her own stardom with her role on TV's "Charlie's Angels" and they have a daughter of their own.)

The Big Haircut's title was changed to *Wild Harvest,* a

switch that pleased all of us. After all, how many barber and hairdresser jokes can one company take? It was a rough picture, especially for Alan, who had a long brawl scene with Pres, a riot scene in a dance hall (again involving Pres, plus Jenkins and Erdman) that took forever to film; a wild automobile chase in which he deliberately wrecks and explodes one of the huge combines, and a spectacular fire in the wheat field, in which he orders the combines driven into the river to escape the flames. The wheat field fire scene was accomplished by studio technicians without burning one stalk of wheat; the blaze was photographed in miniature on the studio's model stage. But it was pretty darned hot when it came to the close-ups on our regular sound stage!

Both Alan and Pres worked very hard to make their big fight scene a classic. For the kayo punch, Ladd sent Pres sailing into a big potbellied stove in the corner. It collapsed, the chimney conking Pres on the noggin and covering him with a steady stream of soot. Looking like he was in blackface, he chuckled, "Boy. This part really 'sooted' me, didn't it?"

Everyone asks about Alan Ladd's height. Yes, he was short compared to most leading men, but he had a great sense of humor about it.

Director Tay Garnett summed up Alan in his delightful book, *Light Your Torches and Pull Up Your Tights:*

> *He was generous, gentle, considerate, possessed of both a fantastic screen personality and a delightful spontaneous wit. He wasn't the tallest man ever to face a camera, but he was superbly built—an Atlas in miniature. Like many a talented man who feels Nature has shortchanged him, Alan had a hangup about his height. When he did a scene with a big guy, Bob Preston, for instance, we laid down planks three inches high for Alan to stand on. Those planks were the equalizer.*
>
> *When "Harvest" wound up, we tossed a big bash in one of our bar sets on the sound stage. Naturally, the excellent free chow and limitless grog drew a full quota of crashers. Most were studio people whom we knew, visiting from other sets; but one unknown giant of a man with a beat-up puss leaned*

> *on the bar and started to belt 'em down. With each fresh drink, he demanded more elbow room.*
>
> *I told Alan, "That big mug is bad trouble, and nobody has a line on him."*
>
> *Said Alan, "I know who he is. He's the big bastard who's leaving as of now!"*
>
> *Before anyone could stop him, Alan strode up to the surly monster, and reaching up, tapped him on the shoulder. The behemoth turned around and grinned down at Ladd, saying, "Hi, Shorty."*
>
> *That didn't get him any votes.*
>
> *Alan said, "You weren't invited to this party." By that time Nolan, Preston and I had moved in, close behind Alan as Gargantua sneered, "And you intend to do something about it, huh?"*
>
> *Alan nodded emphatically, then turned toward the crew and yelled, "Get my planks!"*
>
> *It got a helluva laugh from all hands except Mac Colossal. Before the bewildered crasher could recover, Bob Preston had locked the guy's arms from behind. Possibly the troublemaker had heard of Bob's exploits as a heavyweight in the service. In any case, he cooperated in his fast trip to the door.*

That's a quote from a man who *knew* Ladd, not a story written by someone who didn't even known him. I always knew Alan to be a happy guy, and it really burns me up to read some of the stories written about him when he's not around to defend himself.

As soon as we finished *Wild Harvest,* Alan and I were asked to do a number in *Variety Girl*, Paramount's latest all-star musical revue. If Alan was a nervous wreck awaiting David's birth, that was nothing compared to his stagefright at making his singing debut.

Every star on the Paramount lot either did a walk-on or performed in this film, which chronicled the good work being done by Variety Clubs International for underprivileged children around the world. The only way they could get us all together to appear in the finale was to shoot the sequence on a Sunday afternoon. Autograph hounds had a field day as Bing,

Bob, Gary Cooper, Ray Milland, Barbara Stanwyck, Paulette Goddard, Veronica Lake, Sonny Tufts, Joan Caulfield, Bill Holden, Lizabeth Scott, Burt Lancaster, Gail Russell, Diana Lynn, Sterling Hayden, Bob Preston, John Lund, William Bendix, Barry Fitzgerald, Cass Daley, Howard Da Silva, Billy De Wolfe, MacDonald Carey, Arleen Whelan, Patric Knowles, Mona Freeman, Virginia Field, Cecil Kellaway, Pearl Bailey, George Reeves, Wanda Hendrix, directors Cecil B. DeMille, Mitch Leisen, Frank Butler, and George Marshall (who also directed the film), plus Spike Jones and his City Slickers pulled into the Paramount lot. The only Paramount contractee not present was Betty Hutton, who was having a baby at the time.

Seventeen-year-old Mary Hatcher, who played the "Variety Girl," took a lot of kidding from the rest of the cast. "Okay," George Marshall announced to the crew, "let's get going. Miss Hatcher has to finish by 5:30."

"That right," Hope piped up. "Little Mary has to rush back to her incubator."

In one skit Alan and I played a pilot and a stewardess who decide to highjack a plane—in those days, a funny idea and not a cold reality—and take it to "Tallahassee" (the title of the song). At the end of the number, Alan let out a deep "Whew!!" that was so funny, George left it in the final print. The song "Tallahassee" was written by Frank Loesser, who had scored a big hit with "Praise the Lord and Pass the Ammunition." Bing and the Andrews Sisters did "Tallahassee" on Decca, and Columbia released a Dinah Shore/Woody Herman version. No, we didn't put out a single, but I expect to see it as a black market record any day now.

The premiere of *Variety Girl* was held at the downtown Paramount Theater and offered an all-star live show, with all proceeds going to the $100,000 East Side Boys' Club that the Variety Club was building on Cincinnati Street. That night raised a whopping $27,500 toward that worthy cause. Hope and George Jessel shared the M.C. chores, and Jimmy Durante, Eddie Cantor, Red Skelton, Billy De Wolfe, Eddie Bracken, and Danny Thomas each did comedy turns. Olga San Juan, Jane Russell, Jo Stafford, and I appeared in skits with Jerry Colonna, Bill Bendix,

Alan Ladd, Bill Demarest, and Edgar Bergen with Charlie McCarthy.

Music was provided by Dave Rose and his fabulous orchestra. Colonna broke up the crowd outside by grabbing the microphone and doing his fractured version of "The Road to Mandalay." Inside, Jessel and Cantor convulsed the audience with tales of the good old days (39 years earlier) when they worked together in vaudeville. Each star had been scheduled to one song or skit, but the audience kept giving Cantor standing ovations. After "Ida," he sang "Whoopee," then "Margie," and of course, "If You Knew Susie." Again the house went wild, but the fourth time he didn't come back. "You might as well stop," Jessel told the audience, "After all that exertion, Cantor had to go lie down."

Paramount next booked Bob, Bing, and me on the *Road to Rio,* our fifth adventure together. This time, however, Bing and Bob each put together a production company and joined Paramount in producing this one, so it was a three-way split.

They could have considered a four-way split, but no one even asked me. My feelings were hurt. (And, as it would prove later, so was my pocketbook.) They later gave me a tiny percentage, and one of my proudest possessions is a check for a profit-sharing residual from *Road to Rio* for 16 cents. Instead of bothering to cash it, I framed it. But when interviewed about the new "Road," I simply said, "People seem to be always asking me if I don't get tired of all these 'Road' films. The answer is no. And what's more, I'd feel hurt if Bob and Bing were to appear in a 'Road' picture without me. This one is my fifth, and I like them immensely. So many of us in the cast and crew have worked together that we know each other well and it's easier to work with people you know. Another reason is that Bob and Bing are great ones for jokes and gags. I never know when they will pull one off, and it's nice to anticipate having a laugh or two somewhere along the line."

In this one, the Andrews Sisters, whose Decca recordings with Bing had exceeded a sales total of 5 million platters, made their screen debut in a concert with Crosby aboard the luxury liner en route to Rio. (I never had a scene with them, but later got to know them well.) The super-crazy Wiere Brothers, whom Earl Carroll had signed to perform in his famed Vanities Club for two weeks (and who stayed for five years), played a group of Brazilian musicians who couldn't speak a word of English. They darned near stole every scene they were in.

On the first day of filming I received a very long, cumbersome bundle with a note from Bing and Bob: "For Dottie, who doesn't need any help stopping traffic on any *Road*!" When I opened it, there was a boulevard stop sign!

Now that they were our producers, they checked out a few things a little more closely. One day, Bob teased me about the low cleavage of my Edith Head creation, and really embarrassed me all through the first take. After fluffing my line, I yelled, "Stop everything until Mr. Hope has had a good look!"

Well, he took a good look—at the dress itself—and called Bing over. "How much do you think this dress cost, partner?"

"Somewhere around $4,000," I cut in.

"Well," Bob said when they recovered, "we'll rent it out to at least six more gals before we're through with it. In fact," he added, "before we throw it away we can even alter it to fit Margaret O'Brien."

In spite of their investment, Bing kept breaking up during a take one day and Bob yelled, "This man is crazy! Do you know how much this is costing us?"

"Yeah," Bing came back, "but we'll go broke laughing!"

A few days after we started shooting was Ridge's first birthday, and the first heavy package we opened was a gross of safety pins with a card: "Happy Birthday to our favorite pin-up boy from Uncle Bing and Uncle Bob." The foreign department at Paramount gave Ridge a handsome Morocco-bound book of press clippings on him gathered from all over the world.

Throughout most of the picture I was supposed to be hypnotized by an evil aunt (played by that splendid actress, Gale Sondergaard). This made for some very interesting scenes, because my mood would change as I was given different orders. For example, I walked up to Bing with a big smile on my face, and said, "I hate you. I loathe you. I despise you," then whacked him right across the face!

"But Baby," Bing interjects.

"That sounds like Bogey," threw in Bob, and I turned to him with a right to the jaw!

"This dame is slap-happy!" Hope yelled out.

"Cut!" called director Norman McLeod. "Let's try that again!"

Bob came over, rubbing his jaw. "Look, Dottie, the sound department can put in that loud smack. So you know you don't really have to hit me that hard."

"Yeah," Bing agreed, "or else you'll be known as Rocky Graziano Lamour."

Paramount bought KTLA, the first television station west of Chicago, under their subsidiary of Television Production, Inc. Industry executives hoped its first commercial TV program at 8:30 P.M., January 15, 1947, would launch Hollywood on its way to becoming the television center of the country. A select audience of Hollywood personalities and Los Angeles state and civic leaders arrived to see the newest entertainment premiere. Bob Hope, Willian Bendix, Bill Demarest, Jerry Colonna, Peter Lind Hayes, John Brown, the Rhythmaires, Ann Rutherford, and I were the guests on that first history-making show, sponsored by Tupman Motors of Los Angeles.

Columnist Sheilah Graham came to visit on the *Rio* set one day and asked Bing and me where Bob was.

"He always plays golf in the afternoons," said Bing with a straight face. "You see, we can't use him in the afternoons because of the bags under his eyes, and there isn't enough makeup to fix him up."

On Bob's radio show around this time, guest June Haver commented that she was going to star in *Scudda-Hoo! Scudda-Hay!* a story about two mules. "Why," Hope asked, "is Twentieth Century Fox starring such a beautiful girl like you with two jackasses?"

She replied, "I don't know, but it didn't hurt Dorothy Lamour at Paramount."

On the "Road" films, publicity stills were almost impossible to get because the boys never wanted to sit still for them. Both Bing and Bob kept putting off going to the portrait gallery to pose, and soon my part in the film was finished. Sure enough, a couple of days later I received an urgent call from the studio. Would I please come in and get into makeup and costume so they could get some stills taken? Naturally, I said yes. The next day I was asked to wait in the dressing room until the boys were ready. But they were in such a big hurry to get somewhere (probably to the golf course) that they ran out. The stills ended up being our three heads, superimposed on other bodies sitting on a donkey—and they *looked* superimposed!

For Hollywood's Press Photographers Ball, the stars would get all dolled up in their favorite costumes to party all night. I was surprised when I won first prize as a bearded lady, wearing one of my costumes from *Road to Morocco*; Bill went as a circus barker. Sonny Tufts donned the full regalia of a deep sea diver, Jackie Cooper dressed as The Kid, and Shirley Temple was Alice in Wonderland. Zachary Scott and his wife Elaine came as white bunnies with long pink ears. Greer Garson was Lillian Russell, and her husband Richard Ney was Tom Mix for the night. Ann Rutherford was a perfect can-can dancer, while Carmen Miranda came as herself.

Bob Hope always joked about never getting an Oscar, so after the Academy Awards that year I presented him with a special Oscarette for "Clean living, for unflinching devotion to jokes about Kilroy, the governors of Georgia, and Crosby's horses. Also for consistent bravery in front of hostile audiences. In short, for being the kind of person you are, I present you with the highest award any actor can get . . . for three dollars and fifty cents . . . the coveted Lamour award for loud losers . . . . " It was a ceramic figure of me in a sarong.

For several weeks I had been suffering constant earaches, and finally the doctor told me that I had to go to the hospital for a tonsillectomy and adenoidectomy! I felt like a little girl being admitted for such procedures, but it's a good thing I caught up on some rest. As soon as I came home, I was asked to do a radio show called "Front and Center" to stimulate interest in recruiting for the Armed Forces. The number of volunteers had dwindled, and men were needed for the peacetime armies. NBC donated the time and the Music Corporation of America provided the talent, accepting a token payment for their services. It was a heavy job for me to be announcer, singer, and actress in the skits, but I liked the idea. Glenhall Taylor was set as the program director and Henry Russell conducted the orchestra.

We went on the air July 6, 1947, as the summer replacement for Fred Allen—so to keep the audience, we had to be good. Our time slot was 7:30 to 8:00 P.M. I sang duets with Lionel Barrymore, Jimmy Stewart, and Frank Morgan; did comedy sketches with Boris Karloff, George Murphy, Gregory Peck, Charles Laughton, Lloyd Nolan, Brian Donlevy, Ronald Colman, and Ronald Reagan; and traded quips with Burns and Allen, George Jessel, Abbott and Costello, Victor Moore, Eddie Bracken, Martin and Lewis, and Jerry Colonna. At summer's end, we were picked up as a regular series, with the name changed to "The Sealtest Variety Theater." But my career was in for some other changes, some good and some not.

15. The Queen of the Hollywood Islands

For years I'd been asking Paramount to let me make films for other studios during my twelve-week annual vacation; finally they agreed. So when Benedict Bogeaus offered me a role in his new film, *A Miracle Can Happen,* I said yes. He made it sound especially appealing when he told me that Frank Loesser, one of my favorite composers, was writing a special song for me called "The Queen of the Hollywood Islands," that poked fun at the story of my life.

The movie itself was more or less a revue tied together by Burgess Meredith, who played an inquiring reporter checking out different stories. Paulette Goddard, Buzz Meredith's real wife, played his reel wife. Henry Fonda and James Stewart were a pair of hepcats who played the cornet and piano respectively,

With Jimmy Durante

while Fred MacMurray and Bill Demarest acted in another vignette (they later teamed up again for the successful television series, "My Three Sons"). But the best part of the movie was working with big, lovable Victor Moore again.

Quite a few films were being released or planned with the word "miracle" in their titles (among them, *Miracle on 34th Street*). So our title was first changed to *Along Came Baby* and then to *On Our Merry Way.*

Meredith co-produced with Ben Bogeaus, but obviously they didn't have the best working relationship in town; in June 1950 Meredith sued Bogeaus for his $14,000 salary, which had never been paid. When Bogeaus went into bankruptcy, Meredith ended up paying $1,900 for the rights to the film. But I had no quarrel with Bogeaus, so I moved over to Columbia to do his *Lulu Belle,* based on a Broadway play that David Belasco had produced in 1926 starring the beautiful Lenore Ulric. They had been trying to film it ever since, but the story was a bit too seamy for the movie censors: a "colored chippy" lures the hero George from his wife, then leaves him to marry a prizefighter. After a few more affairs, she returns to the hero—who strangles her!

Not exactly the delight of the Hays office, so Ben did some laundering. In our version, I lure George from a sweetheart (not a wife), then marry him. Due to a misunderstanding, I divorce George and marry a prizefighter, then leave *him* for a producer who makes me a big Broadway star. After finding a new sugar daddy, I realize that I will always love George. Enter the sugar daddy's ex-wife, who shoots both of us. Sugar daddy dies, and when George comes to see me in the hospital, he considers the havoc I've created and decides he couldn't find happiness with a woman like me. He leaves. Fade out . . . The End.

George Montgomery was my leading man and Albert Dekker, Otto Kruger, and Greg McClure, the other men in my life. I sang some lovely songs, such as "I Can't Tell Why I Love You But I Do," "The Ace in the Hole," "Sweetie Pie," and the title song, "Lulu Belle," with a chorus of handsome male dancers. . . . a forerunner to "Hello, Dolly" and "Mame."

Bill brought Ridge to visit me on the set, and one day I

sat him on my lap to watch the daily rushes, since he had never seen me on screen before. When I came on the screen, he looked at the real me (I was wearing the same costume I'd worn during the previous day's shooting), then back at the screen. When I started to explain to him, my screen image also started talking! Ridge let out a shocked scream, and I had to take him outside the studio and calm him down.

After all the cleaning up that the storyline had undergone, I had to smile when the adds for *Lulu Belle* came out:

> *Men are sure to talk about Lulu Belle! Women are sure to gossip about Lulu Belle!*
> *The Belle of an Era!! The Toast of the Town!! The tempestuous siren who became the flame of New Orleans . . . the rage of New York!!*
> *Men called it . . . "Lulu Belle Fever"!!*
> *There was something about the way she looked at a man that rang bells!*
> *Ask George . . . he went to prison for her*
> *Ask Randolph . . . he broke up his home for her*
> *Ask Brady . . . he made her the toast of the New Orleans Latin Quarter*
> *Ask Butch . . . he threw away the title for her*
> *Her torch songs were the rage of New Orleans . . . her love affairs were the talk of New York!!*
> *Everyone knew why she was the Toast of New York . . . but nobody dared say it out loud!*
> *Why did scandal always follow Lulu Belle?????*

Since Paramount had nothing ready for me, I stayed on at Columbia to do *Slightly French*, a remake of an old Ann Sothern film, *Let's Make Love* (1934). Adele Jergens played Yvonne LaTour, a French actress who collapses, leaving producer Don Ameche without a star for his new musical. Searching for a new French leading lady he settles for me, little Irish Mary O'Leary, who knows only one Gallic phrase, "French fries, please!" Clever Don hires a tutor to turn me into a French chanteuse named Rochelle Olivia in no time flat; Janis Carter, Willard Parker, and Jeanne Manet joined us. (We didn't use the original title, so Twentieth

Century Fox used it for their 1960 Marilyn Monroe/Yves Montand picture.)

When I first came to Hollywood, Howard Hughes used to send me dozens of yellow roses with invitations to dine with him. I always refused politely. But now that Howard heard I was available for outside films, he began to woo me to sign with RKO Pictures, his new pet project. He offered $400,000 per picture for four pictures to be made over a period of several years, with story and director approval—an actress's dream. Yet the whole time I was negotiating this at RKO, I never once saw Howard himself."

Neither RKO nor Paramount had a script ready, so back to Columbia for *The Girl From Manhattan,* with George Montgomery, Charles Laughton, and the most incredible group of character actors in the business. You might not recognize all the names, Ernest Truex, Constance Collier, Hugh Herbert, Sara Allgood, Frank Orth, Howard Freeman, George Chandler, Adelaide de Walt Reynolds, and Maurice Cass, but their faces would be familiar. Working with a group of noted scene stealers like that keeps a gal on her toes.

Through the years Jack Benny and I had acquired the same attorney (Loyd Wright), same business manager (Myrt Blom), and the same agency (MCA) representing both of us. They all got together and asked me to appear in *The Lucky Stiff,* Jack's first venture as a producer for his Amusement Enterprises. I was never crazy about the script, but said that I would consider it if they made some changes. They agreed, and while I was in Baltimore visiting Bill's mother, Leo McCarey called to say that he was considering directing. Well, with Benny and McCarey also considering, how could I say no?

But since the budget was low and this was the company's first film, would I defer $125,000 of my salary? Of course. Well, Benny didn't appear in the film; McCarey didn't direct. Brian Donlevy and Claire Trevor, two fine performers, co-starred with me, but *The Lucky Stiff* never set the movie theaters afire.

Jack later sold his company to CBS, who sold it to

someone else, *ad nauseam.* Even though I have written to everyone concerned notifying them that I'm a creditor, I've been completely ignored. Even an attorney I hired hasn't been able to collect my deferred $125,000, but the picture still plays on television constantly on the Late Show. I see it everywhere I travel. Wonder who does get the money?

Myrt Blom's wife Babe is Mary Livingstone Benny's sister. The four of us—Myrt, Babe, Bill, and I—used to exchange elaborate or crazy Christmas gifts. One year they kept asking me for an autographed picture, so I took an inexpensive toilet seat from the hardware store over to Beverly Hills furrier, Al Teitelbaum to be upholstered completely in white mink. I then put my picture under the seat so that when you opened up the mink-lined lid, there I was. I inscribed the photo: "To Myrt, my favorite B.M. [business manager, of course!].

This became my "no way to treat a lady" period. In *Slightly French* I'd been pushed down a fight of stairs; in my new Paramount film I was to be smacked around by Dan Duryea, who then tries to push me off a rooftop. Appropriately called *Manhandled,* it was originally called *Betrayal* and then *The Man Who Stole a Dream,* neither of which was menacing enough.

Blond Sterling Hayden played the good guy, and George Reeves (yesteryear's Superman), an extremely sinister cad. Duryea played such a villain that they made him dye his blond hair black. He gave out an interview that would cause an uproar with today's women. After *Scarlett Street*,, in which he slapped Joan Bennett around, he got letters from women who said he reminded them of their husbands or boyfriends. A psychiatrist told Duryea that a startling 80 percent of the women in this country were masochists who enjoyed being dominated!

Bill and I wanted another child very badly and had been trying since Ridge was a year old. Finally in January 1949 Dr. McBurney gave me word that I was expectant once again. After telling Bill, I immediately notified Paramount and RKO that I would be willing to work approximately until June. From past experience with Ridge, I knew that I would not begin to get heavy until my fifth month. Since neither studio had a picture ready, I concentrated on "The Sealtest Variety Theater." Regular guest Eddie Bracken used to warmup the studio audiences, then introduce me as "Dorothy Lamour and Company."

Texas oilman Glenn McCarthy had a dream of building a really spectacular hotel in Houston, so he took $20 million of his vast fortune to make that dream come true. A total Irishman, he named his hotel The Shamrock; opening day would be St. Patrick's Day, 1949. Bill had taken a job as an ad executive at Ruthrauff and Ryan Advertising Agency, which Glenn hired to promote the opening festivities. Bill was assigned the Shamrock account and before long, he and Glenn became the best of buddies. Would I like to do my radio show live from the Shamrock? Glenn asked. I spoke to Sealtest, who agreed it would be terrific publicity for all of us, and Bill began to organize a huge press junket to Houston.

McCarthy had also just finished producing his first motion picture, *The Green Promise,* starring Walter Brennan, Marguerite Chapman, Robert Paige and a 10-year-old Natalie Wood; and he decided to premiere it at the same time. He leased planes and trains to bring press and celebrities to Houston and even leased the Santa Fe's 16-car Super Chief, and renamed it the "Shamrock Special." The Pullman equipment consisted of bedrooms and drawing rooms only, no berths or roomettes, a diner, and two club cars, each equipped with a piano for continuous entertainment throughout the round trip. The menu listed fresh Hawaiian pineapple, giant mushrooms, hot buttered artichoke hearts, oysters, and two-and-a-quarter-inch steaks (more favored guests would later be presented with Western boots made from the hides of the cattle that provided the steaks).

The Shamrock Special cost McCarthy $14,000 a day for a full week, including the return trip to Hollywood. The beverage bill was $41,000. Consumed were 12 loins of beef (12 steaks to a loin) and 15 racks of lamb (5 chops to a rack). Tips amounted to $3,500 and the junket's total cost was $425,000.

Among the 200 aboard the Shamrock Special were at least 40 press representatives from Hollywood and some 50 celebrities: MacDonald Carey, Andy Devine, Rhonda Fleming,

Alan Hale, Van Heflin, Chester Morris, Pat O'Brien, Dennis O'Keefe, Robert Paige, and Ruth Warrick. From the East by plane came Walter Brennan, Kirk Douglas, Ellen Drew, Kathryn Grayson, Sonja Henie, Constance Moore, Robert Preston, Buddy Rogers, and Ginger Rogers.

They had arranged a parade route for us in Houston. Onlookers were lined up three and four deep to greet the caravan of convertibles and limousines edging itself toward the Shamrock. Together with three connecting promenades, the lobby wall contained 22,000 square feet of Honduras mahogany, all taken from one giant tree so that the burls were perfectly matched. Decorative trees in the lobby were trimmed with over $1,000 worth of orchids. The hotel contained 20 acres of wall-to-wall carpeting as well as original oils and water colors in each of the 1,100 rooms. It was an exciting day, with absolutely no premonition of the fireworks to follow the next evening.

Glennhall Taylor, the director of our program, had worked very hard making the proper broadcasting arrangements. During the broadcast, no food or beverages would be served; the dining room doors would be closed and guests would remain seated. Our rehearsal went very smoothly. My guests were Van Heflin and Ed Gardner (Archie from *Duffy's Tavern*) and Henry Russell's Orchestra never sounded better.

Almost an hour before the broadcast began, Glennhall, Van, Ed, the announcer, the sound effects man, the orchestra and I were all on stage attending to details. Suddenly, the doors to the Emerald Room (where we were to do the show) burst open and in rushed a wave of jewels, evening gowns, and tuxedoes. It seems that in a room that held 1,000, they had sold 1,600 seats for $42 apiece. The hotel staff was going crazy trying to appease people rightly demanding their tables. Amid this bedlam, 8:30 arrived. Glennhall gave the cue. Announcer John Laing proclaimed, "Yes, it's Sealtest Variety Theater . . . starring Dorothy Lamour!"

Our microphones were patched through the hotel's public address system, causing a tinny sound that was picked up for broadcast. Van Heflin and I were standing only two feet apart, but we couldn't hear each other's dialogue over the noise of the crowd. Glennhall had to cue each one of us as we completed our speeches. To add to the confusion, guests began taking shortcuts across the stage. When Glennhall told a matron we were on the air, she grabbed the mike and said, "I don't give a damn about your broadcast, I want my dinner table!"

That was mild compared to what happened when telephone line trouble compounded the melee. In Chicago, where the lines from Houston connected with those feeding the East and the West, a panic-stricken engineer asked for the NBC producer. Crossed wires caused his query to go out over the air. So did Karel Pearson's futile shouting: "*This* is the NBC Producer . . . This *is* the NBC Producer."

The Chicago engineer shook his head ruefully. "They're fucking it up," he muttered. That remark was winged coast to coast. The plugs were pulled immediately, and the show went off the air.

Next day, the front page of the *Houston Press* blazoned a banner headline: "LAMOUR LOSES BATTLE OF BEDLAM."

I was stunned, but all I could say to the press was, "I'm not mad at anybody. I just hope a lot of people had a good time." My main concern was the sponsor. The program, in addition to network charges, cost $15,000 to produce, but Sealtest had received inestimable publicity as a result. Magazines like *Newsweek* and *Time* featured stories on the opening while *Life* spread its account over five full pages. News items mentioning the show appeared in every city in the United States with a population of 11,000 or more. Even more importantly, Glenn McCarthy became a very dear friend. When Tommy Howard was born, in fact, Glenn was one of his godfathers.

In June 1949 the Los Angeles *Times* revealed the salaries of Hollywood's top money-makers. Charles P. Skouras, president of National Theaters and of Fox West Coast Agency was the highest paid male, with $810,000 yearly pay, and Betty Grable topped the females at $208,000. According to the Treasury Department, my salary that year was $150,916. (In comparison to today's million-dollar deals, these salaries seem pretty small, but it was a lot of money in those days.)

That summer Ann Sheridan, Denise Darcel, Bob Hope, Jimmy Durante, and I sponsored a festive tea and cocktail party for the Mickey Finn Foundation; the proceeds went to build a Boy's Town in Chatsworth. Many big stars showed up to support the cause. During a fund-raising auction, I started bidding on a lovely mother-to-be's nightgown. Someone on the other side of the room bid against me. Back and forth we went until the bid reached $100, and I passed. When I saw the winner walk up to pay for it, I couldn't believe he was my Bill. We had been bidding against each other without knowing it.

Pauline Kessinger hosted a baby shower for me at the Paramount commissary, and all my friends on the crew showed up—electricians, grips, makeup, hairdressers. Hope sent me a wire saying, "Sorry I can't make it, but I'm laid up with a bad case of overacting."

I was now in my sixth month. There had been some talk about a musical for me. RKO told me that the script was finished and the score written, but a starting date had never materialized. Then I received a legal notice from them insisting that their doctor examine me to see if I were really pregnant! "If you examine this woman," my doctor told them, "and anything happens to either her or the baby, I will sue you personally."

So RKO decided to send their doctor to my doctor's office. To confirm my condition, they ended up by measuring the size of my stomach. I never heard another word from them until after the baby was born.

On October 20, 1949, I was blessed with a 6-pound, 8½-ounce boy. Had it been a girl, Bill would have named her Dorothy Lamour Howard. I wanted to name him after his great-grandfather—Bill's mother's father, whose name, I thought, was David Thomson Howard. But Bill kept insisting the man's name was *Richard* Thomson Howard. Being prepared, I had made up two telegrams, and now sent Bill's Mother the "boy-gram": "MISS LOU DEAR, YOU NOW HAVE ANOTHER HANDSOME GRANDSON. WE HAVE NAMED HIM RICHARD THOMSON HOWARD AFTER YOUR FATHER."

"THANK YOU, DOTTIE DEAR," she wired back,

"AND MANY THANKS FOR NAMING THE NEW BABY AFTER MY FATHER. BUT WHERE DID YOU GET THE NAME RICHARD?" It was too late to change it, but it didn't really matter, we would always call him Tommy.

Bing's wife Dixie was the mother of four boys. When she heard I had a second son, she telegraphed me: "THIS REMINDS ME OF A FUNNY STORY . . . MINE!!"

The morning after Tommy was born, someone knocked at the door of my room at the Good Samaritan Hospital. "Come in," I said, thinking it was the nurse bringing Tommy for his feeding. But it was a man holding a piece of paper: "Are you Dorothy Lamour?"

When I said, "Yes," he handed me an official notice from RKO informing me that they were canceling my contract!

I immediately called my attorney Loyd Wright. He had done work for Hughes also, but he was so incensed that he called Hughes personally and told him off. He then called Helen Hayes' attorneys in New York. Helen had once been slapped with a similar suit; she won her case on the grounds that her daughter was "a gift of God." Our countersuit used that argument, plus the fact that I had notified RKO of my pregnancy in plenty of time. While Mr. Hughes and RKO could suspend me for one picture had I *not* notified them of the pregnancy, we stated, he could surely not cancel the contract. Therefore, we sued him for the entire amount of my contract.

I came out winning a little better than half a million dollars. Most went to legal fees and income tax, but I did manage to beat Howard Hughes—no mean feat!

16. From the Palladium to the Big Top

Just before I found I was pregnant with Tommy, my London agent Lew Grade (now Lord Lew Grade) had called with an offer to play the famed London Palladium—the dream of most performers. But because of my impending motherhood I had to decline, promising to fulfill my engagement as soon as the baby was born. When Tommy was six months old, I called Lew to say I was ready—and hoped the Palladium was ready for me.

We signed Sam Mineo to be my musical director and I asked Doris Durkus to come along as my hairdresser. The night before we sailed on the *Queen Elizabeth,* Sherman Billingsley invited most of New York to attend a big wingding at the Stork Club. The champagne corks popped all night long with enough toasts of *bon voyage* to float us to the Palladium. The next day, our

Danny Kaye welcomes me to the London Palladium; my friend Doris Durkus looks on

stateroom was filled with flowers, fruit, candy, and more champagne! I kind of miss that in today's traveling. Everything is rushed and a lot of the fun and luxury are gone.

First stop Cherbourg, where we were greeted by the French press and by a group of English reporters who planned to board ship and cross the English Channel with us. I never gave so many interviews and posed for so many pictures in such a short time. At Southampton, more press joined us on the boat train to Victoria Station where were greeted by even more press. By the time we arrived at the Savoy Hotel, I knew why everyone wants to play London.

The next day we began rehearsals. Danny Kaye, who the English consider one of their most beloved performers and who had just completed an engagement at the Palladium, dropped by to give me a few suggestions. I had only met him once or twice socially in Hollywood but I was quite touched that he would take the time. At our first meeting with Val Parnell, who owned the Palladium, we showed him the knockout wardrobe Jean Louis had designed for me. We hadn't planned to include a sarong, thinking it was old hat, but Parnell was so disappointed that we whipped one up. The appropriate place to wear it was in the finale, but for that number Jean Louis had designed a white strapless gown with a form-fitting bodice with over 200 yards of very fine tulle making up the skirt. Both the skirt and top were silver beaded. Now the problem was how to make a quick change. I could wear the sarong under the gown, but they decided to split the gown up the back so I could get out of it fast enough. It broke my heart to see them cut that dress, but the show must go on!

Opening night was sensational. (I still get a lot of fan mail from England.) The British applauded madly after each song, and soon it was time for the finale. I had worn my hair in chignon. As I walked offstage, Doris pulled the pins out of my hair and it fell down, she then stuck a flower in my hair and quickly unsnapped the back of the gown and I pulled up the top of the sarong, which had been folded under my skirt. I returned to the stage and began "Queen of the Hollywood Island." Pandemonium broke out, they were just wonderful!

At the end of each performance it is the custom to sing "God Save the King" and there I was standing in a very short sarong. But Jean Louis had also made me a long skirt to put on when I sang the anthem.

Parnell also asked us to take the show up to his Empire Theater in Scotland. Val had given me a chauffeured Rolls Royce, but the roads in those days weren't the best so he advised us to take the train; he'd send the car ahead. In spite of a rainstorm, huge crowds at the Glasgow train station all carried cards reading "Welcome." Twelve came dressed in kilts, playing bagpipes. The hotel was connected to the train station, so we went right over to meet the press. Crowds gathered outside kept chanting, "We want Dottie!" I went to the window and waved, but some couldn't see me so I stood up on the wet ledge with Doris holding my waist.

We toured the Pringle of Scotland's factory, where they gave us samples of their fine tartans. Since Bill's middle name is Ross, they made him a vest in the Ross tartan and both our boys received a tam and a kilt. Speaking of kilts, one night a man in the audience kept shouting, "Hey, Dottie. What's under your sarong?" I tried to ignore him, but soon more of the audience picked up the chant. I put out my arm and stopped the show.

"I'll tell you my secret about the sarong," I said, "if you'll tell me your secret about the kilt?"

The audience broke up, but I never did get an answer from him. Rumor has it that they wear nothing under those kilts. (Confidentially, I wore bikini panties under my sarong.)

Each night after the show I went outside the theater to say hello to the thousands of fans who congregated there. The police escort would take me to the Rolls, and once inside, I would open the sunroof, sign autographs, and sing, "I Belong to Glascow," a song that Harry Lauder had introduced many years before and was practically the Scots' national anthem. Sometimes the crowd shouting "More!" began to push too much and the car swayed back and forth. One night, I had just handed an autograph to a little boy about 12 years old when the crowd moved the car even though the brake was on. The boy fell down and got pinned under the back wheel. He wasn't hurt, just scared, but his clothes were torn and his shoes damaged. We drove him to the hospital to make sure he was fine. The next day, I had someone from the theater deliver some new clothes and shoes to his house.

The Army had asked Lew Grade if I would entertain the British and American servicemen still stationed in Germany. We had planned to go to Paris and Rome anyway, so we trained back to London. Ambassador Douglas flew us to Hamburg in his private plane. Over Holland I'll never forget seeing acres upon acres of tulips, blooming in red, blue, purple, yellow, pink, every color imaginable.

We did shows all over Germany, in fact, we even went into the Russian zone where the boys hadn't seen any entertainment for a long time, let alone a woman in a sarong.

In Landshut, Germany, Sam was griping that he needed a haircut, but we were so busy he couldn't squeeze it in. When I suggested a military barber he said, "Oh, no. They'll cut too much off."

That night while Sam was playing the piano, I arranged for a barber to come onstage, put a sheet around Sam's neck and calmly begin to cut his hair. Sam was shaking with laughter, but he never missed a note.

I hadn't been feeling too good but chalked it up to working so hard. The day I arrived in Hamburg, I began to hemorrhage and had to have a doctor give me a shot to stop the bleeding. From that day on, my period came quite often and one night, I had to receive another shot in the middle of a performance. Determined not to let the servicemen down, I continued the tour with a military doctor with me at all times.

When we did the last show, I was a nervous wreck with worries of cancer. I thought the trip to Rome would relax me. In Rome we went directly to the Excelsior Hotel. My doctor had advised me to spend a lot of time in bed, but this was Doris' and Sam's first trip to Rome, so I sent them out to see the sights for me. Bill and I sat on the balcony of the Excelsior, people watching the Via Veneto. My appetite hadn't been the greatest, but one night I had a craving for spaghetti so I called room service. The spaghetti was overcooked, so Bill went down to tell the chef how to cook spaghetti properly.

Frank Leahy had arranged an audience with the Pope and I didn't want to miss that. I put on a simple black dress with a lace headscarf. Bill, Doris, Sam and I had to wait in several different rooms as we progressed through the Vatican. The guards followed me and put down a chair each time we had to stop. It was worth all the trouble because I really enjoyed speaking with His Holiness.

My condition wasn't getting any better. The doctor in Rome wanted to operate but I first wanted to talk to Dr. McBurney at home. He advised me to fly immediately to Paris where an American doctor could examine me. I hated to fly but wasn't in any mood to take my time. Doris and I flew out the next day.

Sam had to return home because of a previous commitment, so Bill had to accompany all the heavy luggage on the train to Paris. At the Italian border, the guards began to go through everyone's baggage. Opening my trunks, the customs men kept looking from Bill, who spoke neither French nor Italian, to the costumes, sarongs, gowns and long hair pieces (halfwigs). I'd love to know exactly what they thought was going on.

The doctor said that I could take the *Queen Elizabeth* home if I took it easy. I did manage to make a small trip to Chanel's and Madame Schiaparelli's salons, but most of my time in Paris I spent in bed. After docking in New York, we went directly to the train station. In Pasadena an ambulance met the train and took me straight to the Good Samaritan Hospital where Dr. McBurney examined me.

At first they thought it might have been a miscarriage, but I had to stay in the hospital for a week awaiting the results of several other tests. Dr. McBurney told me I needed a hysterectomy. I was very unhappy because we wanted more children, but Bill told me right now my health was more important.

After a successful operation, I went home to recuperate. And it certainly spurred my recovery when Bing asked if I would do a cameo role in his new film, *Here Comes the Groom,* singing "Misto Cristofo Columbo" with the great Satchmo, Phil Harris, Cass Daley, and Bing himself. The money was certainly right, and that crazy scene took only one day to film, so I agreed.

The Paramount publicity department, headed up by Jerry Pickman and Herbie Steinberg, decided to hold the premiere in Elko, Nevada, where Bing happened to own a very large ranch. How they talked Bing into it I don't know, because he absolutely loathed any large affair, and this was to be a three-day event with planeloads of press being flown in from all over the country.

Elko was a small town with a population of only 5,000, but news travels fast in Nevada. Soon tourists were pouring into town to take a peek at the motion picture stars. Alexis Smith, Jane Wyman, Connee Boswell, and Cass Daley joined us for the festivities, and the town was completely decorated for the fun, though a local gun shop's sign took top honors: "Here Comes the Groom, Let's Make It a Shotgun Wedding."

Since Bing kept refusing to go to the airport, Herbie and Jerry asked me to keep up good relations with the press. I got decked out in my cowgirl outfit, ten-gallon hat and Western boots and escorted the press back to the hotel, and then set off for the airport to meet the next group—a tiring job, but enjoyable.

The first night there was a cocktail party and dinner party for our 200 visitors. Bing politely but firmly refused to attend either function. When he came in from the ranch to discuss the schedule for the next three days, Jerry and Herbie tried to get him just to stick his head in and say hello, but Bing was adamant.

Finally, Herbie excused himself and called me. "Dottie, is there anything you can do to talk Bing into it, and believe me, this is very important to the picture, the studio—and Bing."

Quickly I called the hotel and invited Bing to have an early dinner with Bill and me at our motel. As soon as we sat down for drinks, I started the pitch: how important it was to the picture that he attend the press parties.

"I thought I smelled a rat," Bing laughed. "Right after Herbie leaves the room, I get an invitation to have dinner with you. But no thanks, I really don't want to go. I hate those kinds of affairs.

When Bing finished his drink, I quickly had Bill order another round and whispered, "Have the waiter keep Bing's glass full. Then go call Herbie and Jerry and alert them that I'll be over soon with Mr. Crosby in tow."

A couple of drinks later Bing began to get a little mellow. I looked around and asked, "Now where do you suppose Bill disappeared to? Listen, Bing, I have to get over to the reception, and Bill's run off someplace. I know you don't even want to go near the hotel, but I'd certainly appreciate it if you could drive me over there."

The gentleman in Bing came out and he agreed—but under no circumstances was he going into that reception! We finished our last drink, and off we went.

When we pulled up to the hotel, I said, "Bing, it just isn't ladylike to walk through the casino by myself. Would you mind just escorting me to the door of the ballroom?"

Reluctantly he agreed, again insisting he wasn't going further than the door. But once we got to the door, of course, Bill, Herbie, and Jerry and a couple of reporters grabbed Bing and handed him a drink. He ended up staying the whole evening and charming everyone in sight. I thought he might be a bit upset with me, but he just laughed and told the press some wonderful stories about the "Road" pictures.

It seemed that every few hours there was a banquet, buffet breakfast, buffet lunch, tea, or after-theater snack. I'd never seen so much food in my life. Breakfast started out with silver fizzes and we seemed to eat and drink all day long. The second day featured an enormous barbecue, and contests galore! The studio had managed a publicity tie-in with a national shirt company, so each reporter was dolled up in western garb. Cass Daley and I entered the greased pig contest and, between the two of us, got covered with enough grease to service the fleet of limousines we arrived in.

Boston reporter Marjorie Adams was a tiny lady with a very dignified Boston accent. When Bing picked a winning raffle ticket out of a ten-gallon hat and called out "Marjorie Adams!" she dropped her New England reserve and let out a whoop of joy. Turning to me, she whispered, "What the heck did I win?"

Bing placed the end of a rope in her hand, then

stepped aside to let her see what was on the other end: an enormous steer. Her face turned as red as a beet, but she thanked him in a most dignified manner. Paramount had the steer shipped to her in Boston. What she did with it, I never did find out but I would love to have seen her face when they delivered it.

Bing was named Honorary Mayor of Elko, and I was tabbed Honorary Governor of Nevada, for 48 hours. Connee Boswell sang, and Bing and Jane Wyman reprised their "In the Cool, Cool, Cool of the Evening" (which copped an Oscar for Best Song that year), even though in those days he never liked to get up on stage. As I look back, I think he was a very shy, insecure man. The world looked upon him as one of the great talents, he just never saw himself in that light.

After the premiere, my musical conductor, Sam Mineo, Bill, and I realized we hadn't spent much time gambling, so we headed for the casinos, which are legal throughout the state of Nevada. I played my favorite game, blackjack, until I couldn't see the cards anymore and my feet felt swollen. I had lost Sam completely, but finally came upon Bill, who was on a winning streak. Would I mind, he asked, if he stayed up a little longer? "Go ahead," I told him, "but I have to get to bed."

Up in our suite I got off my cowgirl clothes but for the life of me I couldn't get those damned boots off! Finally, I had Bill paged but was informed that Mr. Howard did not like to be disturbed while gambling! Too embarrassed to explain why I wanted to talk to him, I gave up.

When Bill finally came upstairs, he let himself in, tiptoed across the room, and turned on the bed lamp. Then he burst out laughing. There in bed was his glamorous wife wearing a filmy baby blue negligee and cowboy boots.

For several years Cecil B. DeMille had been very interested in doing a circus picture but knew that David O. Selznick had already made a deal with Ringling Brothers and Barnum and Bailey for the title, *The Greatest Show on Earth.* As always, Cecil loved the title with the word "greatest" in it. One afternoon, he read in the trades that Selznick had given up his option and that John Ringling North was seeking another producer. C. B. called North immediately, and shortly afterwards they held a joint press conference to announce plans to film *The Greatest Show on Earth* with an all-star cast. Mr. DeMille paid North $250,000 for the use of his slogan, talent, and equipment. Paramount designers Edith Head, Dorothy Jeakins and Miles White were told to design brand-new costumes, that would then be donated to the circus for their next season.

Betty Hutton was the first to be signed after her zealous campaign to get the role of Holly, the trapeze artist. Mr. DeMille then asked if I would be Phyllis, the Girl with the Iron Jaw. I asked Dr. Raymond McBurney if he approved of such a role.

"Yes, Dorothy," he said, "I think it would be all right as long as it isn't too strenuous. What kind of role is it?"

I looked at him. "I have to hang by my teeth."

Dr. McBurney finally agreed. He figured that it would take me some time to learn the feat, so by the time the cameras started to roll, I would be in pretty good shape.

Lucille Ball was then signed to play Angel the Elephant Girl (a role that Paulette Goddard had tried her darnedest to snare) but had to withdraw because of impending motherhood. Replacing Lucy was Gloria Grahame (who would win an Oscar for her work in *The Bad and the Beautiful* in 1952). Charlton Heston, fresh from his film debut in *Dark City,* was cast as the circus manager. And Cornel Wilde and Lyle Bettger were assigned top roles.

"I had always loved the circus," Jimmy Stewart recalled, "and when I heard that DeMille was making a circus film, I sent a wire and asked if I could be in it and play a clown. You see, everyone wanted to do this picture. We all had our dreams about running away and joining the circus. Making this film was a joyous time for everybody, much more than just a movie." Jimmy was set for the role of Buttons the Clown—a character with a past that would eventually catch up with him—and was coached in his role by the classic clown Emmett Kelly. "Dottie, I think more than anybody entered into the spirit of the circus wholeheartedly. Circus people are a breed apart, and they appreciated her enthusiasm and accepted her as one of their own. We actually did performances in front of live audiences to get the feel of it. It didn't take long before we all felt that we were a part of the circus family. There's something about the circus life; you get engulfed in it. We all really became circus people, and I must say it was a very nice feeling."

We all worked very hard on this film, going into the circus version of "basic training" for weeks before shooting actually started. Paramount sent me to a dentist who took an impression of my teeth and made upper and lower plates, into which my own teeth fitted perfectly. Then both plates were tightly attached to a wide leather strip. Get the picture? At the end of the strap was a swivel device that hooked onto the rope that would lift me 40 feet into the air . . . without a net!

The great Antoinette Consello trained me by starting me on a ladder. Each day I went up a couple of rungs. On the day I reached the top of the ladder, a studio photographer climbed up in the catwalk high above me to get some good publicity shots. That particular photographer had worked with me many times before, and before tripping the shutter, he always reminded me to smile. Now, from force of habit, he called down, "Dottie, smile!" "*No*!" screamed Antoinette, in a near faint. Had I smiled, every tooth in my head would have come out with the pressure.

Slowly, they pulled me up as I froze into a ballet pose. When I reached the top, I had to spread my arms and legs and turn, then twirl like crazy. I've always had a terrific fear of heights, but this didn't bother me too much. All I could see was the top of the tent, and I was pretty close to it.

Mr. DeMille wanted complete authenticity, so we planned to go to Sarasota, Florida—Ringling Brothers' winter training grounds—and then go out on the road with the circus, shooting scenes in different cities.

This film was going to take several months, and since I didn't want to be away from my family, we *all* went to Florida—Bill, Mother, Ridge, Tommy, Louise, our houseman Amos, and me. We rented a beautiful home on the water, complete with a boat and fishing pier. Ridge was already entered in a Beverly Hills kindergarten, but his teacher felt he would be all right in a Florida school for the duration. His brother Tommy was only about 18 months old so there were no schooling problems for him.

There were no phones on the set, but we all had portable walkie-talkies. One morning hearing that an epidemic of measles had broken out in Ridge's school, I got Mother on the walkie-talkie and asked her to bring Ridge home. She called back and told me not to worry: Ridge seemed to be in perfect health.

The next day, unfortunately, he had all the symptoms, and soon came down with a bad case. But after the measles ran their normal course, he wouldn't eat, and his speech pattern began to change.

"Probably a mild case of encephalitis, a kind of sleeping sickness," the doctor assured me. "The boy will be okay in a day or so."

But that "day or so" was too long in coming. I called our good friend Dr. Barney Kully, an ear, nose, and throat specialist in California, who advised me to get Ridge on a plane immediately. By this time the cast and crew were about to return to the Coast to film the big train-wreck sequence, so a couple of the workmen gave up their seats for Ridge and me on one of the chartered planes. Bill flew back by commercial airline, and Mother took Tommy on the train.

The studio had a limousine ready when we landed in Los Angeles. I held Ridge on my lap all the way to the doctor. Ridge wanted to fight and tried to bite me. The poor child had no control over his bladder or bowels, and his speech was very slurred. As soon as Dr. Kully saw him, he advised us to take him to Children's Hospital.

The other doctors agreed that if Ridge lived, he would be crippled for life. But he needed a blood transfusion immediately. Ridge's blood type was a rare one, and the transfusion had to be taken directly from another person who had not had the measles.

The first person to volunteer was my makeup man Harry Ray, who came dragging into the hospital. No, he told the doctors, he'd never had measles, but he had been out late "celebrating" with some of the girls in the circus so they had better take some tests first. Fortunately he passed with flying colors.

Bing, Bob, and I had nicknamed Harry "No-Blood" because he was so thin, but he was the one who gave the transfusion that really saved Ridge's life.

Finally the doctors told me to go home and rest. As soon as Bill and I walked in the door, the phone rang. I picked up the receiver, only to hear the *plunk* of coins being dropped into a pay phone. My circus friends back in Florida had heard the news on the radio. Someone in Ringling Brothers had Ridge's blood type, and they wanted to pitch in and fly him out to Los Angeles. When Jimmy Stewart said we became part of the circus family, he was absolutely right.

For the next couple of days Ridge was still a very sick little boy, but DeMille insisted that I report each day and get into makeup, whether I worked or not. I know *now* it was his way of keeping me from sitting at home, brooding over Ridge's illness. During lunch I would throw a coat over my circus costume and drive to the hospital, which wasn't too far from Paramount. After work Bill would pick me up at the studio and we'd go back to see Ridge, together. From all over the country I received thousands of letters, cards, and phone calls, which I genuinely appreciated. Red Skelton's son Richard was seriously ill at the time, and Red and I would call each other and pray for each other's child.

One day Mother went shopping in Beverly Hills and ran into Bill Boyd, who played Hopalong Cassidy. Like any other boy, Ridge was crazy about Hoppy and had met him at a few children's functions in Hollywood.

Mother walked right up to Bill, who was dressed in an ordinary business suit, "I'm Dorothy Lamour's mother, and my little grandson is very ill. Could you possibly send him a card? It would mean so much to him."

Hoppy, looked at his watch. "I'll do better than that. I have some free time, so I'll drop by and see him. Where is he?"

At the hospital, I was just leaning over to kiss Ridge good-bye when he stiffened up. He pulled himself up on the bars of the bed, to a sitting position, looked over my shoulder and tried to say something. I turned, and there was Hoppy in full western regalia, his arms filled with all kinds of cowboy toys.

Ridge's eyes were glowing with happiness. He began

to talk and you could *almost* understand what he was saying. His hero. Of course, the word spread all over Children's Hospital that Hoppy was there. So Bill, being the sweet human being that he was, stayed with Ridge a while, then visited many other children. I only wish I could describe the faces of those desperately ill children when Hoppy came into their rooms.

The following day when I got off the hospital elevator, there was Ridge, sitting on a chair down the hall. Obviously waiting for me, he stood up, screamed, "Mommie, Mommie," and tried to run to me. Right then and there I wanted to fall on my knees and thank God for that miracle. Was it the medicine? Hoppy's visit? No matter—He answered all our prayers and I was one grateful lady!

About three months after Ridge's complete recovery, Ringling Brothers and Barnum and Bailey came to Los Angeles, and I decided to throw them a big party. But they worked such wild and long hours that I couldn't figure out when they'd all be able to attend. Bill suggested that we throw the bash on a Sunday morning before their matinee. But they would have to come by bus, and in those days, parking a bus (let alone six of them) on a Beverly Hills street was illegal. I called Chief Anderson of the Beverly Hills Police Department, told him who our special guests were, and asked how I could get permits to allow the parking. "You have permission to park them in front of your house on Palm Drive," he answered, "under one condition."

"What's that condition?"

"Only if you invite me. Sounds like a lot of fun!"

We held the party out in the back gardens and on the tennis court. Everyone showed up: Chief Anderson, the Singer Midget Family, the fat lady, the bearded ladies, the *real* Iron Jaw girls, the trapeze artists, and clowns. As my good friend Jimmie, a dwarf, rode around on Ridge's bike, Ridge yelled out, "Jimmie, why didn't you grow up to be a big man like my Daddy?"

"Because," said Jimmie with a straight face, "I didn't eat my spinach and all the good things my Mommie wanted me to eat."

The next night Mr. DeMille invited *Greatest Show*'s cast and crew, friends and family, to the circus. Bill and I had seats right in the first row, and we had invited two friends of Ridge to join him and Tommy. All four boys were in seventh heaven, and every time a vendor came by, Bill or I would buy the boys something to eat. Neither of us was keeping track of all the food they were consuming.

When the elephants came by, they weren't too polite. Right in front of Mr. DeMille they did what comes naturally . . . every one of them! C.B. looked in every direction, trying to keep his dignity intact as the whole audience started to titter. Unfortunately, too much popcorn and cotton candy and peanuts had taken their toll on the boys, and all four of them threw up, all over the front of my dress!

The audience laughed even harder as I made my unglamorous exit with Bill and the four green-faced little boys. At home, I look off my clothes, put my favorite bath oil in the tub and took a long, hot bath, so happy to have my two boys *well* enough to get sick. Dresses can always go to the cleaners, and I knew I would get out of the tub smelling like a rose.

17. Live and In Person

It had been several years since the last "Road" picture, but the public was still writing and asking for another. So Paramount rounded the three of us up again for the *Road to Hollywood,* in Technicolor for the first time.

The script kept changing so that I was on the film for three months before I finally found out the plot. By that time the title had been changed to *Road to Bali,* though we never did make it to Bali in the film. (Hope used the original title for one of his books.)

Because someone suggested that Bob and Bing do a bagpipe routine, they were going to call me Princess MacTavish. (Why MacTavish? Very simple—they had already decided to make one of my six sarongs out of authentic Scotch plaid, and of

A publicity still for Road to Bali

the several tartans they screen-tested, the MacTavish plaid turned out best in Technicolor.) In the finished product, however, I ended up as Princess Lalah.

In another scene, Bing and I put Bob (who always had to do the dirty work) in a diver's suit so that he can search for some sunken treasure. I was supposed to open the door in his helmet, and give him a kiss for luck. I tried it twice, then turned to director Hal Walker.

"This window is just too small. I can't reach Bob's mouth."

"Turn in your sarong and get out!" Bob shouted. "We should have hired a Ubangi for this part!"

Finally, he got into the water. After a pause, Bing calls to him over the intercom, "Have you found any treasure?"

"No," ad-libbed Bob, "but I just tripped over your old money belt down here."

In another scene, both Bob and Bing were fumbling with their lines.

"Hal," I called, "better warm up Martin and Lewis. They're not only funnier, but younger."

Everybody laughed except the boys. "*You'd* better be careful how you talk to us," Bob said, "You can always be replaced by an actress."

As with *Road to Rio,* Hope, Crosby, and Paramount each owned a third of the picture, but since I was still under contract to Paramount, I was just an employee. The boys asked me to cut an album of songs from the film, but I didn't think it fair that I get less for the album than they did, and told them so. It was never mentioned again. One day Bob and Bing showed up for work quite late, and not until later did I learn that they had recorded some songs from the film with Peggy Lee singing my parts. It would have been nice if I had been informed.

When the studios started using Cinemascope, Panavision, Todd-A-O, and Vistavision to draw the public away from television, good roles were hard to get, so I decided to accept some of the nightclub offers I was getting. Throughout the years, I had learned two rules about live audiences: (1) Never talk back to a heckler, because you make him feel important, and he'll heckle all the more. (2) If the audience keeps talking when you're singing, take a slight pause. When they realize what you're doing, they get embarrassed and start to pay attention.

One of my first engagements was at Batista's in Cuba. Mitch Leisen designed my wardrobe and staged my act; he and Sam Mineo accompanied me to Havana on the *S. S. Floridian.* (The plane would have taken only one hour, but I wasn't too fond of flying in those days.) I first experienced Castro's touch when Batista's military stopped the ship in the harbor and came aboard to search for guns and ammunition.

When we finally docked, we were whisked off to the hotel for a look at its huge main room, seating 1,500. I'm happy to say we packed the place every night of the engagement. But my music was marked in Spanish by the boys in the Cuban band, and so later, when I went to work in an American club, I had to have it done all over again—one expensive chore.

One of my favorite engagements was at the old El Rancho Vegas, where Bill and I had spent our Las Vegas honeymoon. Sam Mineo came with me, of course, and in my act I had three native Hawaiians, Bernie Kaii Lewis, Buddy Silva, and Danny Kuanna played the electric guitar, ukelele, and regular guitar. I opened the act by singing some of the songs written for my films: "I Remember You," "The Moon of Manakoora," "Personality," "It Could Happen to You," "Sunday, Monday, and Always." Then I rushed backstage for a quick change to a sarong for a Hawaiian songfest.

Nightclubs turn your whole sleeping schedule around. In the old Paramount days, we got up at 4:30 or 5:00 so we could be at the studio in makeup at 6:00 A.M. and sometimes we'd work until midnight. Now a lot of people tell me, "I'd never dream of calling you before 1:00 P.M. You sleep so late!" However, don't they stop to think that *I* don't start work until 8:00 or 9:00 P.M. They don't go straight to bed after work, and neither do I. I stay up until 2:00 or 3:00. Like many Vegas entertainers, I liked playing blackjack after the show. Bill loved the crap tables, and I would stand by, watching very quietly (one never talks to husbands when they are gambling). One night I was suddenly lifted into the air and set down right in the middle of the table, with chips and money flying everywhere. (Thankfully I was wearing a dress with a very full skirt; otherwise the gamblers would have seen more of Lamour than ever before.) Someone screamed, "Put her on the hard way eight!" I turned and saw Harry, Al, and Jimmy, the Ritz Brothers, laughing their fool heads off. They had come over from their show, spotted me by the table, and impulsively decided to "bet" me.

Every night a newsboy went through the casino trying to sell his papers, but usually no one paid him any attention. One night I was in a pretty good mood and decided to help him out. Taking his papers from him, I sauntered through the casino, calling, "Paper? Paper anyone? Get your red hot papers!" I would only accept silver dollars for the ten-cent paper, so that night my little pal made out all right.

A couple of years later, I was on my way up to my suite at the Frontier Hotel when I bumped into a man carrying a brown paper bag and wearing tennis shoes. When I started to apologize, he looked up and said, "Dottie!"

"Howard!" I answered, surprised to say the least. It was, of course, Howard Hughes, who would later buy up some of Las Vegas's biggest hotels. When I came down from my room, I spotted him at one of the tables. The brown sack he was carrying contained silver dollars, and he was gambling—*almost* like everyone else.

Then there was the time I was booked into "a very high-class nightclub" in Detroit by an agent who had obviously never seen the place. My first instinct was to turn it down, but I was restless and wanted to work. Bill and I and the kids drove to Detroit and found a motel with a pool that the boys loved. I unpacked and then went down to the club to report for rehearsal.

In the words of Bette Davis (and later Elizabeth Taylor), "What a dump!" The club was dingy, and my dressing room very small. Behind a drapery, I found a large hole in the wall where a urinal had been removed; I later found that my dressing room had once been a men's room. I would have walked out immediately, if I hadn't signed a contract. I got "stuck" a couple of times in places like that because I listened to agents, but I soon learned my lesson.

I had never done live theater before, so an offer to do a stage play called *Roger the Sixth* seemed very exciting. Robert Alda was signed to be my leading man, and we were to open on the Straw Hat Circuit in New Hampshire and then, we hoped on Broadway.

Rehearsal wouldn't start for several weeks so I had time to accept two job offers—one at New Orleans' Monteleone Hotel and the other immediately following in Oklahoma City for a show with Lou Walters' (Barbara's dad) New York revue.

Linda Darnell was appearing at the Roosevelt Hotel in New Orleans, so we went over to see her show. Later she came to see mine, and we became pretty close, taking in the sights together. (It was a terrible shock to hear of Linda's death in a fire in Chicago several years later, but it was just like her to die trying to save someone else's life.) Since we were kids, I had been friends with DeLesseppes Morrison, who was now Mayor of New Orleans. "Chep" invited Bill and me to a late supper, but I had to get to work on the *Roger* script, so we had to decline.

After the show Bill and I went straight upstairs to our suite, two bedrooms, each with its own bath, separated by a huge living room. We slept in one bedroom; the other I had converted into a dressing room and closet for my gowns. Bill's emphysema was acting up, so after taking some medication, he went to bed. Not wanting to disturb him, I decided to take a nice hot bath in the furthest bathroom and study my script.

Stepping out of the bathtub, I fell, twisting my ankle. The pain was excruciating. I limped to the phone and asked the operator to ring the phone in the other bedroom. Bill groggily answered the phone, and when he reached the other bedroom, my ankle was several times its normal size. So at 2:00 A.M. I ended up in the very same hospital I was born in, and where I had done a charity show that very afternoon.

My ankle was broken in three places, so they had to set it and put it in a cast. When I returned to the hotel at 8:00 A.M., the management was waiting for me with tears in their eyes—because my engagement had been sold out. I assured them that if they would give me a few hours to let the medication wear off and get me a wheelchair, I would go on as usual.

I had to do the hula in a wheelchair, I wore out the beads around the fanny of my black beaded gown, but I finished the engagement. Then off for Oklahoma City, where the show was being done in an outdoor theater. Just after I wheeled myself on stage and began my first number a tornado came up. I would have rolled completely off the stage if I hadn't found the brake and stopped the wheelchair just in time.

After Oklahoma City, Bill and I boarded a train for Boston, where Mother and the boys met us, then we continued up to New Hampshire for my debut in *Roger.* When the producer saw the cast up to my knee, he nearly had a stroke, but I assured him it would turn out all right if a few lines in the play were rewritten.

Roger the Sixth was about a woman who has been married six times, with several children from her various marriages. Robert Alda brought with him his young son Alan, a delightful young man who did a very nice job in his acting debut. (As the star of "M*A*S*H," he certainly has turned into one of our better actors.) They rewrote the script so that Bob could carry me onstage and sit me down on a sofa. As my leg got better, I could get up with the aid of a cane, so the crew made me one with my name emblazoned on it in rhinestones. (I'm keeping it for my old age.)

When we hit Syracuse, my cast was removed, and my injured leg looked about one-third the size of my good one. But I used a cane, and we finished the tour. The producers decided not to brave Broadway, but my leg was fine again and so I didn't cry about an experience that had been very rewarding. The boys had had a wonderful time on the tour and loved the large country houses, but it was time to pack up and return to Hollywood.

18. The Road to Baltimore

Sometimes show business associates can be very cruel. It was suddenly difficult for me to reach certain Hollywood people by phone—the same people for whom I had done so many favors when I was "box office magic." You know the routine: Someone would be "in a meeting and simply couldn't be disturbed." "May I ask what this is about?" his secretary would say, or "He's out of town, but when he returns I'll be sure to give him the message."

Real friends like Coley and Pauline Kessinger and Doris and Andy Durkus, always stuck by me, but Bill's health wasn't too good, and we were both worried about the boys. Let's face it, a lot of the children growing up in Hollywood got into trouble. After a long talk, we decided it might be best if we

At the Maryland Shore with Ridge and Tommy (Art Weissman photo)

moved back to Baltimore. Now the boys could be raised in the same environment their father had been, a background of which he was extremely proud.

We settled into a Baltimore suburb called Towson. One of our neighbors was Spiro Agnew (his nickname was Ted) and I used to go shopping with his wife Judy. Mayor Theodore McKeldin (formerly the governor of Maryland, and the man who nominated Dwight D. Eisenhower for President at the Republican Convention) appointed me to Baltimore's brand-new Civic Center Commission. As the only woman on the Commission, keeping all of those businessmen in line was a whole new role for me. One night Bill said, "I never dreamed I'd be sleeping with a Civic Commissioner!"

When Ridge and Tommy first enrolled in school, I kept a very low profile. I wanted them known as the Howard boys, not the Lamour boys. But once they were established, I attended each PTA meeting and joined some committees. I was beginning to get my self-respect back; I hadn't realized just how much that rejection in Hollywood had affected me. One night we were being given a tour of the Towsontown School when Tommy's gym instructor shyly said, "Mrs. Howard, I'd like to show you something." Pulling me aside, he opened the door to his locker, and there was a picture of me that I had sent him while he was overseas in World War II. I was quite flattered, but even more pleased that he had been so discreet about it.

During the ten years that we lived in Maryland, I kept my hand in show biz, so to speak. Occasionally I came to Hollywood to do a television show, such as "I Spy" or the "Joey Bishop Show" but I could never seem to get on "The Tonight Show." I had met Johnny Carson on one of my trips to New York. Totally charming he said he was coming to Baltimore; and I promised that Bill and I would take him out for a real Maryland dinner. When I called his hotel, his secretary answered and was quite rude; I never heard from him again. His secretary is now a fixture on "The Tonight Show" staff, and I've heard quite frequently, whenever my name is brought up as a potential guest, her reply is always, "Don't mention that woman's name to me."

Much as I loved my civic work, church activities, and

PTA committees, I had been in the business too long to get it out of my system. Thank God my Bill understood this, and the boys were learning to understand too. They would go to Bill and say, "Hey, Dad, Mom's getting hard to take; let's get her back to work."

I began to read little items in the columns that another "Road" film was going to be made in London. Next I read that because I had been in retirement for four or five years, Gina Lollobrigida and Sophia Loren were the top choices to take up where I had left off. It was apparent that Bing, Bob, producer Mel Frank, and director Norman Panama had decided that I had been offscreen too long to be a major asset to the film.

Bill Howard, Jr., who was working with the Louis Shurr Agency (who also handled Bob Hope) called to tell me that there was *definitely* going to be another "Road" film. He had kept after them because he knew I was extremely hurt by the silence from everyone concerned. Then one day Louis Shurr finally called to say Norman Panama was on his way to London. Norman wanted to stop off in Baltimore to let me read the "Road" script and listen to a recording of "Softer than a Whisper," a song that Sammy Cahn had written for me. A bit surprised, I asked Louis what kind of a part it was, but he wouldn't commit himself. "Wait until you read the script," he said, "and listen to that wonderful song!"

I told him that I could understand if they wanted a big box office name to play opposite Bing and Bob, but under no circumstances would I play a *bit* part in a "Road" picture. Since all *three* of us had *starred* in those films, I felt it was humiliating to have my contribution minimalized.

But I met with Norman and listened to the recording—a fairly good song, but not one of the greatest that Sammy Cahn ever wrote. Norman left the script with me and rushed off to make his plane, saying he would call from New York to see what I thought of it.

As soon as he left, I skimmed over the script, trying to find me. Finally, I saw a couple of pages of dialogue that an extra could have handled. When Norman called, I told him I was outraged and then called Louis Shurr to tell him the same thing. I did add that I might consider the role if it were built up, but under these circumstances, absolutely not!

After a couple of weeks went by, the phone rang and I heard a terribly British voice ask for me. I thought it was my agent Joe Higgins. We had a standing gag: each time he called, he would use a different corny accent. I began to mimick the accent when I realized that was a genuine call from Mel Frank.

"Dottie," he started, "we are ready to go into production, and we—Bing, Bob, Norm, and I—would greatly appreciate it if you would change your mind and join us in *The Road to Hong Kong*."

I stuck to my guns and told him I'd do it if he'd build up the part. His reply was that it was much too late to make any further additions to the script. On all the other "Road" films, of course, the script changed daily, and those pictures certainly did all right at the box office.

The telephone calls continued. Soon I got to know the English operator so well that we would chat about the weather in England and Maryland before she put Mel on the line. Finally I discovered just why they had been so anxious to get me in the picture: when they made the subsequent distribution deal with United Artists, they had committed my name along with their own. Even though Joan Collins had been signed for the female lead, I was still to be included or the deal was off.

I kept hearing different stories. Crosby didn't want me in the film at all; Crosby did want me, but I didn't have a big enough following to play a major role. I constantly heard that Hope had been fighting for me all along, but I didn't know what to believe. But realizing how important it was that I accept, and remembering all the good times we'd been through together, I came to their rescue—but at a price, with a few zeros attached to it.

Bill and I sailed from New York, both looking forward to England. The day before we docked at Southhampton I received a cable informing me that "some press" would board at Le Havre. There must have been at least 100 of them interviewing me and taking pictures. I hadn't made a film in several years, but I was given the royal treatment. In Victoria Station I was greeted by large crowds of fans who followed us wherever we went. It was terribly exciting and gratifying.

The next day I went out to the studio to lunch with Bing, Bob, Norm, and Mel, and to meet Joan Collins. I knew our first meeting would be strained, especially since one of London's top newspapers had called just before I left New York: Miss Collins had stated that because I was jealous of her getting the larger role in *Hong Kong,* I was looking to start a feud. What was my reaction?

I had to laugh. In all my years in the business I had never been jealous of anyone. My reply was short but sweet: "There is no feud. I have never had a feud with anyone, but *if* I even considered having a feud, it would be with the *stars* of a film."

The luncheon went very well. Again, more press and more pictures. When the papers came out that day, I don't think I've ever seen such coverage—full front-page pictures of me with stories on my arrival, all commenting that it wasn't a very good idea for me not to play the leading role. Those darling Englishmen are so loyal! I later heard that both Bing and Bob's secretaries received quite a bit of mail resenting the fact that I was not the girl in the middle. My tiny scene was never built up, but we did have fun making the film and making jokes. Personally, I was able to forget the hassles and begin to enjoy working with those two guys once again.

When Bob made some silly remark about the old gal in the sarong, I retorted, "If you're not careful, I'll hit you over the head with some of my fan mail!"

From across the set Bing moaned, "You would have to open that can of peas, bub!"

With one free day to call our own, we all decided to go to the races. Bing and his wife, Bob and Dolores, and Bill and I all bet on a horse called Zanzibar, sure he was going to be a winner like the *Road to Zanzibar*. Last I heard, the horse still hasn't crossed the finish line—and for that matter, *Road to Hong Kong* never won either.

Soon we sailed back to America with good feelings toward all. Bill and I received daily cablegrams from Bing and

Bob. One said, "We'll send you water wings, so come back quickly. We miss you." On board ship we ran into several old friends, like Pete Krendler (one of the owners of '21'). Also on board were eight terribly rich Arabs dressed in native garb on their way to Washington to work out some kind of oil deal. One of them gave the steward $100 to get him a razor blade. They would sit in the main ballroom and just stare, fascinated at the way Americans dance close together. One evening as I was dancing with Harvey, they recognized me. First they waved, then one of them who spoke English came over, and soon I was surrounded as I was back on the *Road to Morocco.* They kept asking about "Bob Opee," but shook their heads when I mentioned Bing. I remembered an Arab tumbling act that had been on the bill with me at the Latin Quarter, so when we docked in New York, I asked the acrobats to visit my new friends at the Waldorf-Astoria and guide them around the city.

A few months later, when *Road to Hong Kong* was ready for release, Bob asked me to Hollywood to appear on his television special to promote the film. I was soon sitting in Bob's NBC dressing room reading the trade papers, *Hollywood Reporter* and *Daily Variety*. Each had excerpts from reviews from around the country, whose headlines read, "Bing, Bob and Dottie back on the Road," "Bob, Dottie & Bing Together Again."

"How about that!" Bob kept saying. "They don't even mention Joan, do they?"

I looked up sweetly and said, "I now know how it feels for the cat to swallow the canary."

I was preparing to go back to Maryland when I heard that Bing was also doing a television special to promote the movie. I called him and said that if he wanted me, I would stay over in Hollywood for a few days. Mr. Crosby informed me that it was too late to write me in. When I saw his special, however, I was really shocked to see them using large blowups of me, and they kept talking about me all through the show. I couldn't understand what had happened to Bing. Sometimes—as in England—he could be as sweet as ever, and then an aloofness would set in that had never been there before. And I couldn't forget the sight of him in London. Bing, once the most casual of dressers, all done up in white tie and tails to go to some social function. That certainly wasn't the Bing of yore.

I never did see the accounting books for *Road to Hong Kong*, but reliable sources told me that it never came close to the old "Road" films. The reviews unanimously hated it, and box office wasn't that good. What a terrible end to such a wonderful series!

John Edgar Hoover had been a friend of the family for years, and when Ridge was twelve years old, he and his buddies formed an organization called the Federal Raiders and wrote Uncle Edgar a letter asking him to join too. Edgar sent back a gracious letter of acceptance that became one of Ridge's most prized possessions.

Our sons were so close that Tommy would never leave Ridge's side. "If you aren't careful," I remarked to Ridge, "Tommy'll go along with you on your honeymoon." If they had been in some mischief at school, they could never understand how I could ask them about it as they came in the door. They were convinced that Mother had psychic powers. I never told them until recently that whenever I went to the health spa in the late afternoon for a massage or sauna, I usually ran into a teacher or another mother, and we'd exchange tidbits from A to Z.

I don't think I realized just how great those years were. The beautiful Thanksgiving dinners with the family at our home, then Christmas with snow on the ground, the decorating of the real Christmas tree, the hectic last-minute shopping. "Stores don't put the heart in the wrappings," my mother told me. "If you feel close enough to a friend to give them a gift, always wrap it yourself." And I did. Bill used to tell the boys to hide my gifts under their beds because I'd never look there, and of course I said the same about him.

One day Bill Jr. called to tell me to expect a call from John Ford any minute, because he had just given Ford my number. Sure enough, soon that old familiar voice came over the wire: "Toujy, I'm doing a picture with John Wayne and Lee Marvin called *Donovan's Reef*. There's a wonderful part in it for you."

In those days Lee was known mostly for his television show "M Squad." I had met Wayne only casually, but certainly respected his work and was thrilled at the prospect of working with him, especially with Pappy directing.

You'd think I'd have learned something from the *Hong Kong* fiasco, but I never even asked to see the script. When I finally saw the size of the role, Pappy assured me it would be built up, but it seemed I had heard that song before. Ford's wife Mary and I had been good friends for years; so when they decided that I should wear muumuus in the film, Pappy sent me to his home to try on some of Mary's. I found one that was perfect, so that eliminated wardrobe fittings.

As the days went by, I slowly began to realize that Pappy was not a well man. One afternoon Duke Wayne yelled back at Pappy, an incident that made me very upset. Everyone in the industry knew that Ford was greatly responsible for Wayne's success. Finally I went over to Duke and told him how I felt.

He told me that Ford's thinking wasn't as sharp as it had been, and he couldn't see very well anymore. Every day Duke had to go in and check the rushes to make sure everything was all right. Sometimes the strain got to him, and that was why he blew his stack. Duke assured me that he loved Ford and that everything would come out all right in the end.

It really hit home how ill Pappy was when Lee finished a particularly good sequence playing with an electric train. When the scene was over, Pappy yelled, "Cut!"

"Lee," I said, "that was a really fantastic scene."

Pappy called me down for my remark in front of everyone, saying that he was the director and *he* was supposed to decide whether a scene was good or bad. After those empty promises to build up my role, that was all I needed. I told Pappy off and ran to my dressing room in tears.

He sent his brother-in-law and assistant, Wingate Smith, to calm me down. "Listen," I said, "I don't want *your* apology. I want one from Mr. Ford himself. He embarrassed me in front of the entire cast and crew, and that has never happened to me in all my years in films. You can tell Mr. Ford that I've read the script, and they could certainly finish the rest of my scenes without me."

Within five minutes Pappy was in my dressing room putting his arms around me and apologizing. That man could charm the apples right out of the tree. Angry and indignant as I was, he won me over and soon we both were crying and laughing. I finished the picture and then left for Maryland.

For the first screening, Bob Goodfried, now the vice-president of Paramount's West Coast Publicity, organized a press junket down to Vacation Village in Mission Bay, San Diego, chosen because it was so similar to the *Donovan's Reef* locations. Bob packed them all in buses decorated with leis and tropical flowers. None of the actors or actresses were available, so Hazel Flynn wrote in the *Citizen News,* "None of the actors were able to make the trip with us, so we ate 'em." And then she listed the inventive menu:

Gout Piquant à la Elizabeth Allen
Boula Chantilly à la Jack Warden
Filet of Beef à la Gastronome John Wayne
Légumes à la Cesar Romero
Potatoes à la Dick Foran
Americaine à la Lee Marvin
Omelet Flambée à la Dorothy Lamour
Cafeé Demitasse à la John Ford

The next time I was staying with Pauline Kessinger, in Hollywood, I received a call from a friend of hers, Joe Wonder. He was producing a new movie with Frankie Avalon and Annette Funicello called *Pajama Party*. They had written a cute song for me called "In My Day We Never Did It That Way" and would I listen to it? Since I thought the younger generation ought to know I existed, I took the job. Then I discovered that the original title had been *The Maid and the Martian,* intended to be the first Science Fiction Musical Comedy!

Before I knew it, Ridge was 18. Being a chip off the old military block, he wanted to enlist in the Marines as soon as he graduated from high school. That summer we took Ridge to

Hollywood for a visit. That was the late 1960's, when L.A. was aswarm with long-haired flower children. Many were bearded and heavily into the drug culture. Ridge went out to visit some of his old school friends. He was home within an hour, and said, "Mother, I want to thank you."

"Why?" I asked him.

"We resented it when Dad and you raised hell with us kept us in line. Sometimes we thought you were too strict. But now after seeing the condition of some of my old friends, I understand what you were doing. I wouldn't have wanted to end up like them."

When it came time for Ridge to leave for boot camp, I was a most unhappy woman. Bill had been a very patriotic Air Force man, and we were proud of Ridge for wanting to serve his country, but we both knew that Vietnam wasn't like World War II; we were terrified that something might happen to him.

During his first few months away I tried to keep myself as busy as possible, doing television shows in New York, a summer tour of *Dubarry Was a Lady*, then *Pal Joey* for Lee Guber, who had just married Barbara Walters. I kept watching the news for some sign that the war would end before Ridge left boot camp.

Then I had to prepare for an engagement in the Camellia Room in the Drake Hotel in Chicago. Pauline had just lost her beloved Coley, so we invited her to join us. When we reached Chicago, we immediately called Dorothy Gulman and had ourselves a great time, shopping and lunching in all of Chicago's best places. Pauline, who never wore false eyelashes, kept watching me as I made up for my act every night. Finally I taught her to use them, and now she never takes them off.

It was during this engagement at the Drake that I realized I had fallen in love—with a character in a musical, and knew that I really wanted to play her.

19. Hello to "Dolly"

A few months before my engagement at the Drake I had gone to New York to shop and to see some shows. I got tickets to see *Hello, Dolly.* In some strange way I couldn't explain, I identified with Carol Channing and knew that some day I was going to play the character of Dolly Gallagher Levi. While I was appearing at the Drake, Carol came to Chicago and I took Dorothy Gulman to see a matinee. That did it! After seeing the show a second time, I knew I wanted to play Dolly.

Hearing that Carol wanted a rest and that producer David Merrick was seeking a replacement, I decided to contact him personally and ask for the job. But since he had quite a reputation as a tyrant, I wanted to be sure I did it the right way. I composed a telegram and read it over the phone to Dorothy

The famed staircase sequence from Act II of Hello, Dolly!

Gulman who helped me make a few changes. Then I called Western Union and held my breath.

After closing at the Drake, I returned to Maryland. Weeks passed without any word from Merrick. Finally he called to ask if I would mind coming to New York to audition. Of course I didn't mind, and I liked the way he asked. But arriving in New York a few days later, I was a nervous wreck. It had been years since I had read for any part, and back came all the old fears.

The only people I remember seeing at the audition were Gower Champion and my new agent, Tom Korman. Gower was a doll and hugged me afterwards, assuring me that it was wonderful. But for weeks I heard nothing. In the meantime someone asked me to go for a short straw-hat-circuit tour with *Dubarry Was a Lady*. Rather than sit around waiting for Merrick's call, I accepted.

The tour ended and winter set in, but still no *Hello* from Merrick. That winter the snow really piled high in front of our house. Under these weather conditions, the doctors felt, Bill's emphysema wouldn't get any better. "Honey," Bill asked as we were getting into bed one night, "Do you want to go home?"

I turned to him. "I thought we *were* home."

"No, Momma," he smiled. "I mean our real home in California. The boys are grown, and I think it's time we went back. I know you miss it, and you know, I do too."

As soon as we put our house up for sale and started making plans, naturally a call came from David Merrick asking me to meet with him concerning a national tour of *Hello, Dolly*. Once that was set, I received a call to fly West and do another "Joey Bishop Show." No sooner had I arrived in Hollywood than Bill called: "Our house can be sold—if we can be ready to move out in six weeks."

I gasped. "That means I'd have to get everything packed and find a new home here in California, while learning the *Dolly* script, and then go on tour."

"Don't worry, sweetheart," Bill reassured me. "We'll just ship everything out to the coast and put it in storage for the months you'll be touring."

We didn't know the months were to stretch well into a year. I was to join the Carol Channing company in Syracuse, New York, and go with it to Hartford. Every day I'd rehearse the musical numbers with Terry De Mari (what patience he had!) and watch each performance to review what I was learning. The blocking was the same, but naturally my interpretation was different from Carol's. None of the actresses who played Dolly had to imitate Carol; they just had to have that special "Dolly flavor" and be able to bring something of themselves to the role.

Tommy was in boarding school near Hartford, so Bill and I talked the headmaster into letting him stay the weekend with us at our hotel. I just couldn't seem to learn one long speech that Dolly directs to her deceased husband. Everyone was off doing the matinee, so the only one around to prompt me was Tommy. He was a helpful young gentleman, but such a lousy actor we both got to laughing so hard that tears rolled down our cheeks.

Tommy confided in me that he was not at all happy with his school and because of that, his grades were suffering. I telephoned Gerald Neff, who had been Ridge's headmaster at Hollywood's Black Fox Military Academy and who now ran the Brentwood Military Academy.

"Don't you worry," he promised. "Send Tommy out here and I'll take good care of him." Tom was delighted to be going back to California because he would go to school all week and spend weekends with Aunt Pauline, whom both boys had christened "The Chief." Once again, her home became the Howard West. That's the sign of true friendship, when you can stand your friends—sometimes all four of us—moving in with you. (Mr. Neff kept his word, and Tom eventually graduated with high honors.)

Merrick still hadn't set the opening date of the tour, so we stopped in Maryland long enough to pick up Mother and some clean clothes, and then headed for Ridge's boot camp graduation at Parris Island. Bill had called a friend in Washington and made arrangements for us, asking that there be no publicity. We didn't want to put Ridge in the spotlight.

The camp allowed parents to see their sons for just a few minutes before the ceremony, then brought the boys in with an introductory speech, "You gave us a boy, we give you back a man!" But with their heads shaved, they looked more like ten-year-olds. After a very short five minutes, they marched them away. I couldn't help recalling the day Ridge was born, when the nurse whisked him away after letting me have a peek at him. Now, watching him carry the American flag down the field, brought forth a torrent of tears I had never been able to release before. I thanked God for helping Ridge recover so completely from encephalitis. I thought that Bill and I would burst with pride.

After a short leave, Ridge's first assignment was Guantanamo, Cuba. Still awaiting Mr. Merrick's call, I instead received a call from Ridge via shortwave: "Mom, pack up your sarong and come on down. The guys want to meet you." I knew Ridge never liked publicity, and how could boys his age even know about me? "Mom," he blithely replied, "they all have the new issue of *Playboy*, and you're in it."

I flew to the market to get a copy. When I opened it up, there was a full-page spread of Betty Grable in her famous over-the-shoulder pose, and me in a sarong. One side benefit from being in show business is that if you want to visit your son in the service, you can just call the USO and volunteer to do a show wherever he's stationed. The boys in Guantanamo loved the show, and I think that I made Ridge very proud that night.

At last came the call from Merrick. It took David Merrick long enough to make up his mind, but he was so anxious to get the contracts signed that he had Tom Korman fly a courier to Baltimore. He instructed me to meet him at the airport and sign the contract, then and there so the courier could return to New York on the next plane.

I was very anxious to get to work too, because Ridge had received orders to go to Japan and Vietnam, and work, I knew, was the only way to divert my mind. At last the movers arrived with three of their largest vans, and it cost a fortune to move our furniture, paintings, clothes, and antiques. I still hadn't learned all my lines for *Dolly*, so I had them put a chair in the third van where I sat, out of their way, running lines while they worked.

When they left for California, I flew directly to Seattle, where Ginger Rogers was doing *Dolly*. Merrick wanted me to open in Las Vegas at the Riviera Hotel, alternating performances with Ginger. Doing Vegas meant a back breaking fourteen shows a week, and the only gal that I ever knew to do a "book" show for that many performances was Betty Grable, who had done *Dolly* there the year before.

David Merrick knew what he was doing: Having two stars play *Dolly* at the same time was a very clever stunt that got us all kinds of publicity. I was to work on my lines with Ginger Rogers' understudy, Anne Russell, and rehearse with the principals and dancers during the day. Anne and I worked mainly in my hotel room. I didn't have too much time with the actors because it seemed that Miss Rogers wanted rehearsal time too, even though she'd been playing the show for some time.

I understand that Mr. Merrick and Miss Rogers had quite a few words about doing the show in Las Vegas. With a book show, you usually have to cut the dialogue to fit Las Vegas' desired hour-and-a-half format. Miss Rogers didn't want to do that: she just said her lines faster. Her religious beliefs also conflicted with working in a place where people served liquor and gambled, and she didn't want to perform on Sunday. But a contract is a contract, and besides, she had done her nightclub act there a couple of years before—or so one of the top men at the Riviera told me.

Because all previous Dollys had been towheads, Merrick insisted that I wear a blonde wig. I tried it, but it just wasn't me. I finally persuaded him to let me use own hair, which had been my trademark. (Later, when Pearl Bailey did the show on Broadway, I sent her a telegram saying, "GOOD LUCK TO THE OTHER BRUNETTE DOLLY.")

I had been told we would have a complete runthrough before an audience of relatives, employees of the hotel, and their friends. But lengthy rehearsals prevented it. I opened cold, with the press sitting out front. They had just sat through the first show with Ginger, who had been playing *Dolly* for some time now, and I must say I was one nervous newcomer.

I've always said that God takes me by the hand, and I

can assure you He really held it tightly that night. He also blessed me with a most delightful cast. The chorus kids would whisper reminders to me where to turn right, when to turn left, and sometimes prompt me without the audience hearing them. When I finally came out in that famous white outfit with the big white hat and parasol, I received a standing ovation. The reviews were raves, and I knew that I had made the right choice.

On closing night the cast gave me a silver cigarette case inscribed "To our Dolly with love. Your cast Riviera Hotel, 1967." I knew I'd miss them, but had to dash to New York to catch up on rehearsals with my own company, which had already been in rehearsal for a couple of weeks.

Those rehearsals began some lifelong friendships: that fine actor Eric Brotherson, who was my Horace, and Terry De Mari, who taught me the dances. Dancer Don George doubled as the assistant stage manager, and one of his jobs was to watch over me.

Lucia Victor did a major part of the choreography for *Dolly* and restaged most of the road companies of *Dolly* for Gower Champion. But she was working with Mary Martin and my old beau Bob Preston in *I Do, I Do,* and I could understand Mary was reluctant to let her leave for any length of time. We were very happy, though, when she was able to fly in to help us put the whole thing together in Bloomington for our opening at the University of Indiana.

It took Merrick's office forever to give us our full itinerary. Mother wasn't too well in California, Ridge was in the service, and Tom in school, and I wanted to know where they could reach me at all times. To satisfy me, they sent me the first nine days—and I saw they were all one-nighters. This was going to what's called a bus-and-truck tour, with no one- or two-week stands. Why hadn't someone told me?

My second shock came when I saw the sets, looking so much flimsier than those on Broadway—but that's one way they save money and time. However, they had beautiful duplicates of the original costumes for all of us.

Our entourage included one busload of stagehands, who left each night after the performance, in time to be in the next town when we arrived. Another bus carried the cast and the rest of the crew, followed by one truck with costumes and another with sets. Bill and I drove in our Cadillac because I sometimes had to get into the next town early to meet the press. We zigged around so much that every time we'd get on the Pennsylvania Turnpike, Bill claimed, the tollman would say, "Well, hello, Dottie. Where are you going now?"

Because of *Dolly*'s quick costumes changes, I needed a dressing room as close to the stage as possible. One theater forgot we were booked (how's that for an ego boost?) and a demolition crew had arrived to start tearing it down. Before the goof was discovered, they had knocked out part of the back wall. There was no dressing room near the stage, so the crew put up some flats for me in the corner. Now as soon as a one-night performance is over, the stagehands begin to "strike" the sets and get them ready for packing. That night they began to take down my walls, and there I was in my bra and panties, taking off my makeup. Stagehands are not easily impressed; they just shrugged their shoulders.

Then there was the time I had to dress in a freight elevator. You guessed it, someone pressed the down button, and away I went in the middle of a change.

The Grand Old Opry in Nashville, originally a church, has very small dressing rooms. The only place big enough for my costumes and hats and also close enough to the stage was the ladies' room, which had a long mirror and several sinks. We used each cubicle, putting a hat and a wig atop each commode. There I was one night, putting on my makeup, when a little old lady waltzed in, washed her hands, checked her hair, and said good-bye. It's a wonder she didn't leave me a quarter on the counter.

At Thanksgiving, Bill arranged for Duluth's Ramada Inn to set up four large tables in a private dining room for the entire cast and crew. He insisted that the food be served family-style with large bowls of mashed potatoes, sweet potatoes, vegetables, dressing, and cranberry sauce. It took away the loneliness of being away from home on the holiday.

We were to spend Christmas in Chanute, Kansas, so

Bill called ahead to make sure we would have a hotel dining room open for Christmas dinner. The town was so small that the phone directory had only fourteen pages. I don't know what possessed Merrick's office. Christmas is a notoriously bad time for theater in the larger cities, but in a small town it's murderous. We did the show in the huge auditorium of a building that also housed the fire department, police department, and municipal court. They didn't have any local stagehands, so we used some of the firemen. "What if a fire breaks out in the middle of a performance?" we asked. The chief just shrugged, "Oh, we haven't had a fire in four years."

They didn't have dressing rooms either, so we hung a rope with a couple of sheets over it (just like in *It Happened One Night*). I dressed on one side and the rest of the cast on the other.

I think we played to only 75 to 100 people that night, and I later heard that the check the Merrick office received for that night's performance bounced. David's Christmas gift was a sterling silver cigarette box from Tiffany's, which I did appreciate.

Right after New Year's we opened in Austin, Texas. I was told that LBJ was going to attend the performance and was sworn to secrecy. But when a group of strange men showed up and began to go over our dressing rooms, I think the others became a bit suspicious. The President had asked that his entrance be underplayed, and he planned to arrive just as the lights went down. On the way in, he stopped at the box office and asked our company manager, Boris Bernardi (Herschel's brother), if he could use the phone to check on his sick grandchild. Without looking up, Boris just muttered, "There's a pay phone in the rest room."

"Well," LBJ drawled, "I think I'll be allowed to use this one here. I am the President of the United States."

As we did the first number, "I Put My Hand In," everyone was trying to spot the President. Meanwhile, the secret service men were very busy backstage. The gal who played Ernestina was to walk onstage with a wooden gun, which I'd take away from her. So that no one would substitute a real one, the secret service men held on to the prop gun until she walked on stage.

During intermission, Ladybird and Luci and Pat

Nugent accompanied the President backstage to meet the cast. I felt that I had known LBJ for a long time: many years ago, when he too was just beginning his career, he used to come see me when I was singing with Herbie Kay's band at the old Baker Hotel Roof Garden in Dallas. I'd also had the pleasure of meeting him several times at the White House. We all lined up as they do at a Royal Command Performance in London. The President presented me with a beautifully wrapped package. Inside was a gold charm in the shape of a wishing well, at the bottom of which was the President's insignia.

At the end of the show LBJ jumped to his feet and raised his hands over his head to lead a standing ovation of over 5,000 people. I knew the Merrick office and the press would have liked me to bring the President up on stage, but I respected his wishes to remain low key, and merely said, "Mr. President, Mrs. Johnson, and your lovely family. Thank you for being here, and I, as an American citizen and the mother of a U.S. Marine, would like to thank you for the great job you're doing for our country." Ridge later wrote me telling me that he had read about it in the *Stars and Stripes*, but since he didn't want everyone to know who he was, he couldn't jump up and down saying, "Hey, our boss gave my mom a standing ovation!" These days it has become fashionable to ridicule the White House, but I cannot begin to describe the thrill of having the President of the United States travel miles through the rain just to see your performance.

We did a show in an Illinois armory that had dressing rooms but unfortunately, no stage. They wired together 150 Formica tables, but they were so slippery we couldn't walk on them, let alone do the dance numbers, until the local carpet company covered the tables with the brightest red carpeting I'd ever seen. We weren't able to use the sets, so we did the show with costumes only; but the audience loved it.

To ease the boredom on the road, everyone in the company took up knitting, even the guys. One fellow quipped that if the bus were in an accident, chances are no one would be hurt unless they were stabbed by a flying needle.

While on the road, Bill and I celebrated our twenty-fifth wedding anniversary, and the cast planned a surprise party. Don George had telephoned a friend in Columbus to pick up a big cake for us. The bus made a quick stop for the cake in Ohio, and Don carried it on his lap all the way to Lynchburg, Virginia. We finished the tour in Lambertville, New Jersey, with a long six-week engagement at the Music Circus. It took us a while to adjust to staying in one place; in less than a year we had covered 28,686 miles and played 91 cities. And I heard that Mr. Merrick's coffers were sweetened to the tune of over $7 million, just from our company alone. Right from the beginning the show should have been titled *Hello, Dollars.*

As soon as we arrrived back in Hollywood, Bill and I began looking for a new house. I had always liked the Toluca Lake area, where we found a perfect house on Arcola. As we walked by the pool, I looked and suddenly realized that this neighborhood seemed very familiar. Around the corner was the house that Hope built!

When he took his late-night constitutional, Bob would occasionally see our lights on and stop by. One particular night I was sans makeup in an old bathrobe, watching television, and Bill was in his shorts. Bob rang the doorbell and with him were some friends, among them the syndicated columnist Shirley Eder. Fortunately she was a friend, so didn't print what a slob I am around the house.

My mother's health had been gradually declining. Finally the doctors diagnosed cancer, and she had to be admitted to the same hospital where Bill was being treated for respiratory arrest. I would go up and down between the two floors visiting each of them.

Bill began to get better, but Mother was deteriorating. One day she asked, "How much time do I have left?"

I simply did not know how to answer. My mother, who had practically been my whole life, was dying, and I couldn't help her. As I sat there trying to hold back the tears, all kinds of strange memories hit me.

My mother had never wanted to be a stage mother like so many others, though I'd beg her to come visit me at the studio. Her only concession was to join the Motion Picture Mothers' Club, which did a lot of charity affairs (she also sewed for the Shriner's Crippled Children's Hospital).

My mind went back to the night when I was thirteen and I saw Mother dancing at a party. Afterwards I told her I thought it terrible for a woman with a grown daughter to be dancing like that. She never danced again until 1941, when we were in a nightclub in New York. At the time, a very famous actress used to ask her maid to bring her some strawberry juice, which meant sloe gin, so I asked the maître d' to bring Mother some "strawberry juice" over cracked ice. She thought it really *was* strawberry juice—and so tasty! Before I knew it, she was out on the dance floor dancing up a storm.

Years before, Paramount wanted the two of us to pose for a Mother's Day portrait. They took her to makeup, plucked her eyebrows, and pencilled in Dietrich brows. She always liked looking like a real glamour girl. Two days before she passed away, an old boyfriend of hers called and asked if he could come to visit. She agreed, but had the nurse comb her hair and put some lipstick on her. He brought her red roses, as befitting a lady.

A lot of people don't understand when you say your mother was like a sister to you and was your best friend, but believe me, I miss her terribly even today.

I hadn't worked in a Hollywood nightclub in a long time, but I joined Don Ho for an engagement at the Now Grove (formerly the Cocoanut Grove) in the Ambassador Hotel. The press came out in full force, and it was then that I met Dick McInnes, who was writing for Rona Barrett, acting as her legman and directing her news segment. We became good friends, and when Rona took ill for two weeks, he called me. They had only enough tapes for seven days of reruns: Would I do three shows for Rona? So I made my debut as a television gossip columnist.

The night after the taping, I asked Dick to join Bill and me for dinner and then go on to see Carol Burnett and George Kennedy in *Plaza Suite* at the Huntington Hartford Theater. As we were eating, the waiter gave me a note that read, "Miss Lamour, I've been a terrific fan of yours for a long time. May I come over and say hello? Love, Carol Burnett." We went back after the show to see her.

I was asked to reopen San Diego's Off Broadway Theater, which had been totally refurbished in red velvet and gold. Because I loved the songs and the role was terrific, I decided to do *Anything Goes*. We had a major opening night, with the management flying a planeload of stars down from Hollywood; among them were Lana Turner, Jane Withers, George Jessel, Rudy Vallee, Christine Jorgenson, and some television people.

At the party afterwards Lana told me that she was terrified at having to do *Forty Carats* in stock, her first attempt at live theater. "In the movies," she said, "I'm used to doing several takes if I made a mistake. The stage is so different!"

"How do you think I felt when I did my first play?" I laughed. "In the movies all I ever did was look at Ray Milland or Jon Hall and say, 'Keeess—what is keeess??' "

Asked to do my club act at the Australia's private-membership South Sydney Junior Club, I met another new friend, Tracey Lee, who arranged for this engagement and who did everything he could to make my stay a pleasure. After ten weeks we left to do a show for servicemen stationed in the Philippines, where Bill became extremely ill and had to be rushed back to a stateside hospital. After a very rough time, he beat the illness once again, but I wondered how much he would be able to take.

Ben Pearson, an agent, wanted me to do some dinner theaters, but I didn't really know too much about them. He advised me to ask my pal Betty Grable, who told me that it was a wonderful part of show business, with fabulous audiences. How right she was! While I was searching for a play, an offer came in to join her, Don Ameche, Dennis Day, and Chita Rivera in a musical revue celebrating the Forties.

The St. Louis Municipal Opera is a huge outdoor theater, and the weather was very humid. Betty didn't want anyone to know she was beginning to get sick. She kept breaking out in a sweat and finally became so weak they had to cut the dance number she'd been doing. But unbelievably, she never complained once. I sang my medley, and we sang "I Want to Be Happy" as a duet. We became very close then, and in the last few weeks while she was in a Santa Monica Hospital, we spoke on the phone every day. Her spirits were high, and she wanted to get back to work. I was honored to have been her friend. When she died, it was a major loss, and I only hoped that some of her courage would rub off on me.

For the dinner theaters, I had the choice of any play, but didn't want something that had been done to death. I picked Noel Coward's *Fallen Angels*, which hadn't been done in some time, and was lucky to start work with an excellent cast, Judith Jett, Anne Haney, Bob Larkin, Will Gregory, and Jerry Richards.

The only cloud took up a good deal of the horizon: Bill's health was failing, and this time he had a real battle ahead of him.

20. Farewell . . . Aloha

When you've lived with and loved a man for over 35 years, the key word is *share,* and that's what it was being married to William Ross Howard III. If only I could have the choice of doing it all over again, I would still look up at my handsome lieutenant on April 7, 1943, and say "I will," and still mean every word of the wedding vows.

Bill was an exceptional man. My husband, my best friend, and my lover, he had the wickedest sense of humor of any man around. Even in times of stress, that glint in his eyes would make our problems easier to cope with.

In the years following his discharge from the Air Force, he had recurring bouts with pneumonia. Although Bill had amazing recuperative powers and always bounced back, each

Tommy visiting me backstage

bout took its toll. In later years the attacks became more frequent, and increasingly worse. Since the whole problem was basically touched off by Bill's living conditions in the service, we were advised to petition the Veterans Administration for a disability pension. Bill was informed that his service records had been lost in a big fire in St. Louis, and there actually isn't any proof that a William Ross Howard was ever in the service! Our battle to confirm his enlistment is still going on.

Then came the week I was doing *Fallen Angels* at the Showboat Dinner Theater in Tampa–St. Petersburg. Although he had a slight cold, Bill flew down to join me. Two days later he had to be rushed to the Sun Coast Hospital. At the doctors' strong suggestion, I called the boys in California. Not wanting to scare their father, we decided that only one of them should fly in. They drew straws, and Ridge left immediately. I also called Dick McInnes: since he was in New Orleans for the Mardi Gras at the time, it would make sense for him to "just drop in."

I'll be ever grateful to my bosses at the Showboat, Maurice Shinners and Dow Sherwood, who bent over backwards for me. Bill would have grown suspicious if I canceled a performance (one thing I'd never done), so I kept on with the eight-show-a-week schedule. We were sold out, but believe me, it wasn't easy doing comedy onstage while crying inside.

Before and after each show, I visited the hospital and either Ridge or Dick would sit with Bill to shoot the breeze. It was Bill's sense of humor that carried *us* through, and to everyone's joy and amazement, he began to get well. The doctors just shook their heads in disbelief. He was still very weak, but soon well enough to return to California.

In the early part of 1977 Patrick Baldauff called me to say he was directing *Personal Appearance*, an old play that had been the basis for Mae West's movie with my old pal Randy Scott called *Go West, Young Man.* Could I do it with him? It was to open at the Beverly Dinner Playhouse in New Orleans, owned by my old friends Storer Boone and Charles Wisdom, who had been after me to do something there.

In the Thirties, the Beverly Dinner Playhouse was known as the Beverly Club. Names like Sophie Tucker, Harry

Richman, and Joe E. Lewis used to play the big room, and there was even a hidden salon for illegal gambling. The first day I started rehearsals, it came back to me that this was also where I made my very first public appearance as a singer. (After I was elected Miss New Orleans, the merchants threw a big party for me at the Beverly Club. M.C. George McQueen introduced me and asked me to sing "It Must Be True," a popular song of the time.)

Rehearsals went beautifully, and opening night was a delight. Bill had planned to join me, but he came down with a cold and kept postponing the trip. Storer and Charlie planned a wonderful thirty-fourth anniversary party for us, so finally Bill flew in. He had to go straight to bed, but was able to attend the party.

My next booking was at the Alhambra Theater in Jacksonville, Florida, but Bill just couldn't shake his cold. He wasn't up to joining me right away, so I left Los Angeles to start rehearsals. Each time I spoke to him he'd say "Honey, I read there's a flu epidemic in Florida. I think I'd better stay home a while longer and not take any chances."

There *was* an epidemic, so I didn't think too much about his staying away. I did miss him, but felt sure he'd be better off at home.

After finishing our Florida engagement, Len Hughes—a very dear friend who was playing the chauffeur in the play—and I drove up to Pineville, North Carolina, for our next booking. About halfway there, I began to get a strange foreboding and not wanting Len to think I was cracking up, I told him I had to stop at the next rest room—where I immediately called Bill at home. "Have you been to the doctor as you promised?"

"Momma," he replied, "I'm going to go to Doctor Perry's office right now. Hal Bolin's going to drive me there."

I asked to speak to Hal, another good friend of ours. A contractor by trade, Hal had a lot of experience in nursing, and had taken off work the past few weeks to help Bill. "Hal, you're not taking him to the doctor's, are you?" I asked. "You're taking him to the hospital."

Hal admitted they were taking Bill to the hospital, but for preventive measures only. Obviously, it was time for a full-time staff of nurses. But I hung up the phone knowing the nurses at Hollywood Presbyterian would make sure Bill ate enough to build up his strength.

To put it kindly, it was steaming hot in Pineville, North Carolina, and the theater air conditioning wasn't turned on during the day. At night the theater's dressing rooms remained like ovens, and then when we hit the stage for rehearsals, the theater was ice cold. I had to make a quick change right offstage, and naturally I caught a cold. Unfortunately there were no microphones, and I had to really project if I wanted anyone to hear me. The doctors advised me not to talk except onstage, but I began to lose my voice. I should have left the show, but hated to put the cast out of work. In another theater owned by my bosses, Dan Dailey had recently fallen and broken his hip, and his show had to close. So mine had to go on.

My throat was so bad that it nearly put me in the hospital. Then the doctors found a possibly malignant spot on my vocal chords which worried them—and most certainly me. They insisted I leave the show, so we closed three weeks early. When I arrived back in California, my man was home from the hospital. Weak as he was, he wanted to take care of *me.* I wasn't allowed to talk at all, so Bill took charge of all my business and personal calls. "This is mouthpiece Bill Howard," he would say, "and I'm calling for Dorothy Lamour, the silent star."

The morning I was to go to the doctors for the latest reports on my throat, Bill and I were sitting in the kitchen having a cup of coffee and listening to the all-news radio station. "Bing Crosby drops dead on a golf course in Spain," the announcer said, "Details now coming in."

Bill and I looked at each other in disbelief. Only two days before, Lord Lew Grade had been on the phone from London, asking me to join Bing and Bob in *The Road to the Fountain of Youth*. Yet how appropriate for Bing to make his final exit on a golf course.

I had to get ready for my doctor's appointment. Bill was already late for a haircut appointment at the Beverly Hilton, so I told him to go ahead. The minute that he left, of course, the phone started ringing off the hook. Even though the doctor had told me to keep my mouth shut, I had to answer some of the calls. "Australia calling Miss Lamour." London, Paris, New York . . . I gave a phone interview to ABC's Jerry Dunphy and talked to a few radio stations before realizing the damage I was doing to my throat. By this time, I had missed my doctor's appointment.

I called the doctor to explain why I hadn't shown up. "I know," he replied with slight sarcasm, "you must have been following my orders quite well. I heard you on the car radio while I was driving to the office."

He advised me not to talk any more, but did have some good news. My tests proved conclusively that I *didn't* have throat cancer. I ought to speak in a whisper for the next couple of weeks, but at least I was going to be all right.

Pauline Kessinger came over the next morning. Since we had both been extremely close to Bing, we called his office to ask about funeral arrangements. We were well aware that Bing, a very private man, had always hated funerals, and never attended any, no matter how close he was to the deceased.

I guess stunned is the best word to describe my reaction. Bing's secretary had known me for years. "Dottie, I'm sorry," she said, obviously ill at ease, "but Mrs. Crosby will not allow anyone but the immediate family into the services. I wouldn't want you to be embarrassed if you showed up, because they will not let you in."

Pauline couldn't believe her ears. I had always liked Bing, even though sometimes he was like a stranger. I guess we had been closest when he was married to Dixie Lee, a wonderful lady. Like so many of Bing's old friends, I had never had a chance to really get to know actress Kathryn Grant, the new Mrs. Crosby.

I knew the press was going to wonder why I wasn't at the funeral, but a photo from the wire services hit all over the world with the caption, "Dorothy Lamour attends Crosby services." She happened to be an employee of Bing's who bore a striking resemblance to me—and no one could believe that I wouldn't be there to say good-bye.

Bill felt well enough for us to go to Ridge and Karen's home for Thanksgiving. Tommy was there with his wife Dee Dee, and all his in-laws. Bill and I talked about our upcoming annual pilgrimage to the Royal Hawaiian Hotel. We planned to spend my birthday and Christmas with our good pal Dorothy Mackaill.

A few days before December 9, when we were due to leave, Bill suffered another attack. He knew how important this trip was to both of us. "I can go by ambulance to the airport," he suggested, looking very tired and pale as he lay in his hospital bed. "The porter can meet us with a cart and drive me to the plane. And when we get to Hawaii, the Royal Hawaiian Hotel can meet us with a wheelchair. Don't you worry, Momma, we can still go."

I had to fight back the tears, because I had already cancelled the trip, knowing he would never make it to Hawaii again.

Bill wouldn't eat, and although they had to feed him intravenously, he promised to eat my cooking and kept insisting he was well enough to go home for Christmas. On December 23 the doctors relented and sent him home.

Bill didn't want a nurse around, so I very quickly learned how to be one. When he rang the bell I couldn't always hear him, so I devised a Rube Goldberg device of my own, tying a spoon to the handle of a saucepan. That way, when Bill needed something he could bang on the bottom of the pan, and he'd never lose the spoon, since it was tied on.

One evening I wheeled him to the table so that we could have dinner together. In my old bathrobe, with my hair needing a good washing, I must have looked like Gravel Gertie. I saw Bill staring at me.

"Honey," I asked, "why are you looking at me like that?"

"I'm just thinking about how much I love you," he said simply.

Once in the middle of the night he needed me to help him to the bathroom. As I wheeled him past the mirror on the bathroom door, he glanced at his reflection. "Momma, how in the hell did I get in this shape and bring you all this trouble?"

The following morning he wanted to walk by himself so desperately that he tried it. He made it to the hall before he fell, and with my bad back I just couldn't get him up. Finally I called a young actor friend of ours, Eric Williams, who rushed over to help.

We did spend our last Christmas together. New Year's Eve we stayed up to listen to Guy Lombardo. Right after the New Year, Bill's condition worsened, and he had to return to Hollywood Presbyterian Hospital. It was horrible to watch a handsome man of 6 feet, 3 inches deteriorate day by day. His weight sank to a mere 98 pounds, and sometimes he would ramble on a bit.

But he always came up with some funny remark. One night the doctors said he was really bad, so Pauline, Ridge, Bill, Jr., Tommy, Dick, and I all showed up. Lest he think we were worried, I told him that we had all been out to dinner together.

"Did you pick up the check for that whole group?" he asked.

"No," I said. "Pauline did. She just sold her house today."

"Well, send in Mrs. Rich Bitch. I want to see her."

Ward Grant, who worked for Bob Hope and was always a good friend of ours, was very active in the Episcopal Church I attended. One evening when Bill was particularly low, I called Ward and asked if the minister would come over. He did, and he and Bill discovered they were both native Maryland residents. Bill's condition kept going up and down, and so did our hopes. His spunk and wit made us hope that a miracle would happen.

On Valentine's Day my driver's license had expired, so I called Dick McInnes and asked him to take me to the hospital. I brought Bill a card and a box of candy. The day before, he'd been so low that I asked Dick to wait outside, but today he'd rallied. When I told him Dick was outside, he said, "Send that old S.O.B. in."

This book had always been one of Bill's pet ideas, and so when Dick entered, Bill looked at him and said very lucidly, "Don't procrastinate. Let's get this book done."

He hadn't eaten a crumb of food that day, but he loved chocolates and he ate five from the box. He wasn't able to read the card, so I read it aloud to him. That was one of the hardest things I've had to do.

Dick said good-bye, but I lingered and told Bill I'd come back later in the evening. "No, Momma," he said. "I don't want you to drive in that traffic. Just stay home and get a good night's sleep."

"I love you, Daddy," I said.

He looked at me. "And I love you, my dear."

That "my dear" was so unexpectedly formal; he'd never called me that before. "Well," I remarked, "you certainly are the proper Baltimore gentleman. Where did that 'my dear' come from?"

He just smiled, and I went back and kissed him again.

At 9:00 A.M. the next morning, Dr. Perry called to tell me that Bill had passed away.

My memory of making the funeral arrangements is still a blur. I managed to hold up pretty well for the boys' sakes, and because I knew that Bill would want it that way. So many friends of ours called, sent flowers and cards, and came to the service, and I'll always remember that kindness. Bill had told me that he wanted "The Old Rugged Cross" played at his funeral, and I asked them to play "Aloha."

It's been almost three years now, and I still miss him terribly. There will never be another man like him. I wish I could have had one more chance to say, "Daddy, I love you." But now my life is starting to come back into focus again. I work a lot. The boys are happily married, and I have my new love, my Scottish terrier Coco, to keep me company.

Coco was given to me by Bill, Jr., because he thought I should have something to love and care for now that his father was gone. I told him that this was too difficult a period for me to be raising a dog, but he insisted, and I'm glad he did. I've shocked friends when I told them that I have a new boyfriend and then bring out a photo of that little dog. Coco has such a distinct personality that he's become a most important part of my life and helped pull me through the most difficult period.

I've often said that God has blessed me so much. I had a wonderful mother, a loving husband, three fine sons (and now two lovely daughters-in-law), and a fabulous career. What woman could ask for anything more? I've certainly had the best in life, and it's not over yet.

Recently I have been on the dinner theater circuit with a talented group of actors in Neil Simon's very funny play *Barefoot in the Park.* I've worked for old friends like Maury Shinners and Dow Sherwood at the Showboat Dinner Theater in Tampa-St. Petersburg, for Pat Baldauff and Earl Holliman in their new Fiesta Playhouse in San Antonio, for Storer Boone and Charles Wisdom at the Beverly Dinner Theater in New Orleans; for Bill McHale's Windmill Dinner Theater in Scottsdale, Arizona, and for new friends like Enid Holm at the lovely Mansion Theater in Odessa, Texas. I enjoy playing in revivals of shows I missed when they first opened on Broadway, like *Pal Joey, Can Can*, and *Anything Goes*. Meeting new friends is what keeps me young. I look back on my life not with nostalgic longing, but with a smile on my face.

I'd like to share something with you that I say to my audiences when I'm doing a show. This is for my family, my friends, my fans, the press, Coco, and everyone who's helped contribute to that little girl from New Orleans who became Dorothy Lamour Howard.

"You have all been so wonderful, I don't really know how to thank you. There is a word in the Hawaiian language that says it all, though. It means hello, it means good-bye. It means I love you, and it means I thank you from the bottom of my heart. The word is. . . .

Aloha!
Dorothy Lamour

Filmography*

THE JUNGLE PRINCESS (1936)

Director: William Thiele
Lamour song: "Moonlight and Shadows"
Cast: Dorothy Lamour (Ulah), Ray Milland (Christopher Powell), Akim Tamiroff (Karen Neg), Lynne Overman (Frank)

SWING HIGH, SWING LOW (1937)

Director: Mitchell Leisen
Lamour song: "Panamania"
Cast: Carole Lombard (Maggie King), Fred MacMurray (Skid Johnson), Charles Butterworth (Harry), Jean Dixon (Ella), Dorothy Lamour (Anita Alvarez), Franklyn Pangborn (Henri), Anthony Quinn (The Don), Dennis O'Keefe (Purser)

HIGH, WIDE AND HANDSOME (1937)

Director: Rouben Mamoulian
Lamour song: "The Things I Want"
Cast: Irene Dunne (Sally Watterson), Randolph Scott (Peter Cortlandt), Dorothy Lamour (Molly Fuller), Elizabeth Patterson (Grandma Cortlandt), Raymond Walburn (Doc Watterson), Charles Bickford (Red Scanlon), Akim Tamiroff (Joe Varese), Ben Blue (Zeke), Alan Hale (Walt Brennan), William Frawley (Mac)

THE LAST TRAIN FROM MADRID (1937)

Director: James Hogan
Cast: Dorothy Lamour (Carmelita Castillo), Lew Ayres (Bill Dexter), Gilbert Roland (Eduardo de Soto), Karen Morley (Helen Rafitte) Lionel Atwill (Colonel Vigo), Helen Mack (Lola), Robert Cummings (Juan), Anthony Quinn (Captain Ricardo Alvarez), Lee Bowman (Michael Balk)

THRILL OF A LIFETIME (1937)

Director: George Archainbaud
Lamour song: "Thrill of a Lifetime"
Cast: Yacht Club Boys (Themselves), Judy Canova (Judy), Ben Blue (Skipper), Eleanore Whitney (Betty Jane), Johnny Downs (Stanley), Betty Grable (Gwen), Leif Erickson (Howdy Nelson), Larry Crabbe (Don) Fanchonettes, Dorothy Lamour (Specialities), Zeke Canova, Anne Canova (Themselves), Franklyn Pangborn (Mr. Williams)

*Dates are the year the film was completed
All films are Paramount unless noted

THE HURRICANE (1937) United Artists

Director: John Ford
Cast: Dorothy Lamour (Marama), Jon Hall (Terang), Mary Astor (Madame De Laage), C. Aubrey Smith (Father Paul), Thomas Mitchell (Dr. Kersaint), Raymond Massey (Governor De Laage), John Carradine (Warden), Jerome Cowan (Captain Nagle), Kuulei De Clerq (Tita), Movita Castenada (Ara)

THE BIG BROADCAST OF 1938 (1938)

Director: Mitchell Leisen
Lamour song: "You Took the Words Right Out of My Heart"
Cast: W. C. Fields (T. Frothingill Bellows & S. B. Bellows), Martha Raye (Martha Bellows), Dorothy Lamour (Dorothy Wyndham), Shirley Ross (Cleo Fielding), Lynne Overman (Scoop McPhail), Bob Hope (Buzz Fielding), Leif Erickson (Bob Hayes), Grace Bradley (Grace Fielding), Tito Guizar (Himself), Leonid Kinskey (Ivan), Kirsten Flagstad (Herself), James Craig (Steward), Richard Denning (Officer)

HER JUNGLE LOVE (1938)
Director: George Archainbaud
Lamour songs: "Coffee and Kisses"
"Jungle Love"
"Lovelight in the Starlight"
Cast: Dorothy Lamour (Tura), Ray Milland (Bob Mitchell), Lynne Overman (Jimmy Wallace), J. Carrol Naish (Kuasa), Virginia Vale (Eleanor Martin), Jonathan Hale (J. C. Martin), Richard Denning (Pilot), Jiggs (Gaga, the Chimp), Meewa (Lion Cub)

TROPIC HOLIDAY (1938)
Director: Theodore Reed
Lamour songs: "On a Tropic Night"
"Tonight Will Live"
"My First Love"
Cast: Dorothy Lamour (Manuela), Bob Burns (Breck Jones), Martha Raye (Midge Miller), Ray Milland (Ken Warren), Binnie Barnes (Marilyn Joyce), Tito Guizar (Ramon)

SPAWN OF THE NORTH (1938)

Director: Henry Hathaway
Cast: George Raft (Tyler Dawson), Henry Fonda (Jim Kemmerlee), Dorothy Lamour (Nicky Duval), Akim Tamiroff (Red Skain), John Barrymore (Windy), Louise Platt (Diane), Lynne Overman (Jackson), Fuzzy Knight (Lefty Jones), Duncan Renaldo (Ivan)

ST. LOUIS BLUES (1938)

Director: Raoul Walsh
Lamour songs: "Junior"
"I Go for That"
"Blue Nightfall"

"Let's Dream in the Moonlight"

Cast: Dorothy Lamour (Norma Malone), Lloyd Nolan (Dave Guerney), Tito Guizar (Rafael), Jerome Cowan (Ivan DeBrett), William Frawley (Major Martingale), Sterling Holloway (Boatman)

MAN ABOUT TOWN (1939)

Director: Mark Sandrich
Lamour songs: "That Sentimental Sandwich" with Phil Harris
"Enchantment"
Cast: Jack Benny (Bob Temple), Dorothy Lamour (Diana Wilson), Edward Arnold (Sir John Arlington), Binnie Barnes (Lady Arlington), Phil Harris (Ted Nash), Eddie Anderson (Rochester), Monty Woolley (Monsieur Dubois), Isabel Jeans (Mme. Dubois), Betty Grable (Susan)

DISPUTED PASSAGE (1939)

Director: Frank Borzage
Cast: Dorothy Lamour (Audrey Hilton), Akim Tamiroff (Dr. "Tubby" Forster), John Howard (John Wesley Beaven), Judith Barrett (Winifred Bane), Gordon Jones (Bill Anderson), Keye Luke (Andrew Abbott), Renie Riano (Mrs. Riley), Elisabeth Risdon (Mrs. Cunningham), Richard Denning (Student)

TYPHOON (1939)

Director: Louis King
Lamour song: "Palms of Paradise"
Cast: Dorothy Lamour (Dea), Robert Preston (Johnny Potter), Lynne Overman (Skipper Joe), J. Carrol Naish (Mekaike), Chief Thundercloud (Kehi), Jack Carson (The Mate)

ROAD TO SINGAPORE (1939)

Director: Victor Schertzinger
Lamour songs: "The Moon and the Willow"
"Too Romantic" with Bing
Cast: Bing Crosby (Josh Mallon), Dorothy Lamour (Mima), Bob Hope (Ace Lannigan), Charles Coburn (Joshua Mallon, IV), Judith Barrett (Gloria Wycott), Anthony Quinn (Caesar), Jerry Colonna (Achilles Bombanassa), Pierre Watkin (Morgan Wycott), Monte Blue (High Priest)

JOHNNY APOLLO (1940)

Director: Henry Hathaway
Lamour songs: "This is the Beginning of the End"
"Dancing for Nickels and Dimes"
Cast: Tyrone Power (Bob Cain), Dorothy Lamour ("Lucky" Dubarry), Edward Arnold (Robert Cain, Sr.), Lloyd Nolan (Nicky Dwyer), Charles Grapewin (Judge Emmett F. Brennan), Lionel Atwill (Jim McLaughlin), Marc Lawrence (Bates), Jonathan Hale (Dr. Brown), Russell Hicks (District Attorney) Fuzzy Knight (Cellmate), Charles Lane (Ass't. D.A.), Bess Flowers (Secretary), Milburn Stone (Reporter), James Flavin (Guard)

MOON OVER BURMA (1940)

Director: Louis King
Lamour songs: "Moon Over Burma"
"Mexican Magic"
Cast: Dorothy Lamour (Arla Dean), Robert Preston (Chuck Lane), Preston Foster (Bill Gordon), Doris Nolan (Cynthia Harmon), Albert Basserman (Basil Renner), Addison Richards (Art Bryan)

CHAD HANNA (1940) Twentieth Century Fox

Director: Henry King
Cast: Henry Fonda (Chad Hanna), Dorothy Lamour (Albany Yates), Linda Darnell (Caroline), Guy Kibbee (Huguenine), Jane Darwell (Mrs. Huguenine), John Carradine (Bisbee), Roscoe Ates (Ike Wayfish)

ROAD TO ZANZIBAR (1940)

Director: Victor Schertzinger
Lamour song: "You're Dangerous" with Bing
Cast: Bing Crosby (Chuck Reardon), Bob Hope (Fearless Hubert Frazier) Dorothy Lamour (Donna Latour), Una Merkel (Julia Quimby), Eric Blore (Charles Kimble), Iris Adrian (French Soubrette in Cafe), Leo Gorcey (Boy), Norma Varden (Clara Kimble), Ken Carpenter (Commentator)

CAUGHT IN THE DRAFT (1941)

Director: David Butler
Lamour song: "Love as I Am"
Cast: Bob Hope (Don Gilbert), Dorothy Lamour (Toni Fairbanks), Lynne Overman (Steve), Eddie Bracken (Bert), Clarence Kolb (Col. Peter Fairbanks)

ALOMA OF THE SOUTH SEAS (1941)

Director: Alfred Santell
Lamour song: "The White Blossoms of Tah-Ni"
Cast: Dorothy Lamour (Aloma), Jon Hall (Tanoa), Lynne Overman (Corky), Philip Reed (Revo), Katherine DeMille (Kari), Dona Drake (Nea), Esther Dale (Tarusa), Pedro de Cordoba (Ramita)

BEYOND THE BLUE HORIZON (1941)

Director: Alfred Santell
Lamour songs: "Pagan Lullaby"
"A Full Moon and an Empty Heart"
Cast: Dorothy Lamour (Tama), Richard Denning (Jakra), Jack Haley (Squidge), Patricia Morison (Sylvia), Walter Abel (Thornton), Helen Gilbert (Carol), Elizabeth Patterson (Mrs. Daly), Ann Doran (Margaret Chase), Barbara Britton (Pamela), Frances Gifford (Charlotte)

THE FLEET'S IN (1941)

Director: Victor Schertzinger
Lamour songs: "I Remember You"
"When You Hear the Time Signal"
Cast: Dorothy Lamour (The Countess), William Holden (Casey Kirby), Eddie Bracken (Barney), Betty Hutton (Bessie Dale), Cass Daley (Cissie), Gil Lamb (Spike), Leif Erickson (Jake), Betty Jane Rhodes (Diane Golden), Jack Norton (Kellogg), Jimmy Dorsey and his Band (Themselves), Barbara Britton (Eileen), Dave Willock, Rod Cameron (Sailors)

ROAD TO MOROCCO (1942)

Director: David Butler
Lamour song: "Constantly"
Cast: Bing Crosby (Jeff Peters), Bob Hope (Turkey Jackson), Dorothy Lamour (Princess Shalimar), Anthony Quinn (Mullay Kasim), Dona Drake (Mihirmah), Mikhail Rasumny (Ahmed Fey), Vladimir Sokoloff (Hyder Khan), Monte Blue (Aide to Kasim), Yvonne De Carlo (Handmaiden)

THEY GOT ME COVERED (1942) RKO

Director: David Butler
Cast: Bob Hope (Robert Kittredge), Dorothy Lamour (Christina Hill), Lenore Aubert (Mrs. Vanescu), Otto Preminger (Fauscheim), Eduardo Ciannelli (Baldanacco), Marion Martin (Gloria), Donald Meek (Little Old Man), Philip Ahn (Nichimuro), Donald MacBride (Mason), Mary Treen (Helen), Florence Bates (Gypsy Woman), Walter Catlett (Hotel Manager), George Chandler (Smith), Stanley Clements (Office Boy)

STAR SPANGLED RHYTHM (1942)

Director: George Marshall
Lamour song: "A Sweater, A Sarong and A Peek-a-Boo Bang"
Cast: Betty Hutton (Polly), Eddie Bracken (Jimmy), Victor Moore (Pop Webster), Anne Revere (Sarah), Walter Abel (B. G. De Soto), Cass Daley (Mimi), MacDonald Carey (Louie the Lug), Gil Lamb (Hi-Pockets), Bob Hope (Master of Ceremonies) with the Paramount roster of stars: Marion Martin, William Bendix, Dorothy Lamour, Paulette Goddard, Veronica Lake, Arthur Treacher, Walter Catlett, Sterling Holloway, Vera Zorina, Frank Faylen, Fred MacMurray, Franchot Tone, Ray Milland, Lynne Overman, Susan Hayward, Ernest Truex, Mary Martin, Dick Powell, Cecil B. DeMille, Preston Sturges, Alan Ladd, Marjorie Reynolds, Dona Drake, Bing Crosby, Ellen Drew, Susanna Foster, Frances Gifford and Rochester

DIXIE (1943)

Director: A. Edward Sutherland
Cast: Bing Crosby (Dan Emmett), Dorothy Lamour (Millie Cook), Marjorie Reynolds (Jean Mason), Billy De Wolfe (Mr. Bones), Lynne Overman (Mr. Whitlock), Eddie Foy, Jr. (Mr. Pelham), Raymond Walburn (Mr. Cook), Grant Mitchell (Mr. Mason), Norma Varden (Mrs. La Plant)

RIDING HIGH (1943)

Director: George Marshall
Lamour songs: "Get Your Man"
"Injun Gal Heap Hep"
"I'm the Secretary to the Sultan"
"Whistling in the Light" with Cass Daley
Cast: Dorothy Lamour (Ann Castle), Dick Powell (Steve Baird), Victor Moore (Mortimer J. Slocum), Gil Lamb (Bob "Foggy" Day), Cass Daley (Tess Connors), Bill Geodwin (Chuck), Rod Cameron (Sam Welch), Glenn Langan (Jack), Douglas Fowley (Brown), Pierre Watkin (Masters), Roscoe Karns (Shorty)

AND THE ANGELS SING (1943)

Director: George Marshall
Lamour songs: "For the First Hundred Years"
"Knocking on Your Own Front Door" with Hutton, Lynn and Chandler
"It Could Happen to You"
Cast: Dorothy Lamour (Nancy Angel), Fred MacMurray (Happy Morgan), Betty Hutton (Bobby Angel), Diane Lynn (Josie Angel), Mimi Chandler (Patti Angel), Raymond Walburn (Pop Angel), Eddie Foy, Jr. (Fuzzy Johnson), Frank Albertson (Oliver), Mikhail Rasumny (Schultz), Frank Faylen (Holman) Douglas Fowley (Cafe Manager), Hillary Brooke (Polish Bride), Jack Norton (Drunk)

RAINBOW ISLAND (1943)

Director: Ralph Murphy
Lamour song: "Beloved"
Cast: Dorothy Lamour (Lona), Eddie Bracken (Toby Smith), Gil Lamb (Pete Jenkins), Barry Sullivan (Ken), Anne Revere (Queen Okalana), Reed Hadley (High Priest Kahuna), Marc Lawrence (Alcoa), Elena Verdugo (Moana), Yvonne De Carlo, Noel Neill (Lona's Handmaidens)

ROAD TO UTOPIA (1944) Released in 1945

Director: Hal Walker
Lamour songs: "Would You"
"Personality"
Cast: Bing Crosby (Duke Johnson/Junior Hooten), Bob Hope (Chester Hooten), Dorothy Lamour (Sal Van Hoyden), Hillary Brooke (Kate), Douglass Dumbrille (Ace Larson), Jack LaRue (LeBec), Robert Benchley (Narrator)

A MEDAL FOR BENNY (1944)

Director: Irving Pichel
Cast: Dorothy Lamour (Lolita Sierra), Arturo de Cordova (Joe Morales), J. Carrol Naish (Charley), Mikhail Rasumny (Raphael), Charles Dingle (Zach), Frank McHugh (Edgar Lovekin), Grant Mitchell (Mayor of Pantera), Douglass Dumbrille (General)

MASQUERADE IN MEXICO (1945)

Director: Mitchell Leisen
Lamour songs: "Masquerade In Mexico"
"That's Love"
"Adios and Farewell My Lover"
Cast: Dorothy Lamour (Angel O'Reilly), Arturo de Cordova (Manolo Segovia), Patric Knowles (Thomas), Ann Dvorak (Helen), George Rigaud (Boris), Natalie Schafer (Irene), Mikhail Rasumny (Pablo), Billy Daniels (Rico)

DUFFY'S TAVERN (1945)

Director: Hal Walker
Lamour song: "Swingin' on a Star" with Betty Hutton, Diana Lynn, Bing Crosby, Arturo de Cordova
Cast: Ed Gardner (Archie), Charles Cantor (Finnegan), Ann Thomas (Miss Duffy), Victor Moore (Michael O'Malley), Barry Sullivan (Danny Murphy) with Paramount stars: Bing Crosby, Betty Hutton, Paulette Goddard, Alan Ladd, Dorothy Lamour, Eddie Bracken, Brian Donlevy, Sonny Tufts, Veronica Lake, Arturo de Cordova, Cass Daley, Diana Lynn, Gary Crosby, Phillip Crosby, Dennis Crosby, Lindsay Crosby, William Bendix, Joan Caulfield, Gail Russell, Helen Walker

MY FAVORITE BRUNETTE (1946)

Director: Elliott Nugent
Cast: Bob Hope (Ronnie Jackson), Dorothy Lamour (Carlotta Montay), Peter Lorre (Kismet), Lon Chaney, Jr. (Willie), John Hoyt (Dr. Lundau), Charles Dingle (Major Montague), Reginald Denny (James Colling), Ann Doran (Miss Rogers), Jack La Rue (Tony), Bing Crosby (Executioner) Alan Ladd (Himself)

WILD HARVEST (1946)

Director: Tay Garnett
Cast: Alan Ladd (Joe Madigan), Dorothy Lamour (Fay Rankin), Robert Preston (Jim Davis), Lloyd Nolan (Kink), Dick Erdman (Mark Lewis), Allen Jenkins (Higgins)

VARIETY GIRL (1947)

Director: George Marshall
Lamour song: "Tallahassee" with Alan Ladd
Cast: Mary Hatcher (Catherine Brown), Olga San Juan (Amber LaVonne), DeForest Kelley (Bob Kirby), William Demarest (Barker) Frank Faylen (Stage Manager), Catherine Craig (Secretary), Bing Crosby, Bob Hope, Gary Cooper, Ray Milland, Alan Ladd, Barbara Stanwyck, Paulette Goddard, Dorothy Lamour, Veronica Lake, Sonny Tufts, Joan Caulfield, William Holden, Liz Scott, Burt Lancaster, Gail Russell, Diana Lynn, Sterling Hayden, Robert Preston, John Lund, William Bendix, Barry Fitzgerald, Cass Daley, MacDonald Carey, Billy De Wolfe, Cecil B. DeMille, Pearl Bailey, George Reeves, Spike Jones and his City Slickers

ROAD TO RIO (1947)

Director: Norman Z. McLeod
Lamour song: "Experience"
Cast: Bing Crosby (Scat Sweeney), Bob Hope (Hot Lips Barton), Dorothy Lamour (Lucia Maria De Andrade), Gale Sondergaard (Catherine Vail), Frank Faylen (Trigger), Jerry Colonna (Cavalry Captain), Wiere Brothers, Andrews Sisters

ON OUR MERRY WAY (1947) United Artists

Director: King Vidor
Lamour song: "The Queen of the Hollywood Islands"
Cast: Burgess Meredith (Oliver), Paulette Goddard (Martha), Fred MacMurray (Al), Hugh Herbert (Elisha), James Stewart (Slim) Dorothy Lamour (Gloria Manners), Victor Moore (Ashton Carrington) Henry Fonda (Lank), William Demarest (Floyd), Nana Bryant (Housekeeper)

LULU BELLE (1947) Columbia

Director: Leslie Fenton
Lamour songs: "Lulu Belle"
"Sweetie Pie"
"Ace in the Hole"
"I Can't Tell Why I Love You But I Do"
Cast: Dorothy Lamour (Lulu Belle), George Montgomery (George Davis), Albert Dekker (Mark Brady), Otto Kruger (Harry), Glenda Farrell (Molly Benson), Greg McClure (Butch Cooper)

SLIGHTLY FRENCH (1948) Columbia

Director: Douglas Sirk
Lamour songs: "I Want to Learn About Love"
"Let's Fall In Love"
Cast: Dorothy Lamour (Mary O'Leary), Don Ameche (John Gayle), Janis Carter (Louise Gayle), Willard Parker (Douglas), Adele Jergens (Yvonne LaTour), Patricia Barry (Hilda), Pierre Watkin (P.R. Man)

THE GIRL FROM MANHATTAN (1948) United Artists

Director: Alfred E. Green
Cast: Dorothy Lamour (Carol Maynard), George Montgomery (Rev. Tom Walker), Charles Laughton (The Bishop), Ernest Truex (Homer Purdy) Hugh Herbert (Aaron), Constance Collier (Mrs. Brooke), William Frawley (Mr. Bernouti), Sara Allgood (Mrs. Beeler), Howard Freeman (Sam), Frank Orth (Oscar), George Chandler (Monty), Adeline de Walt Reynolds (Old woman)

THE LUCKY STIFF (1948) United Artists

Director: Lewis R. Foster
Lamour song: "Loveliness"
Cast: Dorothy Lamour (Anna Marie St. Claire), Brian Donlevy, (John J. Malone), Claire Trevor (Marguerite), Irene Hervey (Mrs. Childers), Marjorie Rambeau (Hattie Hatfield)

MANHANDLED (1948)

Director: Lewis R. Foster
Cast: Dorothy Lamour (Meri Kramer), Dan Duryea (Karl Benson), Sterling Hayden (Joe Cooper), Irene Hervey (Mrs. Bennet), Philip Reed (Guy) Alan Napier (Mr. Bennet)

HERE COMES THE GROOM (1951)

Director: Frank Capra
Lamour song: "Misto Christofo Columbo" with Crosby, Cass Daley, Phil Harris & Louis Armstrong
Cast: Bing Crosby (Pete) Jane Wyman (Emmadel), Alexis Smith (Winifred), Franchot Tone (Wilbur), Dorothy Lamour, Cass Daley, Phil Harris Frank Fontaine & Louie Armstrong (Themselves)

THE GREATEST SHOW ON EARTH (1951)
Director: Cecil B. DeMille
Lamour song: "Lovely Luawanna Lady"
Cast: Betty Hutton (Holly), Cornel Wilde (Sebastian), Charlton Heston (Brad), Dorothy Lamour (Phyllis), Gloria Grahame (Angel), James Stewart (Buttons), Emmett Kelly (Himself), Lyle Bettger (Klaus), John Ringling North (Himself)

ROAD TO BALI (1952)

Director: Hal Walker
Lamour song: "Moonflowers"
Cast: Bob Hope (Harold Gridley), Bing Crosby (George Cochran), Dorothy Lamour (Lalah), Murvyn Vye (Ken), Jane Russell, Dean Martin, Jerry Lewis, Bob Crosby (Themselves) Carolyn Jones (Eunice), Michael Ansara (Guard)

ROAD TO HONG KONG (1961) United Artists

Director: Norman Panama
Lamour song: "Warmer than a Whisper"
Cast: Bing Crosby (Hary Turner), Bob Hope (Chester Babcock), Joan Collins (Diane), Dorothy Lamour (Herself), Robert Morley (The Leader), Felix Aylmer (Grand Lama), Peter Sellers, Frank Sinatra, Dean Martin, David Niven and Zsa Zsa Gabor (Themselves)

DONOVAN'S REEF (1962)

Director: John Ford
Cast: John Wayne (Guns), Lee Marvin (Gilhooley), Elizabeth Allen (Amelia), Jack Warden (Dr. Dedham), Cesar Romero (The Governor), Dick Foran (Sean), Dorothy Lamour (Fleur), Mike Mazurki (Sgt. Menkowicz)

PAJAMA PARTY (1964) AIP

Director: Don Weiss
Lamour song: "In My Day We Never Did It Like That"
Cast: Tommy Kirk (Go-Go), Annette Funicello (Connie), Elsa Lanchester (Aunt Wendy), Harvey Lembeck (Eric Von Zipper), Jesse White (J. Sinister Hulk), Dorothy Lamour (Head Saleslady), Buster Keaton (Chief Rotten Eagle), Jody McCrea (Big Lunk)

Index